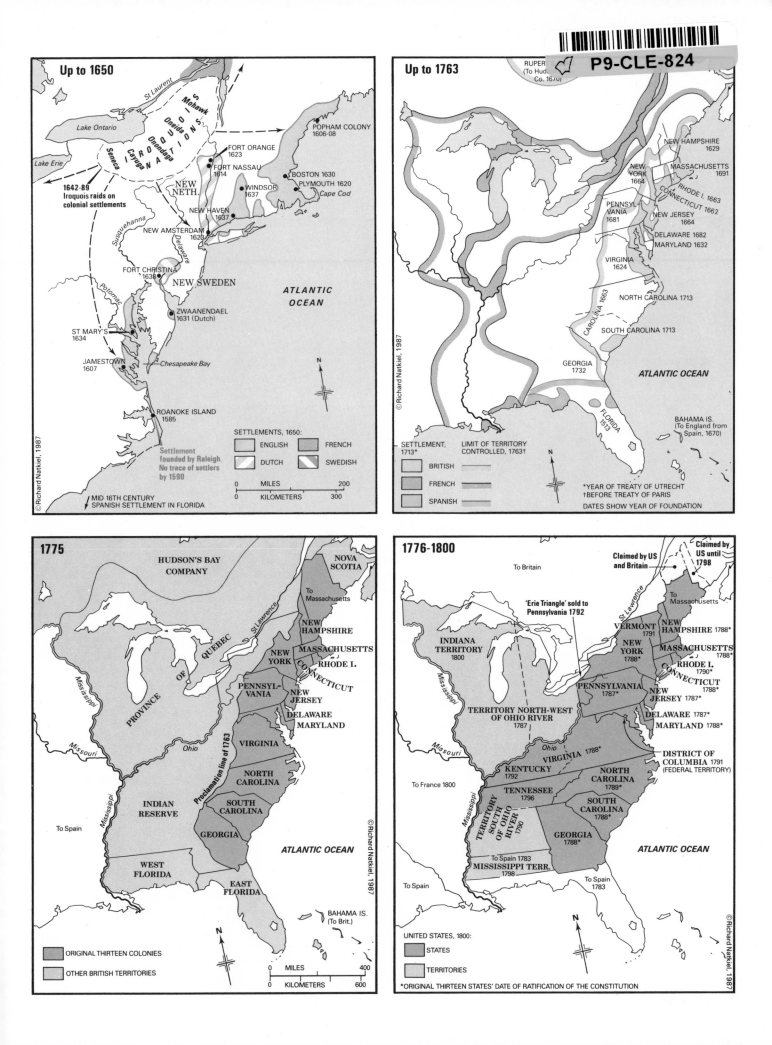

Up to 1650

Lake Ontario

Lake Erie

IROQUOIS NATIONS
Mohawk
Oneida
Onondaga
Cayuga
Seneca

St Laurent

1642-89
Iroquois raids on
colonial settlements

POPHAM COLONY
1606-08

FORT ORANGE
1623

FORT NASSAU
1614

NEW
NETH.

Susquehanna

Delaware

BOSTON 1630
WINDSOR
1637
PLYMOUTH 1620
Cape Cod

NEW HAVEN
1637

NEW AMSTERDAM
1626

FORT CHRISTINA
1638

NEW SWEDEN

Potomac

ZWAANENDAEL
1631 (Dutch)

ST MARY'S
1634

JAMESTOWN
1607

Chesapeake Bay

ATLANTIC
OCEAN

ROANOKE ISLAND
1585

Settlement
founded by Raleigh.
No trace of settlers
by 1590

© Richard Natkiel, 1987

MID 16TH CENTURY
SPANISH SETTLEMENT IN FLORIDA

SETTLEMENTS, 1650:
ENGLISH | FRENCH
DUTCH | SWEDISH

MILES 200
KILOMETERS 300

Up to 1763

RUPER
(To Hud.
Co. 1670)

NEW HAMPSHIRE
1629

NEW YORK
1664

MASSACHUSETTS
1691

RHODE I. 1663
CONNECTICUT 1662

PENNSYL-
VANIA
1681

NEW JERSEY
1664

DELAWARE 1682

MARYLAND 1632

VIRGINIA
1624

CAROLINA 1663

NORTH CAROLINA 1713

SOUTH CAROLINA 1713

GEORGIA
1732

FLORIDA
1513

ATLANTIC OCEAN

BAHAMA IS.
(To England from
Spain, 1670)

© Richard Natkiel, 1987

SETTLEMENT,
1713*
BRITISH
FRENCH
SPANISH

LIMIT OF TERRITORY
CONTROLLED, 1763†

*YEAR OF TREATY OF UTRECHT
†BEFORE TREATY OF PARIS

DATES SHOW YEAR OF FOUNDATION

1775

HUDSON'S BAY
COMPANY

NOVA
SCOTIA

To
Massachusetts

QUEBEC

PROVINCE OF

St Lawrence

Mississippi

Missouri

Ohio

Proclamation line of 1763

NEW
HAMPSHIRE

NEW
YORK

MASSACHUSETTS

RHODE I.

CONNECTICUT

PENNSYL-
VANIA

NEW
JERSEY

DELAWARE

MARYLAND

VIRGINIA

NORTH
CAROLINA

SOUTH
CAROLINA

GEORGIA

INDIAN
RESERVE

To Spain

WEST
FLORIDA

EAST
FLORIDA

ATLANTIC OCEAN

BAHAMA IS.
(To Brit.)

© Richard Natkiel, 1987

ORIGINAL THIRTEEN COLONIES
OTHER BRITISH TERRITORIES

MILES 400
KILOMETERS 600

1776-1800

To Britain

Claimed by US
and Britain

Claimed by
US until
1798

To
Massachusetts

'Erie Triangle' sold to
Pennsylvania 1792

St Lawrence

INDIANA
TERRITORY
1800

Mississippi

Missouri

Ohio

TERRITORY NORTH-WEST
OF OHIO RIVER
1787

VERMONT
1791

NEW HAMPSHIRE 1788*

NEW
YORK
1788*

MASSACHUSETTS
1788*

RHODE I.
1790*

CONNECTICUT
1788*

PENNSYLVANIA
1787*

NEW JERSEY 1787*

DELAWARE 1787*

MARYLAND 1788*

VIRGINIA 1788*

DISTRICT OF
COLUMBIA 1791
(FEDERAL TERRITORY)

KENTUCKY
1792

TENNESSEE
1796

TERRITORY
SOUTH
OF OHIO
RIVER
1790

NORTH
CAROLINA
1789*

SOUTH
CAROLINA
1788*

GEORGIA
1788*

To France 1800

To Spain

MISSISSIPPI TERR.
1798

To Spain 1783

To Spain 1783

ATLANTIC OCEAN

© Richard Natkiel, 1987

UNITED STATES, 1800:
STATES
TERRITORIES

*ORIGINAL THIRTEEN STATES' DATE OF RATIFICATION OF THE CONSTITUTION

P9-CLE-824

Atlas of
AMERICAN
HISTORY

Atlas of
AMERICAN
HISTORY

ROBERT H. FERRELL
RICHARD NATKIEL

Facts On File Publications
New York, New York ● Oxford, England

Produced by
Bison Books Corp
15 Sherwood Place
Greenwich
CT 06830

Published by
Facts on File, Inc.
460 Park Avenue South
New York
NY 10016

Printed in Hong Kong

Library of Congress Cataloging-in-Publication Data

Ferrell, Robert H.
    Atlas of American history.

    Includes index.
    1. United States—Historical geography—Maps.
I. Natkiel, Richard.   II. Title.
G1201.S1F4   1987   911'.73   87-675628
ISBN 0-8160-1028-5

10 9 8 7 6 5 4 3 2 1

Richard Natkiel would like to thank his assistant David Burles for his
help in preparing the maps for this book.

Page 1: A cowboy is silhouetted against the big sky of the
American West.
Page 2: George Washington, first President of the United States of
America.
This page: The immigrant landing station at Ellis Island, New York,
photographed in 1905.

Contents

The Mayflower enters Plymouth Harbor, 1620.

The Colonial Era

When the first European explorers arrived in North America, they did not find an unpopulated wilderness. Some 2,000,000 indigenous people were widely scattered across the so-called New World, comprising hundreds of distinct tribes speaking about 500 different languages. These native Americans were the descendants of early Asiatic peoples who apparently crossed the Bering Strait land bridge between 40,000 and 8000 BC, when the sea level was low because of the great glacial ice sheets. These newcomers moved southward and ultimately spread widely over the North and South American continents. They were essentially hunters, fishers, and gatherers, although those who migrated into the area from present-day Mexico to Peru later developed complex civilizations. Those who remained north of the Rio Grande River were primarily nomadic or the inhabitants of relatively small towns. Only the Mound Builders of the Mississippi River Valley, who were sedentary farmers, created the kind of monumental earthworks, temples and tombs that were commonplace in Central and South America.

The first Americans were mistakenly described as Indians by the Genoese explorer Christopher Columbus, who believed he had sailed to the Orient rather than discovered a New World. The native peoples regarded the newcomers from Europe with a combination of astonishment, awe, animosity and downright confusion. They first welcomed, then resisted, the settlers at Jamestown, Plymouth, and Massachusetts Bay. From the late fifteenth century onward, the Indians were gradually dispossessed by the advancing whites. By the nineteenth century, survivors found themselves penned in Western reservations and relegated to a life of mere subsistence, and sometimes less than that.

The slow retreat of the native Americans reflected the extension of white settlement, the advance of Western European ways. In the years after the American Civil War, when the Indians had been forced across the Mississippi, they fought back with the accoutrements of Western Europe. These included the horse (which had come to America from the Old World and which the Indians found running wild in the West) and the rifle, one of the prime devices of Western civilization.

The number of Indians slaughtered and eventually subdued by the European settlers has been variously estimated, and probably did not surpass a million, although no one will ever know for certain. The complexity of their social organization – the degree of Indian culture within the North American subcontinent – in no sense equalled the Indian societies of Mexico and Peru, which were obliterated by the Spanish *conquistadores*. Some Indian tribes in the present-day area of the United States achieved substantial developments, including the Mound Builders of southern Ohio and the Iroquois in what is now New York State. At best, however, these Indian groupings constituted pale reflections of the Aztec and Inca Empires. Most European settlers scorned the North American Indians as savages. Their totemistic religions were another source of aversion, but the key factor in their removal was their lands, which the settlers coveted.

At the outset of discovery and exploration, the exploitation of the original Americans was hardly anticipated by their supplanters. The uncertainties of the moment – including the prospect of sailing west from Europe until they dropped off the edge of the world (still widely believed to be flat) – proved almost overwhelming. In their small and often unseaworthy ships, the discoverers sailed west for weeks, sometimes months on end, in hope of 'gold and glory' and in any case adventure.

The initial discoverers and explorers were surely the Vikings, who came to America by the northern route and settled Iceland in AD 874. A century later, in 986, the Norsemen established a colony in Greenland. Bjarni Herjulfsson probably discovered North America that same year, when blown off course en route to Greenland. Other Norsemen worked their ships to America via Greenland, according to Norse sagas, although no settlers survived, even in Greenland, into the last year of the fifteenth century.

By that time, the Admiral of the Ocean Sea, Christopher Columbus, had begun his voyages of discovery. The explorations of Columbus commenced with the sighting of what was probably Watlings Island in the Bahamas on 12 October, 1492, which prefaced the discoveries of Cuba and Santo Domingo (present-day Haiti and the Dominican Republic). Then came the discoveries resulting from the other voyages, four in all, including navigation of the Honduran coast to central Panama. The last expedition took place in 1504, and Columbus died two years later.

Meanwhile, the work of successors brought knowledge of the New World to the Old. John Cabot, an Italian, migrated to England and went out from Bristol on 2 May, 1497; he made a second voyage the next year, exploring the North American coast as far south as the Delaware River and Chesapeake Bay. Amerigo Vespucci sailed westward between 1499 and 1501 in the service of Spain. Ferdinand Magellan, a Portuguese sailing under the Spanish flag, circumnavigated the world, although it was his fellow seamen, rather than the captain, who returned to Europe by this long westward route. Magellan was killed in 1521 in the Philippines, and the remnants of his expedition returned over a year later – a three-year odyssey that twentieth-century spacemen accomplish within hours. While Magellan was en route, the adventurer Hernando Cortés conquered the Aztecs of Mexico and began sending galleons filled with silver back to Spain. They enriched the Spanish court for generations. Giovanni de Verrazano, in 1523-4, reached what was to become New York Harbor – across the narrows of which, centuries later, a great bridge would bear his name. In the 1530s the French explorer Jacques Cartier explored Canada. Beginning in 1539 the Spaniard Hernando de Soto, governor of Cuba, sailed northward to Florida. In the next few years he reached the Blue Ridge Mountains, crossed the Mississippi south of Memphis, continued west through the Ozarks, and wintered in 1541-2 in eastern Oklahoma. Francisco Vásquez de Coronado left Mexico at the same time and discovered the Grand Canyon, New Mexico, and the Texas Panhandle. He passed north into Kansas before returning to Mexico City.

As befitted a small and not very significant island kingdom, England came late to the business and adventure of exploration. Francis Drake reached the Pacific via the Strait of Magellan only in 1578, whence he seems to have discovered what became known as San Francisco Bay (1579), returning home the next year. Sailing for Holland, the Englishman Henry Hudson voyaged into Delaware Bay and the Hudson River (named for him) in 1609. Poor Hudson did not make it home from a later voyage; his men returned in 1611, but set their captain adrift before setting off on the way back.

Every American schoolchild learns about the consequent settlement of the Eastern seaboard, the colonizing that began

Above right: *The building of a settlement gets under way on the first day at Jamestown.*

Right: *Unloading supplies at an early settlement on the Delaware.*

even before Hudson's epochal discoveries. Sir Walter Raleigh had planted the first colony a generation earlier, after reaching a land he called Virginia – for Elizabeth I, his sovereign. This colony on Roanoke Island survived uncertainly from its foundation in 1585 and disappeared some time after 1587, leaving only two signs: the cryptic letters *CRO* carved in a tree and the word *CROATOAN* cut into a doorpost. Raleigh dispatched an expedition seeking survivors as late as 1602, but none was found. Then came a settlement that lasted – Jamestown, which resulted from the landing of the *Susan Constant* and two other ships sent by a private group of speculators known as the London Company. The first permanent settlers disembarked on 24 May, 1607. Their vicissitudes were many, but the blunders of the first English Americans were redeemed by the decisiveness of Captain John Smith. Virginia became a royal colony, under control of the King, in 1624.

Gold, curiously, proved far less important than two other factors in the settlement of English North America. Contrary to popular belief then and later, even into the twentieth century, it was the desire for land (so difficult to obtain in England) conjoined with the desire for freedom of religion that populated what became the Thirteen Colonies. Both land and freedom of worship drew the Puritans to Plymouth in 1620, despite the long and exhausting passage, which they regarded as a pilgrimage. This episode in the settlement of North America may have received more attention than it deserves, although it did occur before the far more important settlement of the Puritans in Massachusetts Bay, beginning in 1630. At best, the Pilgrim settlers numbered in the dozens; the Puritans of the Bay came over in the thousands. In the first decade, 1630-40, 20,000 settlers emigrated to New England.

Maryland was founded in 1634 by the two Lords Baltimore, George Calvert and his son, Cecil, with a charter from Charles I. The Calverts were Roman Catholics – a persecuted minority in seventeenth-century England – and their colony legislated religious freedom (for professing Christians only, however) as early as 1649.

Rhode Island was created by a group of exiles from Boston between 1636 and 1656: they were banished for protesting the religious intolerance of the Massachusetts Puritans, which was expressed in both religious and civil discrimination. Under the leadership of Roger Williams, Rhode Island's laws became an exemplar of justice and tolerance. The colony was the first to welcome both Jews and Quakers.

New Haven, which became the principal city of Connecticut in colonial times, was organized in 1637, a year after clergyman Thomas Hooker and his followers arrived in Hartford from Newton, Massachusetts. They founded the first church in the territory and declared their freedom from all but divine authority. In 1643 the Connecticut towns of Guilford, Stamford and Milford united with the New Haven colony under a single government.

Another emigration from Boston – the Puritans were not easy to live with – established New Hampshire in 1638 under the leadership of John Wheelwright. Settlers there signed the Exeter Compact, patterned on the Mayflower Compact, on 14 July. That same year, a royal charter named Sir Ferdinand Gorges proprietor and governor of Maine, confirming a grant from the Council for New England. Maine soon sought independence from Massachusetts, but its autonomy came only after organization of a Federal Government following the Revolution – and even then, not until 1820.

Settlement of the so-called middle colonies of New York, New Jersey, Delaware, and Pennsylvania came about the same time as that of Massachusetts. The purchase of Manhattan Island from native Indian chiefs by the Dutch representative Peter Minuit was made in 1626 for 60 guilders (about $20). This capital of New Netherland, named New Amsterdam at its founding under the auspices of the Dutch West India Company, was governed by Dutchmen, most notably Peter Stuyvesant, until New Netherland's conquest by the English in 1664. They renamed the city and colony in honor of the Duke of York, who made a proprietary grant of land between the Hudson and Delaware Rivers that same year to Sir George Cartaret and John, Lord Berkeley. This territory, originally settled by the Dutch, was appropriated from New Netherland and renamed New Jersey in honor of Cartaret, who had served as governor of the Isle of Jersey. Cartaret and Berkeley expected to profit from sales of their rich North American land holdings, and they were not disappointed.

Pennsylvania was founded in 1682 by William Penn, the Quaker son of an English admiral. Its capital was Philadelphia, 'the city of brotherly love,' a name that expressed the ideal underlying the Society of Friends. The Quakers had been persecuted harshly in their native land, and many emigrated to the Penn family's proprietary colony. In 1701, William Penn granted it a charter of liberties that became its constitution until the American Revolution.

Meanwhile, the colony of New Sweden had been established by Swedish and Finnish immigrants at Fort Christina, on the present site of Wilmington, Delaware, in 1638. This territory was seized by the Dutch in 1644 and subsequently passed to England with the other Dutch holdings 20 years later. It was renamed for Thomas West, Lord Delaware, first lord-governor and captain-general of the Virginia colony.

Englishmen founded the Carolinas, North and South, in the 1660s, under a charter issued by Charles II. In 1664, William Drummond was appointed governor of Albemarle, or present-day North Carolina. Subsequently, the Carolina proprietors compiled a list of Concessions and Agreements providing for representative assembly, freedom of conscience, and liberal land grants. In 1732, the Colony of Georgia was formed from part of the South Carolina proprietorship, which had been taken over by the English Crown in 1729. Georgia's proprietor, James Edward Oglethorpe, was a humanitarian who wished to recruit colonists from English debtors' prisons and to provide a haven for persecuted Protestants. Georgia was the last of the 13 original colonies, whose foundation spanned almost a century and a half, from 1607 until 1752, when Georgia passed under royal control. This extension of English rule was often haphazard, occurring through organization of proprietorships, efforts of royal companies, or conquest of Swedish and Dutch colonies. Happenstance seemed to govern, but the underlying and unifying force was the energy of the people who emigrated from England, Scotland, and Wales (known after the Act of Union of 1707 as Great Britain). Migration to the New World came at the same time that British traders went out to India and other lands formerly little known to Western civilization.

Anglo-French rivalry in the New World had a long history, beginning in the sixteenth century with a dispute over the fisheries of Newfoundland. John Cabot had reported the waters 'swarming with fish,' and both countries desired to take and dry these fish for consumption or for sale in Mediterranean ports. Similarly, the rich fur trade of the New World, inspired less by vanity (as it would be later) than by the need for warmth, attracted nationals of both countries. Eventually, the Englishmen's overriding desire for land led to conflict. In addition to such reasons for rivalry as fish, furs and land, there was the immeasurable quality known as glory – sought in part for monarchs, in part for the explorers themselves.

While Englishmen, largely as individuals and small groups, were settling the eastern fringe of what is now the United States, Frenchmen roamed farther to the west. Having journeyed up the great Mississippi, they also ventured up the mouth of the other great North American river, the St Lawrence. Thus the Mississippi and St Lawrence Valleys became nominal provinces of France, threatening to limit English expansion on the North American continent. Before long the French intrigued with the Indians for their assistance. The imperial wars that followed ended in a great British victory and eventual division of the continent itself.

Problems in Europe were the initial occasions of war between England and France. But by 1756 the occasion was rivalry in North America itself – perhaps displaying the true source of the ongoing conflict. In the great European wars for empire, the first major engagement – small frictions were almost constant – came in 1689 and lasted until 1697. William of Orange, soon to become William III of England, joined the League of Augsburg to resist the invasion of the Rhenish Palatinate, a portion of latter-day Germany, by the French monarch Louis XIV. Known in Europe as the War of the League of Augsburg, in America as King William's War, it ended inconclusively with the Treaty of Ryswick in 1697, with everything returned to the status quo ante – conditions as they stood before hostilities. Only a few years later, in 1702, war broke out again and lasted until 1713. In Europe this second of the great wars for empire was known as the War of the Spanish Succession. At issue was whether the French royal family, the Bourbons, would succeed to the throne of Spain, raising the specter of alliance between Spain and France, which enemies of the succession believed would produce an overweening Bourbon power. In America this second war was known for the monarch on the British throne, Queen Anne. Unlike the first of the great wars, the second ended with a major change in European territorial arrangements: the Treaty of Utrecht. In the New World, Newfoundland, Acadia and Hudson Bay were ceded to Britain, a change that anticipated further conflict and eventual passage of all Canada to British control.

Four more wars followed between Britain and France – making six altogether. The second-to-last occurred during the American Revolution. The last began in 1793 and wore on until 1815 and the final defeat of Napoleon. The third and fourth, however, were to prove crucial for stirring the embers of revolt in the Thirteen Colonies of British North America.

The third in the procession of great conflicts originated in a problem that was so trivial one must suspect it was not the problem at all – except to the unfortunate fellow who started it, Captain Robert Jenkins. A British merchant seaman, Captain Jenkins claimed in 1739 that a French naval captain had not only captured his ship but also cut off his ear. To prove his point Jenkins exhibited a severed ear to such members of the British Parliament as desired to see it; the ear was floating in a bottle of formaldehyde. The likelier reason is the invasion of Silesia by Frederick II ('the Great') of Prussia, after the death of Emperor Charles VI of Austria, which touched off a series of Continental wars that came to include France, Spain and Britain. This war, King George's War in America, resulted in the inconclusive Treaty of Aix-la-Chapelle in 1748, which restored everything to the status quo ante – Fort Louisbourg, captured by the British colonists, was returned to France. Aside from this expedition, little had happened in North America beyond the raiding of towns in Maine by French and Indians and, in New York, raids on Saratoga and Albany.

The fourth war in the Anglo-French series turned out very differently from its predecessors. Not only did it begin in the New World, but its resolution saw far-reaching changes there with the conquest of French Canada and Nova Scotia by British and American colonial forces. The cause of this war was also expansionist: the westward movement of Pennsylvanians and Virginians into the Ohio Valley, where they came up against the forces of imperial France. The 21-year-old George Washington was dispatched by the lieutenant governor of Virginia to protest French movements in Pennsylvania and ascertain French intentions. Washington reported in 1754 that the French planned to take the entire Ohio, and only force would remove them. Next year occurred the ill-fated campaign of the British General Edward Braddock. The combined British regulars under Braddock and colonials under Washington were ignominiously defeated by 900 French and Indians at the Battle of the Monongahela. The war spread quickly to Canada. Thence its enmities translated to Europe. In 1759 occurred the cardinal disaster for France in the New World: defeat of the Marquis de Montcalm by the British General James Wolfe on the Plains of Abraham, outside the city of Quebec. Wolfe's expedition had been part of the new strategy of Prime Minister William Pitt, who had come to power in Britain in 1757. Pitt was determined to prosecute this war without the lassitude and leniency that had marked previous Anglo-French conflicts. The dream of empire pervaded all his actions, as he pursued the French in America, in Europe and in the Mediterranean. The resultant Treaty of Paris – ending what was described in America as the French and Indian War, in Europe as the Seven Years' War – took all of Canada from France, except for the minuscule islands of St Pierre and Miquelon. France also yielded all territory east of the Mississippi except the city of New Orleans.

Below: *General Braddock falls from his horse, mortally wounded, as the rout of his army begins at the Battle of the Monongahela, also known as the Battle of the Wilderness.*

The Discovery of America

MAP right: Notable voyages of discovery. The Pope's division of the Western Hemisphere into two parts, one to be developed by the Spanish and the other by the Portuguese, meant that the English and the Dutch came on the scene only after the break with Rome and the wresting of naval mastery from the Spanish.

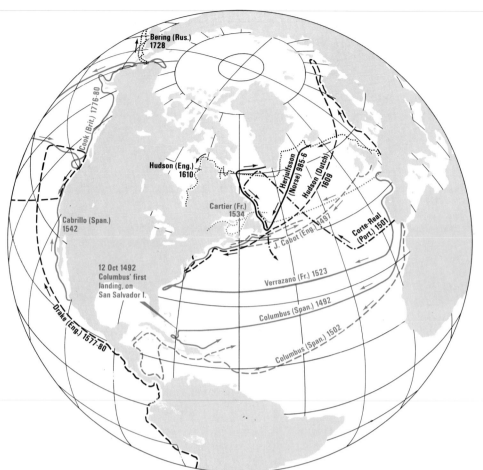

Bering (Rus.) 1728

Cook (Brit.) 1776-80

Hudson (Eng.) 1610

Herjulfsson (Norse) 985-6

Hudson (Dutch) 1609

Cartier (Fr.) 1534

Cabrillo (Span.) 1542

Corte-Real (Port.) 1501

J. Cabot (Eng.) 1497

12 Oct 1492 Columbus' first landing, on San Salvador I.

Verrazano (Fr.) 1523

Columbus (Span.) 1492

Columbus (Span.) 1502

Drake (Eng.) 1577-80

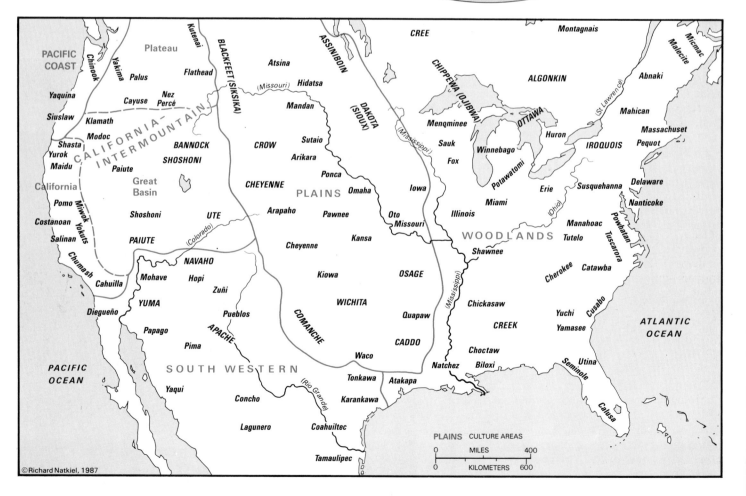

PLAINS CULTURE AREAS

0 MILES 400

0 KILOMETERS 600

©Richard Natkiel, 1987

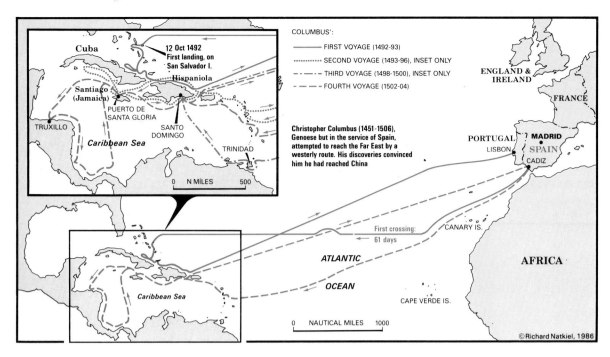

MAP above: The expeditions of Christopher Columbus. Although the popular belief that Columbus discovered America is incorrect, his reputation is deserved, for in his four expeditions he explored 'the Indies' (the Caribbean) and discovered the main islands of what are now called the West Indies (to distinguish them from the original, or eastern Indies, which is what he thought he had discovered). Although Columbus is generally believed to have landed on San Salvador (now known as Watlings Island) recent research suggests another nearby island may in fact have been the first.

MAP left: The distribution of Indian tribes at the time of the first European settlement. The way of life, or culture, of Indians living on the plains, who were nomadic, varied considerably from that of the woods Indians, and the Indians of the arid South-West and of the western mountains likewise were distinctive. In general, however, adjacent tribes inhabiting similar terrain were very alike in customs and language, but this only rarely resulted in alliances between them.

Right: *An idealized, but accurate in detail, print of Columbus landing in the Western Hemisphere, then popularly known as the New World.*

Exploration and First Settlement

MAP below: Exploration of the North American interior. In the 17th century, except in the Far West, seaborne exploration had been superseded by epic overland treks, with the Spanish moving up from the south and the French descending from their footholds in Canada to take the Great Lakes and Middle West territories into their empire.

Die Indianer giessen den Spaniern zuersättigung ihres Geitzes geschmeltzt Goldt in den Mund.   XX.

Right: *A German print which successfully combines suspicion of the Spanish, popular beliefs about the savagery of the Indians, and the conviction that the New World was filled with gold; the inscription reads 'Indians pour molten gold down the throats of the Spanish, to satisfy their avarice.'*

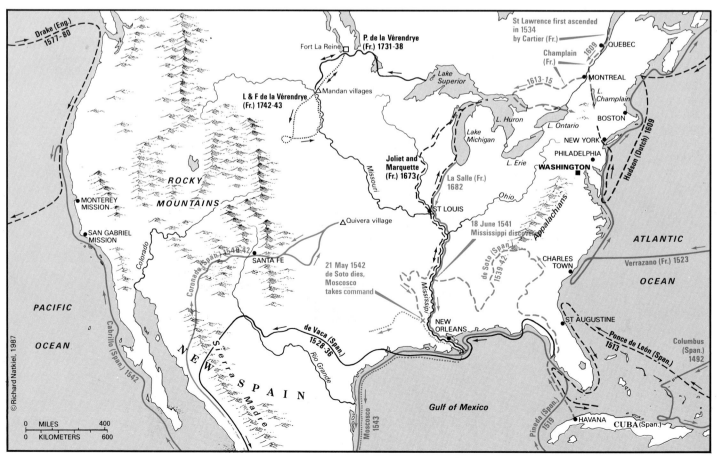

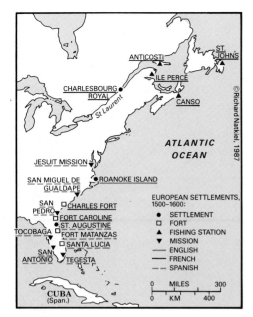

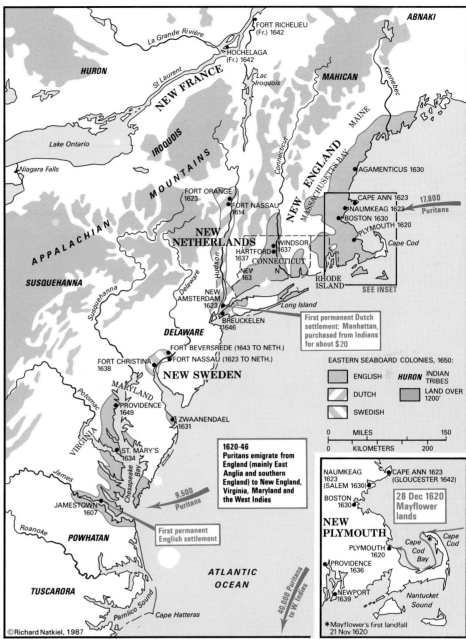

MAP above: The earliest settlements. In the 16th century it was the Spanish who led the way in settling the New World, although most of their energies were devoted to Central and South America. The English settlement at Roanoke was doomed to failure, probably because it was the work of an individual (Walter Raleigh) in a situation when large resources were required for success, such resources being only obtainable from the state, or from private investors joined together in a company.

MAP right: Settlement in the first half of the 17th century. In this period, the idea of starting settlements (that is, colonization as opposed to the search for fabulous riches) took hold of the European imagination. The quest of minorities, like the famed Pilgrim Fathers of 1620 (see inset), for religious freedom, and the over-population of large parts of western Europe, were among the stimulants of this interest.

Right: *One of many prints which perpetuated the belief that Indians were savages. Here the massacre of settlers in Virginia is portrayed; such massacres did occur, but modern historians consider that Indians were more often the victims rather than the instigators of violence.*

The Colonial Era

© Richard Natkiel, 1987

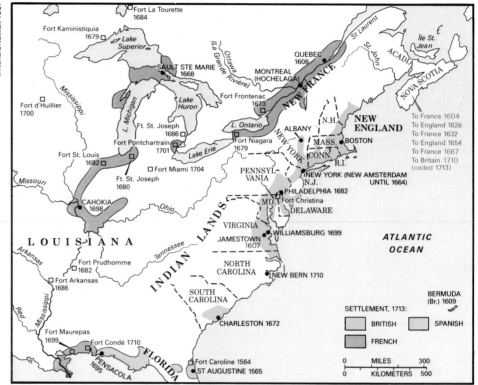

MAP above: The European 'spheres of influence' in North America before the great transformations wrought by the 18th century wars. This division left a permanent mark on the culture of the continent, as the eventual disappearance of the French and Spanish flags did not mean the disappearance of the French and Spanish inhabitants.

MAP above right: The areas of settlement at the beginning of the 18th century. These should be distinguished from the areas of claimed or presumed possession, which were much more extensive and frequently disputed between the French, Spanish and English (not to speak of the Indians, who regarded all the land as their own).

MAP right: The British capture of Louisbourg. After an initial failure, this naval base on Ile Royale, commanding the Gulf of St Lawrence, fell to the British in 1758, thereby paving the way to the assault on Quebec, the nucleus of French power in North America.

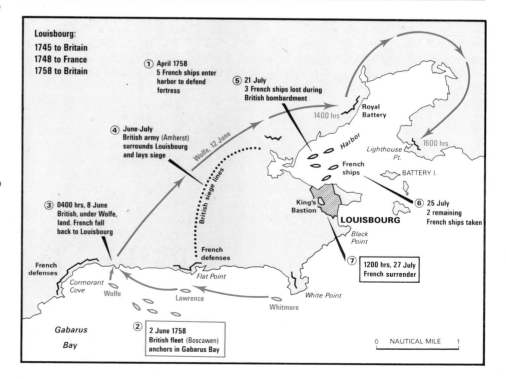

The French and Indian War

MAP below: The course of the French and Indian War, in which the two European powers fought for mastery in Canada and the North-East. The British planned four campaigns, toward and against Niagara, the Lake Erie settlements, Ticonderoga, and Quebec, but they began badly, with the defeat of Braddock's expedition at the crossing of the Monongahela, also known as the Battle of the Wilderness. However, with the French surrender of Quebec the strategic picture changed, and the British emerged as winners.

Left: Lieutenant-Colonel George Washington raises the British flag at Fort Duquesne on the Ohio River in 1758. The capture of this settlement by the French in 1754 had been one of the incidents which caused Anglo-French rivalry in this region to increase.

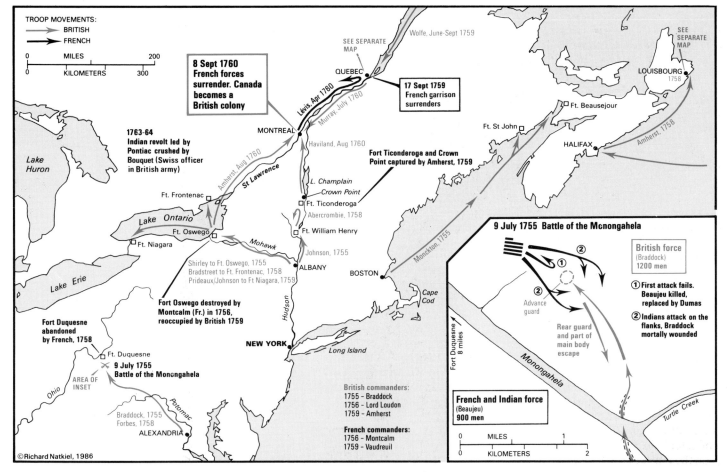

TROOP MOVEMENTS:
BRITISH
FRENCH

MILES 200
KILOMETERS 300

Wolfe, June-Sept 1759

SEE SEPARATE MAP

SEE SEPARATE MAP

QUEBEC

LOUISBOURG 1758

8 Sept 1760 French forces surrender. Canada becomes a British colony

Lévis, Apr 1760

Murray, July 1760

17 Sept 1759 French garrison surrenders

Ft. Beausejour

MONTREAL

Haviland, Aug 1760

Ft. St John

HALIFAX

1763-64 Indian revolt led by Pontiac crushed by Bouquet (Swiss officer in British army)

Amherst, Aug 1760

St Lawrence

Amherst, 1758

Lake Huron

Fort Ticonderoga and Crown Point captured by Amherst, 1759

L. Champlain
Crown Point

Ft. Frontenac

Ft. Ticonderoga
Abercrombie, 1758

Lake Ontario

Ft. Oswego

Mohawk

Ft. William Henry

Ft. Niagara

Johnson, 1755

Monckton, 1755

Shirley to Ft. Oswego, 1755 Bradstreet to Ft. Frontenac, 1758 Prideaux/Johnson to Ft Niagara, 1759

ALBANY

BOSTON

Lake Erie

Fort Oswego destroyed by Montcalm (Fr.) in 1756, reoccupied by British 1759

Hudson

Cape Cod

Fort Duquesne abandoned by French, 1758

NEW YORK

Long Island

Ft. Duquesne

9 July 1755 Battle of the Monongahela

AREA OF INSET

Ohio

Braddock, 1755
Forbes, 1758

Potomac

ALEXANDRIA

British commanders:
1755 – Braddock
1756 – Lord Loudon
1759 – Amherst

French commanders:
1756 – Montcalm
1759 – Vaudreuil

©Richard Natkiel, 1986

9 July 1755 Battle of the Monongahela

British force (Braddock) 1200 men

① First attack fails. Beaujeu killed, replaced by Dumas
② Indians attack on the flanks, Braddock mortally wounded

Advance guard

Rear guard and part of main body escape

Fort Duquesne 8 miles

Monongahela

Turtle Creek

French and Indian force (Beaujeu) 900 men

MILES 1
KILOMETERS 2

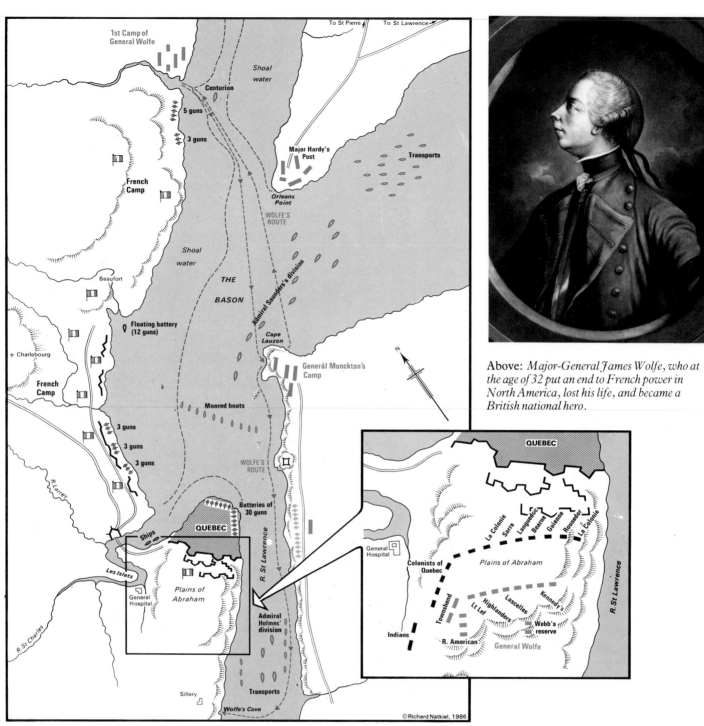

Above: *Major-General James Wolfe, who at the age of 32 put an end to French power in North America, lost his life, and became a British national hero.*

©Richard Natkiel, 1986

MAP above: The capture of Quebec in 1759. This is regarded as one of the classic battles of modern history, deserving its reputation because of its result, which was British predominance in North America, and because of its tactics, which were bold. The British General Wolfe, confronted with an apparently impregnable defense, situated on high ground overlooking the river, had the advantage of command over the water, and used it to land troops stealthily at night. These scaled the cliffs, took the French in the rear, and won the Battle of the Plains of Abraham.

Public imagination was gripped by the circumstance that the rival commanders, Wolfe and Montcalm, were both mortally wounded. One interesting sidelight was that the officer who charted the course for the British fleet to make the tricky passage up the St Lawrence to Quebec was the future Captain James Cook who was to make many pioneering explorations in the Pacific and Australasian waters.

The Eve of the Revolution

MAP below: The division of North America after the Seven Years' War. Britain now predominates, with the British crown possessing most of the North-East, and the British Hudson's Bay Company administering the far northern territories. Spain still holds the greater part of the South, a region known as Louisiana, but because of her weakness at home is vulnerable. The West is still in the undisturbed possession of the Indians, while in faraway Alaska a few Russians have moved in from Siberia.

MAP below right: The pattern of settlement after the Seven Years' War. Very evident is the role of rivers, and especially of the St Lawrence and Mississippi, as paths for colonization.

Right: *British ships bombarding French positions at Quebec. The strength of the French position, high above the assaulting forces, is evident.*

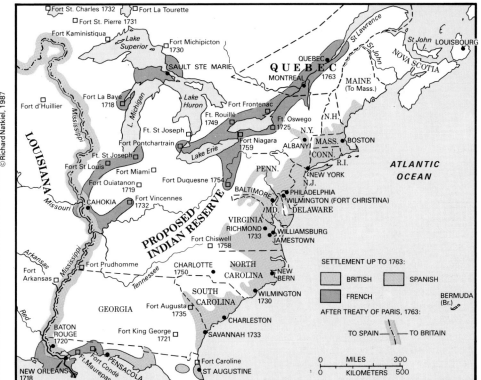

Founding a Nation

President Jackson celebrates his re-election in 1832 with a gathering at the White House.

After 1763, the newly acquired territory in North America became a heavy financial burden on the British Government. The cost of policing vast areas from Canada to Florida and west to the Mississippi was added to the prohibitive £137-million war debt incurred in the previous seven years. Not unnaturally, the British Government looked to its North American colonies for revenue to help defray these costs. During the mid-1760s, the British Parliament enacted a series of measures designed to tighten colonial administration and to reverse a half-century of what Edmund Burke had called 'salutary neglect' of its colonies.

The Sugar Act of 1764 added duties to a number of products imported into the colonies and closer supervision of shipping made colonial evasion of such duties more difficult. The following year brought the Stamp Act, the first direct tax on America ever levied by Parliament. It provoked such antagonism and protest in the colonies that it was repealed in 1766. In 1767, under the leadership of Charles Townshend, Chancellor of the Exchequer, the British Government renewed its efforts to raise revenue through customs duties. At the same time, the empire's bureaucracy was strengthened, and British troops in North America were moved from scattered frontier posts into the coastal ports. The angry colonists agreed not to import British goods until the duties were withdrawn.

After an armed clash between colonists and British troops in Boston (1770), Britain eventually repealed all the Townshend duties except that on tea, which remained a source of resentment. Committees of correspondence were formed to consolidate the colonies vis-à-vis the Mother Country. On 16 December 1773, the colonists dumped £10,000 worth of tea into Boston Harbor, precipitating a series of coercive acts by the British Government that included closing the port of Boston. On 19 April 1775, an armed clash between colonists and British troops at Lexington and Concord inaugurated the eight-year Revolutionary War between Britain and its North American colonies. Distance and misunderstanding had combined with nascent American patriotism to produce open rebellion.

On the British side, the government was assailed by critics led by Pitt the Elder and other Britons who found the pretensions of the friends of George III intolerable. Their constant strictures against a war that they saw as fratricidal forced the British Government into strategies and tactics that were too weak and too limited to prevail. On the American side, there was little unity of either sentiment or action. In fact, Americans were so divided in their loyalties that John Adams made the well-known statement that everything was in thirds – a third of the country was ardent for the war, another third favored the British, and the remainder was indifferent. Adams's opinion has reverberated over the years, impossible either to prove or disprove. It is enough to say that not all Americans, by any means, fought the British.

Lexington and Concord, the calculated show of power whereby British troops marched out of Boston to capture supplies stored by the Revolutionists, opened the epochal struggle on 19 April 1775. The Battle of Bunker Hill (17 June) soon followed. Two weeks later General George Washington arrived in Cambridge, Massachusetts, to take formal command of 14,500 men, a force sufficiently large to necessitate reinforcement of the British Army from the faraway British Isles.

Muddle and lack of vision had produced the war, and British troops failed to cover themselves with glory. Overall strategy was set in London and tactics by commanders in the field, with predictable results. Many British soldiers were reluctant to fight people so like themselves – common people inspired by dislike for monarchy and the desire for liberty. What reflective observers beheld in America was a society devoted to individual freedom. There, men and women who worked hard might get ahead by owning and tilling their land, operating small businesses in villages and towns, shipbuilding and trading with Europe, the Mediterranean, and other areas. British soldiers were adventurers who liked the American spirit, or conscripts who found themselves inspired by it. When the government in London imported professional soldiers, mercenaries, from the German province of Hesse, such soldiers were no more enthusiastic for fighting; many of them deserted. In any event, the constant dispatch of troops did not seem to bring results. Apart from garrisoning the major towns and cities – Boston, New York, Philadelphia, Charleston – the British made few marches into the interior: the expanses of the Thirteen Colonies were large enough to swallow their armies. And always the Americans, whatever their ragamuffin uniforms, short-term enlistments and frequent defeats, proved elusive. Invasion of one self-proclaimed state might provoke the departure of volunteers from another state, who preferred to fight for their home soil, but it raised up an equal number of locals who anticipated the sacking of their own houses and barns. It was not guerrilla warfare as we know it today, but it was enough like it to bewilder British regulars accustomed to setpiece battles waged in formation.

Good fortune had undoubtedly played a large part in the rapid accumulation of the first British Empire. With the appearance of William Pitt the Elder (his son William was also prime minister for most of the period 1783-1806), another factor was added to the foundation of British imperial greatness. Pitt knew what he was doing: he refused to allow events to go out of control, military campaigns to wallow in indecision, or decisions to be revoked by bursts of remorse. In the mind of this statesman, who was created Earl of Chatham for his role in the Seven Years' War, a vision of empire dominated the affairs of state. Pitt sensed the energies of Englishmen everywhere, not merely in Britain. He felt that the world belonged to them, and his duty as the King's first minister was to extend the sway of the imperial sceptre.

The vision of Pitt triumphed in 1763, but within a few short years the feeble imagination of his successors produced a vacuum rather than a strategy, resorts to law rather than to reason, stupidity instead of overarching ideas. Petty bureaucrats in London, and autocratic ambitions on the part of Britain's monarch, George III, threw empire to the winds. It was then that Americans themselves, no longer colonists, became the new imperialists, sensing a grand opportunity to extend their sway across a largely uninhabited continent. In the nineteenth and early twentieth centuries they succumbed to a vision of empire as heady as that of Pitt himself. They aspired not merely to 'A More Perfect Union embracing the entire North American Continent' (as Senator Daniel S Dickinson described in 1848) but to something far beyond that. An Irish American of the 1840s named John L O'Sullivan – of the company of Irish dreamers – believed that the United States should by no means confine its territorial ambitions to the continent of North America. 'Its floor shall be a hemisphere,' he declaimed, 'its roof the firmament of the star-studded heavens, and its congregation an Union of many Republics, comprising hundreds of happy millions....' But this dream, of course, perhaps fortunately, was not to be.

The military balance sheet alternated between the black ink of victory and the red of defeat for several years after 1775. The next year the British Army evacuated Boston. Vastly encouraged, the colonists, 'in Congress assembled,' voted their independence. The document was signed in Philadelphia on 4 July, thenceforth the birthday of the new American Republic. The achievement of independence, however, required more than a piece of paper. The British Government took New York City later that year and held it until the end of the Revolution. The year 1776, when independence was announced, ended with a mixture of revolutionary defeat and victory. Some 2400 of General Washington's ragtag troops retreated into Pennsylvania, then attacked and seized the Hessian garrison at Trenton after crossing the ice-choked Delaware.

The next year, 1777, was in a real sense decisive, though this did not become apparent until later. In 1777, American representatives in Paris made a concerted effort to bring France into what would become the fifth great Anglo-French war for empire. This time the objective was to overcome British opposition to the American Revolution. In this same year, the British Government assented to a proposal from the inept General John Burgoyne for a three-pronged attack to isolate New England. 'Gentleman Johnny,' as he was known, suggested that a main army should push southward down Lake Champlain and the upper Hudson. An auxiliary force was to operate from Oswego through the Mohawk Valley. A strong force under Howe, now commanding in New York, was to move up the Hudson to join the descending forces. Mean-while, Howe undertook to take Philadelphia before returning to New York to move troops up the Hudson.

Some responsibility for the failure of Burgoyne's ill-conceived plan lay with Howe, who moved too slowly against Philadelphia. It was not occupied until 26 September, too late in the year for facile movement of forces back to New York and then up the Hudson. Thus Howe failed to extricate Burgoyne's army from what turned out to be serious trouble with the Americans. Part of the blame for overall failure lay with the bungled British expedition coming down from Oswego. Most of the responsibility, however, lay with Burgoyne, originator of the plan, who seems to have had no clear idea of the enormous problems of a campaign through the American wilderness. His model, apparently, was the conduct of warfare in the settled areas of Europe, with all the conveniences that implied. The process of moving a large body of troops through the trackless American forests was something very different from marching along the highways of the European continent. Burgoyne's 7200 troops, British and German, Canadian and Indian, left Canada with a huge baggage train, including 138 pieces of artillery. Perhaps never had the forest seen such a panoply of color, as the uniformed men moved out. Yet the color could be no advantage in the wilderness – it merely identified targets – and the baggage was to prove only a

Below: *The death of Richard Montgomery, the Irish general of the colonists' Continental Army, who captured Montreal but was defeated and killed in 1776 while attempting to capture the city of Quebec.*

burden, not an asset. As summer lengthened into fall, the Germans began to desert, and American troops came into constant contact with the British, raiding and shooting, turning suspicion into the certainty that Burgoyne had been surrounded by a huge net of elusive pursuers. Ill supplied, the Americans resorted to ingenuity, removing lead glazing bars from windows and melting them into bullets. The heavy British artillery was useless in the wilderness. The British General was caught in early October in the little New York town of Saratoga. Reduced to 5700 men, surrounded by three times that number, he surrendered on 17 October. The convention signed by Burgoyne and the American General Horatio Gates provided that the British would be marched to Boston and shipped back to England, under a pledge not to serve again during the American War. It was a sorry end to a sorry plan.

The Battle of Saratoga was one of the two decisive engagements of the Revolutionary War, in that it galvanized the French Government into action for the American cause. When word reached the French court at Versailles, the foreign minister of France, the Comte de Vergennes, sought an alliance with Spain against the British. He called upon the court's Bourbon relatives to support the Americans – not to encourage the cause of revolution, but purely in the interest of humbling the British, who had foisted a harsh treaty upon France and Spain after the Seven Years' War. The Spanish delayed doing anything about alliance until June of 1779, for they had their own concern to address. This was Spain's desire to take back the Rock of Gibraltar, lost to Britain in 1713 after Queen Anne's War. The Spanish negotiated this issue for months with the British court, failed to obtain satisfaction, and finally entered the war against Britain. (They failed in war, as they had in peace, to get Gibraltar.) Meanwhile, the French Government decided that it could not wait for Spanish diplomacy: the principal American negotiator in Paris, Benjamin Franklin, received word that the court would enter into an agreement. The Franco-American Treaty of Alliance was signed on 6 February 1778. It meant recognition of the independence of the United States of America by France, although the extent of American territory was left undefined. It also meant embroilment of the British in Europe, as well as America, with all the attendant diversion of resources. France's entry into war resulted in the eventual participation of Spain; Prussia came in against France's weak ally Austria. Thus the outbreak of another European war saw Britain virtually alone against the major nations.

Confused British tactics in America and peace feelers from the Mother Country marked the year 1778. The agony at Valley Forge ended when the British evacuated Philadelphia and marched back to New York. The inconclusive Battle of Monmouth, New Jersey, on 28 June was followed by a British movement north, with Washington in close pursuit. In the West, George Rogers Clark captured the British garrison at Kaskaskia, on the Mississippi River, on 4 July. A Franco-American attack on Newport, Rhode Island, failed in August, and Savannah fell to the British on 29 December.

Next year, on 21 June, Spain entered the war. Captain John Paul Jones raided into British waters from France, and a Franco-American force failed to retake Savannah. In 1780 the Americans watched the fall of Charleston to nearly 14,000

Left: General George Washington acknowledges the salute of his victorious troops after the Battle of Trenton. The Americans took 900 prisoners for only eight casualties.

troops led by General George Clinton; wherever the British acted with such large forces, they took what they wanted. Charleston constituted the largest American defeat of the war, with 5400 men captured. Afterward Clinton departed for New York, leaving General Lord Cornwallis with 8000 men. Cornwallis spent the winter of 1780-81 in South Carolina, perhaps hoping – vainly, as it turned out – for some kind of victory in the year ahead.

The decisive battle of the Revolution was fought in 1781, although the war would wear on for two more years. The rebellious Americans appeared to give little attention to defeat or victory, and the war's length only encouraged them to make their independence more permanent by drawing up a Constitution. Known as the Articles of Confederation, and formulated in 1777, it was not ratified by the states until 1 March 1781. Shortly thereafter, the war in the Carolinas resumed, as Cornwallis moved into North Carolina, then proceeded to Wilmington, Delaware, where he hoped to receive reinforcements by sea. His belief that Virginia was a seedbed for rebellion in the Carolinas finally brought Cornwallis into the Old Dominion. There, at Yorktown, his hopes of reinforcement by sea finally foundered on the dilatoriness of British Admiral George Rodney. Rodney had just captured the rich Caribbean island of St Eustatius, from which the Dutch had been supplying the Americans, and he was in no hurry to leave his new wealth behind. Cornwallis's forces looked to sea only to sight the ships of French Admiral Comte de Grasse. The French sent ships up Chesapeake Bay to bring troops under Washington and the French General de Rochambeau to Williamsburg. The union of these forces (9000 and 7800 strong, respectively) made Cornwallis's position indefensible, and the British general surrendered on 19 October 1781. When Clinton finally arrived off Chesapeake Bay on 24 October with 7000 reinforcements, he had to pull back to New York.

The fall of the intransigent British ministry under Lord North early in 1782 forecast the war's end. Formal peace negotiations opened on 27 September 1782, preliminary articles were signed in Paris on 30 November, and a definitive treaty was signed the next year (3 September 1783). The French court displayed momentary displeasure at negotiation and signature of the preliminary articles of an Anglo-American peace treaty, for one of the terms of the Treaty of Alliance of 1778 was a proviso that neither France nor America would negotiate a separate peace. Franklin admitted slight impropriety. The French foreign minister Vergennes was not too disappointed, for meanwhile he had signed – without consulting the Americans – a treaty with Spain. The Spanish were finding it impossible to retake Gibraltar, but refused to give up, and Vergennes had no desire to continue the war once he had humiliated the hated British. Thus the lack of propriety may have pleased him more than he admitted, as it allowed him to take France out of the war by giving him a lever against the stubborn Spanish.

Peace, then, was convenient for everyone in 1782-3: for the Americans, who obtained thereby a British acknowledgement of their independence; for the French; even for the Spanish, who were saved from their embarrassment over Gibraltar. The British, too, found peace attractive, as many Britons, including the aging Pitt, had opposed both prosecution of the war and George III's effort to control Parliament through the group known as 'the king's friends.' Defeat in 1783 meant the end of this coterie and strengthening of Parliament's authority as against the king, renewing the movement toward Parliamentary dominance that had begun many years before.

Above: *The American frigate* Constitution *defeats the British* Guerrière *in one of several successful naval actions fought by the young US Navy during the War of 1812.*

No serious account of the American Revolution can fail to consider the underlying changes that had supported military action by the colonials against the Mother Country. The independence achieved thereby was not only social and political, but intellectual as well. Full economic independence was still in the future, when American trade would become progressively more diversified and less reliant upon Britain.

Economically, the new United States of America had changed dramatically from the primitive ways of preceding decades. The principal problem of British rule in the eighteenth century, as the colonies matured, was the perennially unfavorable balance of trade – the excess of colonial imports over exports, which rose to $3.5 million annually just before the Revolution. All the colonies except the Carolinas had suffered unfavorable balances. The total from 1700 until the outbreak of revolution was about $100 million. During the war, this 'extraction' of economic goods from the colonies ended, and the former colonials asserted their independence by looking elsewhere for trade. The Revolution marked the beginning of worldwide American trade, and it was not an accident – indeed, it was a plan by the financier of the Revolution, Robert Morris – that the first American trading vessel, the *Empress of China*, went out to Canton in 1784.

Meanwhile, it had become expedient to reorganize American industry: lumbering, shipbuilding, naval stores (tar, pitch, turpentine, potash), fishing, whaling, workshop crafts,

weaving, flourmilling, ironmaking. British capital had financed industry in the colonies, while colonial capital had preferred such conservative investments as real estate or British government securities. Corporate organization had developed very slowly, at first in the form of joint stock companies wherein each member was liable for obligations of the whole enterprise. Commercial corporations made their appearance with a Connecticut trading corporation in 1723, and just before the Revolution other such limited corporations appeared. In the postwar 1780s, such corporations sprang up everywhere. The new nation was rebuilding its economy from the near-chaos of colonial times.

As economics supported the Revolution, so did learning in all its forms. As the colonies grew in the eighteenth century, people lived in closer proximity to one another and had more leisure time from which to benefit. Astronomy was one of the first colonial interests, as was natural history – the investigation of plants, insects, and animals. The American Philosophical Society appeared in the mid-eighteenth century, and Benjamin Franklin reorganized it on the eve of the Revolution in 1769. Meanwhile, colonials made life easier for themselves with inventions, including the long rifle, the flatboat, and the Conestoga wagon. John Stevens patented the multitubular boiler in 1783, the year in which the Revolution ended, and Franklin invented bifocal spectacles. In 1791 John Fitch patented the steamboat – perhaps the single most important device in American exploration of the inland waters, notably the Mississippi, the Ohio and the Missouri.

The eighteenth century also saw many developments in medicine. Dr Zabdiel Boylston began inoculation for smallpox in 1721, a year before a British physician in London inoculated the royal children. American hospitals came into being by mid-century, and medical schools just before the Revolution. William Brown published the first American pharmocopoeia in 1778.

In religion – which had played such a large part in the foundation of the American colonies – Virginia had established the Church of England in 1609. The Pilgrims introduced Congregationalism in 1620, and the Puritans introduced a similar mode of worship a decade later. New Amsterdam witnessed the evolution of a Calvinist group, the Dutch Reformed Church. Roman Catholics appeared in Maryland in 1633; Baptists in Rhode Island in 1639. Lutherans arrived in 1640, Jews in 1654, Quakers in 1656, Mennonites in 1683, and Presbyterians in 1706. Methodists, a major denomination, did not come to the New World from England until 1766; their sect was comparatively late in developing. The post-Revolutionary government ruled that these many groups, some of them competing for adherents, should not have government support. It saw an undesirable precedent in the case of Virginia's Anglicans, who had depended upon taxes, as they did in the Mother Country.

Education was on the increase throughout colonial times. Elementary schools existed from the beginning, and higher education became available with the founding of Harvard College, a Congregational institution, in 1636. Free public schools of the kind familiar to contemporary Americans did not develop until the nineteenth century.

Well before the Revolution, a native literature was emerging, beginning with the *Bay Psalm Book* (1640), which went through 27 editions before the mid-eighteenth century. Books were first written for religious purposes, but before long they were treating of colonial geography, Indians, and other native phenomena. Travel description appeared, to be followed by historical writing. Franklin's *Autobiography*, a prerevolutionary classic, was first published in full form in 1867, almost a century after its completion. Newspapers and periodicals arose in the colonies in the half-century before the Revolution and contributed mightily to dissatisfaction with British rule.

By 1776 fine arts and architecture testified to American rather than European abilities and tastes. A nascent American interest in music, including the manufacture of instruments, also anticipated the imminent coming of age of the new nation.

The Revolution was no simple political movement, but a combination and focusing of trends that began decades earlier and gathered momentum that ultimately swept the New World into a cultural constellation distinct from that of the Old.

The two decades from 1783 to 1803 proved to be full of surprising evidence of American expansion. The fringe of colonies-turned-states that had looked mainly to the Atlantic generated a phalanx of new states, as pioneers passed over the initial barrier to westward settlement, the Appalachians. They moved into the attractive territory that lay between those mountains and the great Mississippi River (then the Far West). Independence from Britain gave the United States the same territory that Britain had extracted from France in 1763, namely, everything south of Canada and along the boundary of the Great Lakes out to the major inland river itself. Even before the Revolution, settlers were passing into what became Kentucky and Tennessee. During and after the Revolution they moved across the mountains in tens of thousands. Most went down the Ohio in flatboats to people the later states of Ohio, Indiana, and

Illinois, as settlers moved north from their early river locations. The turn of the new century saw rapid moves toward statehood for the territories north of the Ohio. Known initially as the Northwest, they became the Old Northwest when the Pacific Coast below Canada became the farthest frontier. The Northwest Ordnance of 1787, passed by the Congress of the Articles of Confederation in the very year that the Constitutional Convention assembled in Philadelphia, established procedures by which new states might be added to the Union. Territorial government could now evolve systematically into statehood. Congress also established an arrangement by which the new territory was to be surveyed into square miles, each containing 640 acres or 16 40-acre parcels. This measurement was, of course, far different from that for land south of the Ohio, where landmarks and crude distinctions prevailed. The settlement of the trans-Appalachian areas up to the Mississippi proved inexorable, although there were some confusions. For example, the transitional state of 'Franklin' was established by settlers who later saw it divided into Kentucky and Tennessee. At first, too, there were claims by citizens of the original Thirteen States that their borders ran westward to the setting sun, or at least as far as the Mississippi River. This was curtailed by the Northwest Ordnance's requirement that all the original states must surrender their claims to western territory for the great good of the Union.

The Indian wars continued. In 1791 a mixed force of American regulars and militia led by General Arthur St Clair was defeated by Indians from the area between the Maumee and Wabash Rivers. St Clair was succeeded by General Anthony Wayne, who conquered the Indians at Fallen Timbers, near present-day Toledo, Ohio (20 August 1794) and secured the Northwest Territory's frontier. On 3 August 1795 12 Indian tribes signed the Treaty of Greenville on the southern border of what is now Ohio and Indiana, setting a boundary in the Northwest Territory between Indian lands and those available to white settlers.

Twenty years after the definitive peace establishing the new nation came the first of two enormous additions to American territory, the Louisiana Purchase. The purchase, of course, was a result of peaceful negotiation, although it succeeded because of the imminence of European war. The second great addition to the territory of the United States of America was to come more than 40 years later, in 1848, after the Mexican War. The acquisitions of 1803 and 1848 virtually tripled the size of the American Republic.

The Louisiana Purchase was complex from the standpoint of negotiations, but culminated at last in a treaty with the France of Napoleon Bonaparte. Its origins were self-evident. The rapid movement of American settlers over the Appalachians, their travels down the Ohio, the growing number of flatboats converging on New Orleans, were outward signs of the innate mobility of hardy American pioneers. American scholars have argued over why this huge territory was yielded to the government of the United States. No one can be certain of the underlying motives and forces, but the Franco-American diplomatic record itself is clear, the fact of purchase beyond dispute. We will never know what the future of continental expansion might have held for European powers: both the Spanish (who held Louisiana from 1763 until 1800) and the French (who obtained it from the Spanish but sold it almost immediately to the eager Americans).

Early in the nineteenth century, a two-fold change in international relations became evident to Thomas Jefferson, the third President of the United States. Jefferson had succeeded

Washington (1789-97) and John Adams (1797-1801). The wars of the French Revolution, begun in 1793, had ended awkwardly in 1801 and were bound to reopen soon. And a French effort to quell a rebellion among the Haitian people – with heavy loss of life on both sides – was failing. The island of Haiti (which includes present-day Haiti and the Dominican Republic) had been coveted as a pearl in the diadem of France. It was to produce sugar for Europe, and Haitian workers, according to the scheme, would be fed by the grain of Louisiana. This territory had been nominally owned by Spain (which had claimed all of the New World except Brazil, since 1493) when the French explorer De la Salle arrived at the mouth of the Mississippi River in 1682. La Salle staked a claim to the region in the name of his King, Louis XIV, for whom he named the territory that would eventually comprise 10 states. Nothing came of the Haitian dream except a costly rebellion soon after France had passed almost completely under Napoleon's control. President Jefferson saw at that time an opportunity to purchase the city of New Orleans, from which American settlers along the Mississippi might ship their produce, mainly agricultural, either to Eastern Seaboard ports or to Europe.

The Jefferson Administration sent James Monroe to Paris early in 1803 to assist the resident American minister, Robert R Livingston, in buying New Orleans from Napoleon. To the surprise of both emissaries, they were offered the entire expanse of Louisiana. This expanse was bounded on the east by the river, on the west by a border whose extent was not clearly defined, but which eventually adjoined Spanish territory in Mexico, New Mexico, and California. (The Louisiana Territory had been formally ceded to France by Spain in the 1 October 1800 treaty of Ildefonso.) Knowing a bargain when they saw one, the envoys bought all of the Louisiana Territory for about $15 million – $11,250,000 plus debts owed by France to United States citizens, which the US Government assumed.

Monroe and Livingston acted without authorization, and Jefferson at first thought he must go not merely to Congress for ratification of the treaty, but to the people for an amendment to the Constitution. (The Constitution made no provision for the addition of territory.) But as he thought over the possibilities of the purchase, he realized that the new territory could be divided into states that would support his own political party rather than that of the Federalists. He also acted from the obvious advantage to his country of such a purchase. For some months the president wavered in apparent indecision, but in the end he did nothing to amend the Constitution and seized the moment for what it was.

The century between 1792 and 1889 was one of continuous expansion. New states formed from the Northwest Territory included: Ohio, 1803; Indiana, 1816; Illinois, 1818; Michigan, 1837; Wisconsin, 1848; Minnesota, 1858. South of the Ohio were four trans-Appalachian admissions: Kentucky, 1792; Tennessee, 1796; Mississippi, 1817; Alabama, 1819. And from the huge Louisiana Purchase came: Louisiana, 1812; Missouri, 1821; Arkansas, 1836; Iowa, 1846; Kansas, 1861; Nebraska, 1867; Colorado, 1876; North Dakota, 1889; South Dakota, 1889.

Even before the Louisiana Purchase, President Jefferson looked toward US expansion. In his message to Congress of January 1803, he requested an appropriation for an exploratory expedition to cultivate relations with the Indians and extend the nation's internal commerce. Meriwether Lewis and William Clark, the brother of George Rogers Clark, were chosen to lead the expedition. The party descended the Ohio beginning 31 August 1804 and on 14 May began to ascend the Missouri. It spent the winter of 1804-05 near present-day Bismarck, North Dakota, and in the spring of 1805 crossed the Rockies, coming within sight of the Pacific on 7 November of that year. Returning to St Louis on 23 September 1806, it proved the feasibility of an overland route to the Far West. All the while Lieutenant Zebulon M Pike was exploring the sources of the Mississippi; he visited Colorado and New Mexico, sighting Pike's Peak, Colorado, in the course of his journeys.

During the heady years after the Louisiana Purchase, the country was looking both westward, to the Far West, and eastward to Europe. The latter interest – which involved a large commerce with Europe and the Mediterranean – led to the War of 1812, which was in a sense a second war for American independence.

A combination of commerce and land hunger drove the country to war, and the comparative force of each factor has never been determined. As in the case of the Louisiana Purchase, the diplomatic process is more measurable than intangible aspects like the pressure from Western settlers in 1803 or the desire for more land in 1812. American shipping volume was large, second only to British, and after resumption of the European war in 1803 shippers demanded that 'free ships make free goods.' This meant that neutral American ships were or should be free to trade anywhere, so long as their cargoes were not declared contraband by any belligerents. British desire to keep contraband (defined very broadly) out of the hands of French rivals, and to regulate and profit from neutral (mainly American) trade with all of Europe, led to a series of American countermeasures. These included an embargo (1807-09) and eventually led to war with Britain. Historians later observed that the West and the South voted for war because of the availability of land and the belief that the British were stirring up the frontier Indians; however, the New England states, for whose commercial interests the war was presumably fought, were against it. The major maritime and commercial states voted for peace in the belief that war could only disrupt trade even further.

The choices of war and peace were confused by the fact that British (and French) rules against neutral ships were not often observed: New England merchants could make money whatever the rules. The War Hawks, men like the young Henry Clay of Kentucky and John C Calhoun of South Carolina, may have voted out of anti-British sentiment – a desire to hurt Britain (and aggrandize the US) by seizing Canada. By most historical measures of the war's perplexing causes, the War Hawks drove President James Madison, Jefferson's successor, into the War of 1812.

As the nation moved uncertainly into war, it fought without plan, then concluded a peace just before the British defeated Napoleon decisively at Waterloo in 1815, with Russian and Prussian help. At the war's outset, an American attack against Upper Canada by General William Hull from Detroit failed, and Hull ended by losing Detroit. A small expedition into Canada from Niagara in New York State also failed. Naval successes by the splendid frigates constructed earlier for use against the Barbary pirates could hardly hide the miserable showing of American arms during the first year. Disaffection in New England was such that talk of secession flourished there. Next year, 1813, the 28-year-old Captain Oliver H Perry won control of the Great Lakes in the Battle of Lake Erie (10 September) enabling General William H Harrison to retake

Detroit. In 1814 the American naval officer Captain Thomas Macdonough seized control of Lake Champlain in the battle of that name on 11 September, preventing an invasion by a British force. Another British command under General Robert Ross, only 4000 men but veterans of the war in Europe, marched on Washington and Baltimore, burning the Executive Mansion and the Capitol on 24-25 August. They attacked Baltimore unsuccessfully on 12-14 September during which battle a British naval bombardment inspired Francis Scott Key to write 'The Star Spangled Banner,' set to the tune of an old English drinking song. Key had watched anxiously all night to see if the flag still flew over the besieged harbor citadel, Fort McHenry; when he looked out 'by dawn's early light,' he saw the beloved flag.

After conclusion of the Peace of Christmas Eve, 1814, signed at Ghent in latter-day Belgium, General Andrew Jackson's force of 5700 troops defeated General Sir Edward Pakenham's force of 8000 veterans just outside New Orleans. The intrepid Jackson deployed his sharpshooters behind breastworks and cut down the British, who attacked in close ranks, with a withering rifle and artillery fire, defeating them in half an hour on 8 January 1815. Neither side, of course, had received news that the war was already over. Because of Jackson's singular victory, Americans ever after liked to believe that they had won what was almost a disastrous war. Their diplomats at Ghent, led by the sensible if prickly John Quincy Adams, managed to extricate them from the European war just before the European nations finally defeated Napoleon. The peace settlement of 1814 restored the *status quo ante bellum*.

An aftermath of the Anglo-American peace was conclusion of the Rush-Bagot Agreement on 28-9 April 1817. Arranged by the British minister in the United States, Charles Bagot, and Acting Secretary of State Richard Rush, it provided for mutual disarmament on the Great Lakes.

More important in its sequel was the clash of American and British policy toward the newly independent nations of Latin America. When a revolution broke out in Spain in 1808, most Spanish colonies in the New World declared their independence of the subsequent regime, which was crudely imposed by Napoleon. When the Bourbons were restored in Spain after Napoleon's defeat, they were unable to resume control of the Latin American provinces. One after another, the New World colonies declared their independence – except for Cuba, which the Spanish described for several generations thereafter as the Ever Faithful Isle. (Cuba's successful revolution came in 1895-8.) European monarchies, including the British Government, hesitated to recognize the new Latin American nations. So did the government of the United States,

Above: *The best-remembered British success of the War of 1812, the burning of Washington. This picture shows the gutted Library of Congress.*

because of the need to obtain a territorial settlement with post-1815 Spain.

Before and after the War of 1812, the Americans had been taking portions of what were known as the Floridas, East and West. The latter was a strip of territory below the 31st parallel, approximately between present-day Florida and Louisiana. President James Monroe's administration looked benignly upon an audacious excursion by General Jackson into what was clearly Spanish territory, and allowed Secretary of State J Q Adams to press the Spanish to give up the Floridas. This they did on 22 February 1819, in the Adams-Onis Transcontinental Treaty, signed with the Spanish minister in Washington, Juan de Onis. Its alternative name refers to the step-like border that the United States obtained in the Far West, defining the line between the Louisiana Purchase and Spain's possessions of New Mexico and California. The settlement extinguished Spanish claims above the 42nd parallel, meaning that the Oregon Territory – present-day Oregon, Washington, and British Columbia – would be disputed only between the United States and Britain.

Having arranged these concessions from Spain, the United States quickly recognized the new Latin American nations. When European nations intimated that they might support a reassertion of Spanish sovereignty in the New World, President Monroe announced the doctrine that would become known by his name after the American Civil War. In his annual message to Congress (December 1823) President Monroe proposed three points: Europe was to stay out of America, America would stay out of Europe, and the American continents were closed to colonization. (The last proviso looked to Russian encroachments on the Pacific Coast that never materialized.) This doctrine was not invoked again by the American Government until 1895 during a crisis with Britain over Venezuela. It was asserted often by President Theodore Roosevelt, less forcefully by his successors, but it has never been renounced and remains a cardinal part of American foreign policy.

Announcement of the Monroe Doctrine in 1823 was in full knowledge that the British Government would not permit Spain to reconquer its American provinces. But the Monroe Administration gloried in its assertion of a New World and an Old, its doctrine of the separate spheres of influence. This announcement marked the end of any perceived American dependence upon, or inferiority to, Europe in the realm of international affairs and brought the chapter of American independence to a suitably assertive conclusion.

Atlantic Trade in 1770

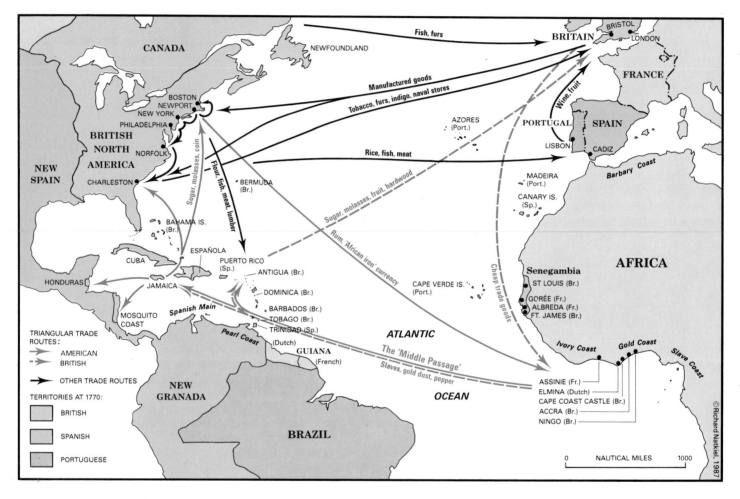

MAP above: Atlantic trade routes on the eve of the Revolution. The highly-developed system of multi-lateral trading, with each participant having several partners, is clearly shown. But attempts by one participant to improve its commercial position at the expense of another could create animosity; the conviction of the American commercial class that British policy was threatening its profits was the main theme of the quarrel which led to the War of Independence.

Right: A view of New York, one of the principal trading ports, in about 1775.

The War of Independence

MAP right: The main battles of the War of Independence. The general north to south movement of the struggle can be discerned, with hostilities starting in Massachusetts but effectively ending five years later with campaigns in the Carolinas culminating in the British defeat at Yorktown in Virginia. The proximity of almost all battlefields to either the sea or a river will also be noted, indicating the as yet generally primitive overland communications.

MAP below: The Battle of Bunker Hill. This was the first major engagement and, although British troops eventually dislodged the colonists from their position, it was at such cost that the Americans derived great encouragement from it. The British made two abortive close-order attacks before their third advance succeeded in overrunning the hill. Most of the colonists escaped simply

to take up new positions nearby. The siege of Boston continued unbroken and the town was eventually evacuated by the British in April 1776.

Below right: *Tarring and feathering an exciseman, the official responsible for collecting London-imposed duties. Tarring and feathering, a cruel but rarely fatal chastisement, was also widely practised by the more radical colonists against those of their fellows who were reluctant to take up arms against the British. Liberty Trees and Liberty Poles were named or erected as symbols of resistance by the Sons of Liberty, radical colonists who instigated and led violent agitation against the Stamp Acts.*

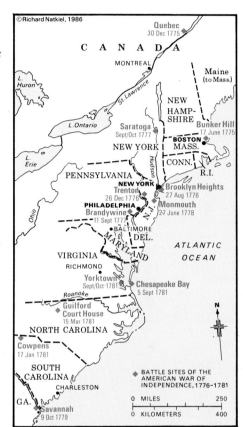

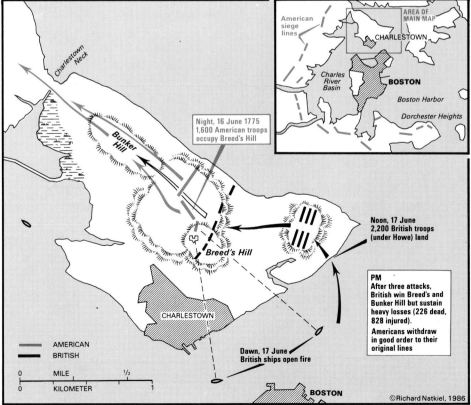

MAP right: The 1776 campaign in New York. This series of engagements was won by the British, but George Washington, who had been appointed commander of the colonists' Continental Army, acquitted himself well and eventually retired in good order into New Jersey.

MAP below right: The Battle of Trenton. After being pursued out of New York by Cornwallis' army, Washington managed to ferry the remnants of his troops across the Delaware River, capture Trenton, and then defeat three of Cornwallis' regiments before sending his weary troops to winter quarters.

Below: A tax-collector being tarred and feathered in 1774; such public events served to encourage the radicals' sympathisers and to cow their opponents.

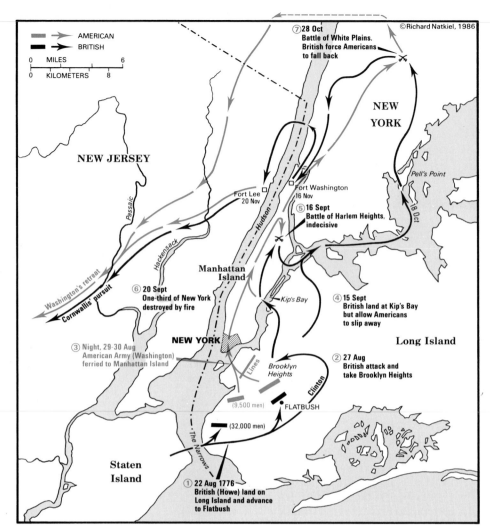

© Richard Natkiel, 1986

AMERICAN
BRITISH

0 MILES 6
0 KILOMETERS 8

NEW JERSEY

NEW YORK

⑦ 28 Oct
Battle of White Plains.
British force Americans
to fall back

Pell's Point

Fort Lee
20 Nov

Fort Washington
16 Nov

⑤ 16 Sept
Battle of Harlem Heights,
indecisive

Passaic

Hackensack

Washington's retreat

Cornwallis' pursuit

Manhattan Island

⑥ 20 Sept
One-third of New York
destroyed by fire

Kip's Bay

④ 15 Sept
British land at Kip's Bay
but allow Americans
to slip away

Long Island

③ Night, 29-30 Aug
American Army (Washington)
ferried to Manhattan Island

NEW YORK

Lines

Brooklyn
Heights

Clinton

② 27 Aug
British attack and
take Brooklyn Heights

(9,500 men)

FLATBUSH

(32,000 men)

Staten Island

The Narrows

① 22 Aug 1776
British (Howe) land on
Long Island and advance
to Flatbush

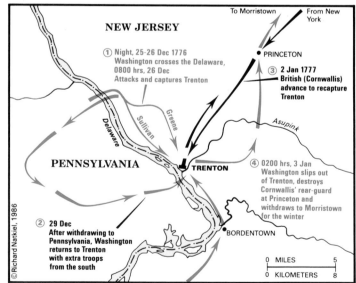

© Richard Natkiel, 1986

NEW JERSEY

To Morristown   From New York

① Night, 25-26 Dec 1776
Washington crosses the Delaware,
0800 hrs, 26 Dec
Attacks and captures Trenton

PRINCETON

③ 2 Jan 1777
British (Cornwallis)
advance to recapture
Trenton

Delaware

Sullivan

Greene

Asupink

PENNSYLVANIA

TRENTON

④ 0200 hrs, 3 Jan
Washington slips out
of Trenton, destroys
Cornwallis' rear-guard
at Princeton and
withdraws to Morristown
for the winter

② 29 Dec
After withdrawing to
Pennsylvania, Washington
returns to Trenton
with extra troops
from the south

BORDENTOWN

0 MILES 5
0 KILOMETERS 8

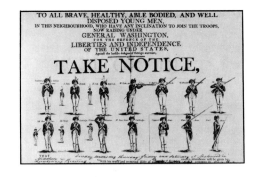

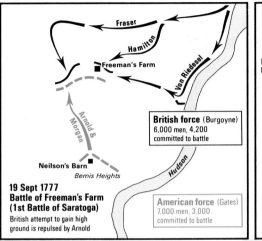

19 Sept 1777
Battle of Freeman's Farm
(1st Battle of Saratoga)
British attempt to gain high
ground is repulsed by Arnold

Fraser

Hamilton

Freeman's Farm

Von Riedesel

Arnold & Morgan

Neilson's Barn

Bemis Heights

Hudson

British force (Burgoyne)
6,000 men, 4,200
committed to battle

American force (Gates)
7,000 men, 3,000
committed to battle

Night, 7 Oct
Burgoyne begins
withdrawal

Saratoga
7 miles

Recon.
Force

Morgan

1 Poor
2 Lerned/Arnold

Bemis Heights

Hudson

7 Oct 1777
Battle of Bemis Heights
(2nd Battle of Saratoga)
British reconnaissance force
checked, and Arnold captures
a key redoubt in the center

0 — MILE — 1
0 — KILOMETERS — 2

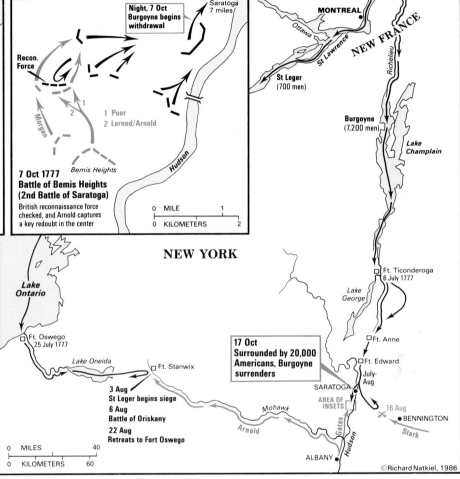

MONTREAL

Ottawa

St Lawrence

NEW FRANCE

Richelieu

St Leger
(700 men)

Burgoyne
(7,200 men)

Lake
Champlain

NEW YORK

Lake
Ontario

Ft. Ticonderoga
6 July 1777

Lake
George

Ft. Anne

Ft. Oswego
25 July 1777

Lake Oneida

Ft. Stanwix

3 Aug
St Leger begins siege
6 Aug
Battle of Oriskany
22 Aug
Retreats to Fort Oswego

Mohawk

Arnold

17 Oct
Surrounded by 20,000
Americans, Burgoyne
surrenders

Ft. Edward

July-
Aug

SARATOGA

AREA OF
INSETS

Gates

Hudson

16 Aug

BENNINGTON

Stark

ALBANY

© Richard Natkiel, 1986

0 — MILES — 40
0 — KILOMETERS — 60

MAP right: The Saratoga campaign of
the British General Burgoyne, who came
south from Canada and aimed to capture
Albany by a pincer movement. The
westerly arm of the pincer, a weak force
under St Leger, was stopped by the
colonists' militia at Oriskany, but
despite this Burgoyne pressed on, to
meet defeat at the two battles of
Saratoga. At Freeman's Farm (inset
above), he was checked, and before he
could again advance the Americans had
brought up overwhelming
reinforcements which, after a series of
engagements, including that of Bemis
Heights (inset above right), forced the
British to surrender.

Top right: *An invitation to enlist in the
American Continental Army. During the war,
the American forces consisted of the Continental
Army, which was a regular, professional, force,
aided by irregulars who included the militiamen,
some Indians, and a variety of independent and
unimportant guerrillas.*

Right: *The Battle of Lexington, the first
engagement of the war, in which eight colonists
died while resisting British troops on Lexington
Green.*

MAP right: The campaign in the South. In 1778 the British transferred their effort to the South, and Cornwallis won a series of victories in the Carolinas and Georgia. A relief force sent by Washington was defeated at Camden, but two small concentrations of the Continental Army remained in being and forced Cornwallis to withdraw to Yorktown in the hope of receiving seaborne supplies and reinforcements.

Below: *The capture of the British* Serapis *by Captain John Paul Jones, America's first naval hero, in 1776.*

Below right: *The death of Joseph Warren at Bunker Hill. Although Warren was an officer at the time, he was a doctor by profession, and had been an intellectual inspiration for those opposed to British rule.*

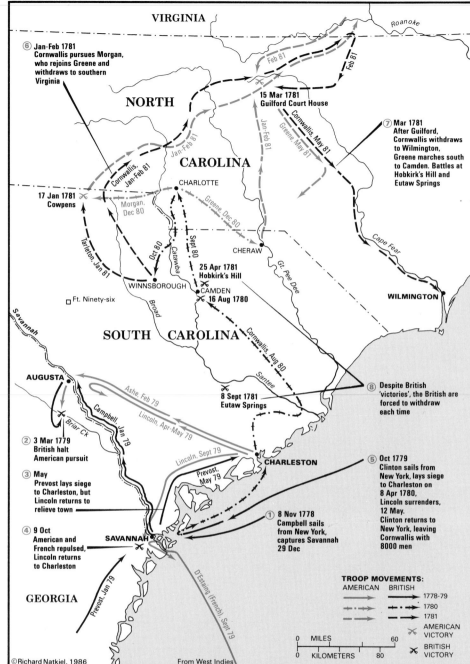

VIRGINIA

Roanoke

⑥ Jan-Feb 1781
Cornwallis pursues Morgan, who rejoins Greene and withdraws to southern Virginia

NORTH

CAROLINA

15 Mar 1781
Guilford Court House

⑦ Mar 1781
After Guilford, Cornwallis withdraws to Wilmington, Greene marches south to Camden. Battles at Hobkirk's Hill and Eutaw Springs

CHARLOTTE

17 Jan 1781
Cowpens

Morgan, Dec 80

Cape Fear

CHERAW

25 Apr 1781
Hobkirk's Hill

Gt. Pee Dee

WINNSBOROUGH

CAMDEN
16 Aug 1780

WILMINGTON

☐ Ft. Ninety-six

SOUTH CAROLINA

Broad

Santee

⑧ Despite British 'victories', the British are forced to withdraw each time

AUGUSTA

Ashe, Feb 79

Lincoln, Apr-May 79

8 Sept 1781
Eutaw Springs

② 3 Mar 1779
British halt American pursuit

Lincoln, Sept 79

⑤ Oct 1779
Clinton sails from New York, lays siege to Charleston on 8 Apr 1780, Lincoln surrenders, 12 May. Clinton returns to New York, leaving Cornwallis with 8000 men

③ May
Prevost lays siege to Charleston, but Lincoln returns to relieve town

CHARLESTON

Prevost, May 79

④ 9 Oct
American and French repulsed, Lincoln returns to Charleston

① 8 Nov 1778
Campbell sails from New York, captures Savannah 29 Dec

SAVANNAH

GEORGIA

Prevost Jan 79

D'Estaing (French) Sept 79

TROOP MOVEMENTS:

AMERICAN	BRITISH	
		1778-79
		1780
		1781
✕		AMERICAN VICTORY
	✕	BRITISH VICTORY

0 MILES 60

0 KILOMETERS 80

©Richard Natkiel, 1986

From West Indies

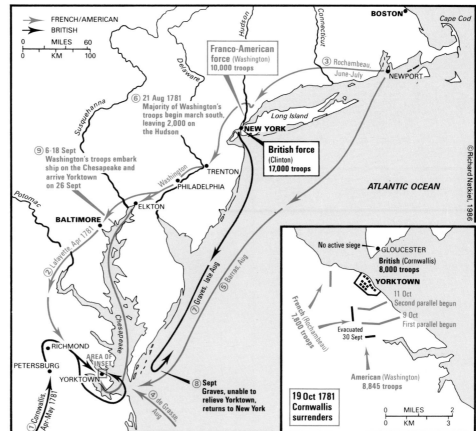

MAP right: The Yorktown campaign. With the help of the French on both land and sea, the Americans were able to transform the British retirement to Yorktown into a decisive defeat. While French and American troops were sent down from the north, the French fleet prevented the British Admiral Graves landing the reinforcements he had brought. The British loss of command of the sea meant that Cornwallis could be neither reinforced nor evacuated, and his surrender became inevitable.

MAP below: The Battle of Chesapeake Bay, in which the French under de Grasse turned back the British reinforcing fleet under Admiral Graves.

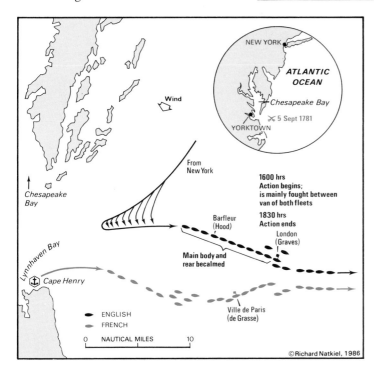

Above right: *The ceremonial commencement by American officers of the decisive but relatively bloodless siege of Yorktown: the first gun is fired.*

Right: *Cornwallis surrenders at Yorktown, bringing the war virtually to a close.*

The New Nation

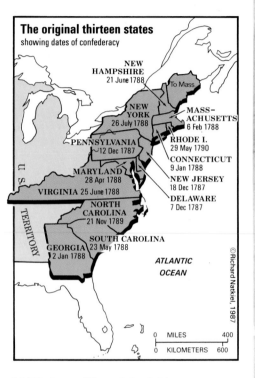

The original thirteen states
showing dates of confederacy

NEW HAMPSHIRE
21 June 1788

To Mass

NEW YORK
26 July 1788

MASS-ACHUSETTS
6 Feb 1788

PENNSYLVANIA
12 Dec 1787

RHODE I.
29 May 1790

CONNECTICUT
9 Jan 1788

MARYLAND
28 Apr 1788

NEW JERSEY
18 Dec 1787

VIRGINIA 25 June 1788

DELAWARE
7 Dec 1787

NORTH CAROLINA
21 Nov 1789

SOUTH CAROLINA
23 May 1788

GEORGIA
2 Jan 1788

ATLANTIC OCEAN

U.S. TERRITORY

© Richard Natkiel, 1987

0 MILES 400
0 KILOMETERS 600

MAP above: The original thirteen states. The formal admission of states into the American confederation was regularized by the three ordinances of 1784-87, which prescribed that public land (that is, land not yet organized as a territory or state) could be granted the status of a territory, and then, provided it had a minimum population and a two-chamber legislature, could become a fully-fledged state.

MAP right: The creation of new states up to 1812. Kentucky and Vermont became states without passing through the intermediate stage of territories.

MAP far right: New states from 1816 to 1821. Although Maine is among the newcomers, having gained statehood without passing through the territory stage, the emphasis now is on westward expansion.

By the KING.

A PROCLAMATION,

Declaring the Cessation of Arms, as well by Sea as Land, agreed upon between His Majesty, the Most Christian King, the King of Spain, the States General of the *United Provinces*, and the United States of *America*, and enjoining the Observance thereof.

GEORGE R.

WHEREAS Provisional Articles were signed at *Paris*, on the Thirtieth Day of *November* last, between Our Commissioner for treating of Peace with the Commissioners of the United States of *America* and the Commissioners of the said States, to be inserted in and to constitute the Treaty of Peace proposed to be concluded between Us and the said United States, when Terms of Peace should be agreed upon between Us and His Most Christian Majesty: And whereas Preliminaries for restoring Peace between Us and His Most Christian Majesty were signed at *Versailles* on the Twentieth Day of *January* last, by the Ministers of Us and the Most Christian King: And whereas Preliminaries for restoring Peace between Us and the King of *Spain* were also signed at *Versailles* on the Twentieth Day of *January* last, between the Ministers of Us and the King of *Spain*: And whereas, for putting an End to the Calamity of War as soon and as far as may be possible, it hath been agreed between Us, His Most Christian Majesty, the King of Spain, the States General of the *United Provinces*, and the United States of *America*, as follows; that is to say,

That such Vessels and Effects as should be taken in the *Channel* and in the *North Seas*, after the Space of Twelve Days, to be computed from the Ratification of the said Preliminary Articles, should be restored on all Sides; That the Term should be One Month from the *Channel* and the *North Seas* as far as the *Canary Islands* inclusively, whether in the Ocean or in the *Mediterranean*; Two Months from the said *Canary Islands* as far as the Equinoctial Line or Equator; and lastly, Five Months in all other Parts of the World, without any Exception, or any other more particular Description of Time or Place.

And whereas the Ratifications of the said Preliminary Articles between Us and the Most Christian King, in due Form, were exchanged by the Ministers of Us and of the Most Christian King, on the Third Day of this instant *February*; and the Ratifications of the said Preliminary Articles between Us and the King of *Spain* were exchanged between the Ministers of Us and of the King of *Spain*, on the Ninth Day of this instant *February*; from which Days respectively the several Terms above-mentioned, of Twelve Days, of One Month, of Two Months, and of Five Months, are to be computed: And whereas it is Our Royal Will and Pleasure that the Cessation of Hostilities between Us and the States General of the *United Provinces*, and the United States of *America*, should be agreeable to the Epochs fixed between Us and the Most Christian King:

We have thought fit, by and with the Advice of Our Privy Council, to notify the same to all Our loving Subjects; and We do declare, that Our Royal Will and Pleasure is, and We do hereby strictly charge and command all Our Officers, both at Sea and Land, and all other Our Subjects whatsoever, to forbear all Acts of Hostility, either by Sea or Land, against His Most Christian Majesty, the King of *Spain*, the States General of the *United Provinces*, and the United States of *America*, their Vassals or Subjects, from and after the respective Times above-mentioned, and under the Penalty of incurring Our highest Displeasure.

Given at Our Court at *Saint James's*, the Fourteenth Day of *February*, in the Twenty-third Year of Our Reign, and in the Year of Our Lord One thousand seven hundred and eighty-three.

God save the King.

LONDON:
Printed by CHARLES EYRE and WILLIAM STRAHAN, Printers to the King's most Excellent Majesty. 1783.

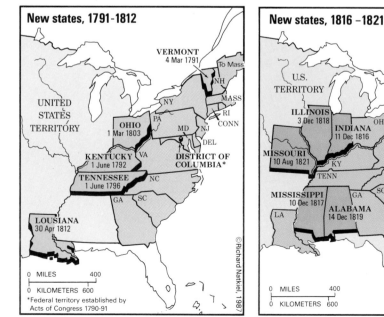

New states, 1791-1812

VERMONT
4 Mar 1791

To Mass

UNITED STATES TERRITORY

OHIO
1 Mar 1803

NH
NY
MASS
RI
CONN
PA
MD
NJ
DEL

KENTUCKY
1 June 1792

VA

DISTRICT OF COLUMBIA*

TENNESSEE
1 June 1796

NC

GA
SC

LOUSIANA
30 Apr 1812

© Richard Natkiel, 1987

0 MILES 400
0 KILOMETERS 600
*Federal territory established by Acts of Congress 1790-91

New states, 1816-1821

MAINE
15 Mar 1820

U.S. TERRITORY

VT
NH
NY
MASS
RI
CONN
PA
OH
MD
NJ
DEL

ILLINOIS
3 Dec 1818

INDIANA
11 Dec 1816

VA
DC

MISSOURI
10 Aug 1821

KY
NC
TENN

MISSISSIPPI
10 Dec 1817

GA
SC

ALABAMA
14 Dec 1819

LA

© Richard Natkiel, 1987

0 MILES 400
0 KILOMETERS 600

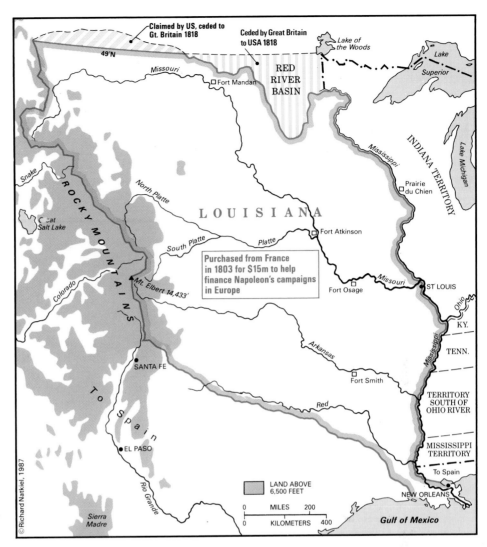

MAP right: The Louisiana Purchase. Louisiana was an expanse far larger than the present state of Louisiana. At about 828,000 square miles, its acquisition made possible the formation of no fewer than thirteen new states. President Jefferson had been alarmed by the French acquisition of this territory from Spain in 1800, feeling French ownership would be a security threat. He accordingly instructed American representatives to obtain navigation and trading guarantees from Napoleon's government. These negotiations unexpectedly ended with the purchase of Louisiana at a price which worked out at four cents per acre. The Senate confirmed the agreement even though this kind of territorial acquisition could be (and was) described as unconstitutional.

Above left: *The royal proclamation announcing the end of Britain's war against America and her French, Dutch and Spanish allies.*

Right: *Napoleon's foreign minister Talleyrand discusses with the Americans James Monroe and Robert Livingston the final details of the agreement. The Americans had earlier offered to purchase New Orleans, and had been surprised when Talleyrand asked 'How much will you give for the whole of Louisiana?' a question which initiated one of history's greatest real estate deals.*

THE LOUISIANA PURCHASE.
MESSRS. MONROE AND LIVINGSTONE COMPLETING NEGOTIATIONS WITH TALLYRAND, APRIL 30, 1803

The Barbary Wars

Painted by T.Sully. Eng. by A.B.Durand from a Copy by James Herring.

MAP below right: America's war against Tripoli. The Barbary states (Algiers, Morocco, Tripoli, Tunis) declared war on the United States in 1801 when the latter decided to cease the customary annual payments of tribute that were, in effect, protection money exacted by the Barbary pirates. After several American ships had been seized, the American navy imposed a blockade of Tripoli, until in 1805 the Pasha agreed to abandon the tribute in exchange for a ransom to be paid for American prisoners. Decatur, the naval officer who had most distinguished himself in this campaign, was despatched a second time in 1813 against Algiers and forced the other Barbary states to accept an end to tribute.

MAP below: The American capture of Derna, a fortress belonging to the Pasha of Tripoli. This victory, achieved by an arduous 600-mile trek across the Libyan Desert, was immediately followed by the peace agreement.

Above right: *Stephen Decatur, who distinguished himself in the two expeditions against the Barbary pirates, won several victories in the War of 1812, and was finally killed in a duel.*

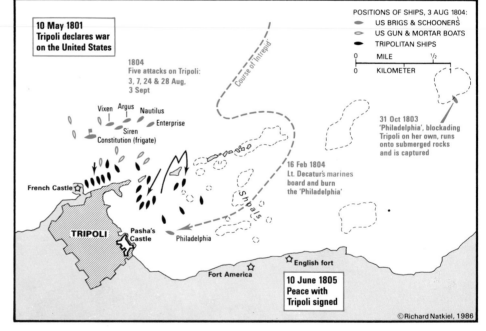

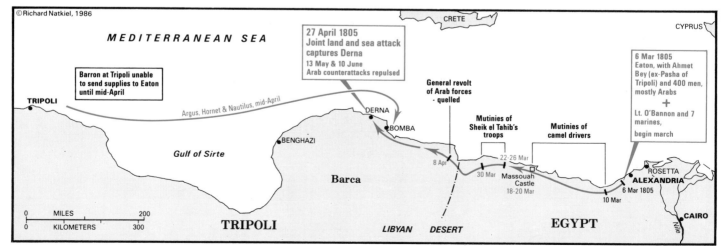

The War of 1812

MAP right: The course of the War of 1812. At first, the small and poorly-trained American army had little success against the British, drives toward Canada being defeated, and territory lost around the Great Lakes. However, morale was sustained by small naval ship-against-ship victories. Despite the latter, Britain kept command of the sea and blockaded America's ports. By 1814, thanks to Perry's naval victory on Lake Erie, the British were in retreat in that region, while the numerous attacks by American privateers on British shipping were persuading the merchants of Britain's largest ports to call for an end to the war.

Above left: *Major General Jacob Brown, one of the American commanders in the War of 1812.*

Below: *A print showing the high point of Commodore Perry's victory on Lake Erie: the flagship* Niagara *breaks through the British line.*

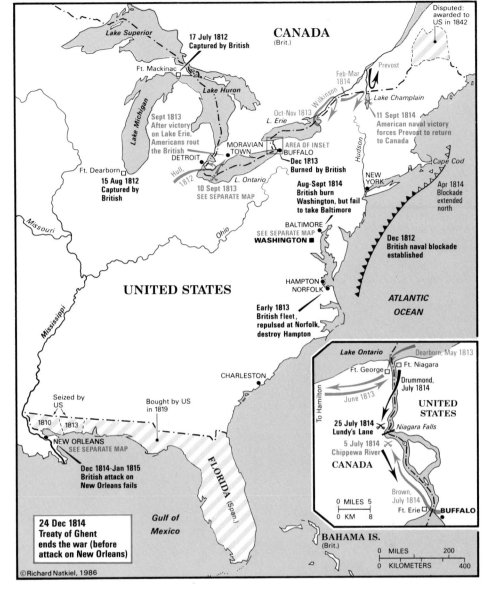

MAPS below: The crucial American naval victory on Lake Erie: Perry clears the British blockade and then goes into battle on 10 September 1813.

Right: *The death of the British commander, General Pakenham, during the costly and unsuccessful frontal assault on New Orleans.*

Bottom: *A British print showing, and somewhat glorifying, the capture of Washington.*

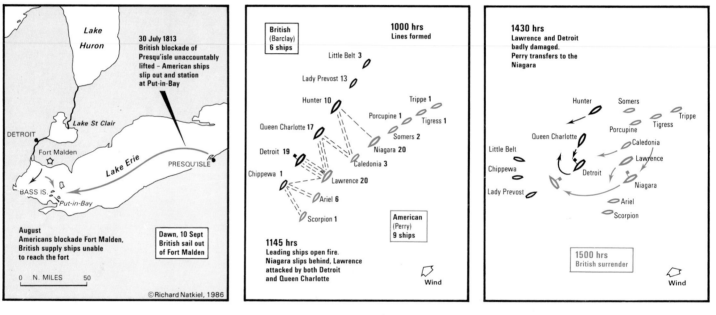

30 July 1813
British blockade of Presqu'isle unaccountably lifted – American ships slip out and station at Put-in-Bay

Lake Huron

Lake St Clair

DETROIT

Fort Malden

Lake Erie

PRESQU'ISLE

BASS IS.

Put-in-Bay

August
Americans blockade Fort Malden, British supply ships unable to reach the fort

Dawn, 10 Sept
British sail out of Fort Malden

0   N. MILES   50

© Richard Natkiel, 1986

British (Barclay) 6 ships

1000 hrs
Lines formed

Little Belt 3
Lady Prevost 13
Hunter 10
Trippe 1
Porcupine 1
Tigress 1
Queen Charlotte 17
Somers 2
Detroit 19
Niagara 20
Caledonia 3
Chippewa 1
Lawrence 20
Ariel 6
Scorpion 1

American (Perry) 9 ships

1145 hrs
Leading ships open fire. Niagara slips behind, Lawrence attacked by both Detroit and Queen Charlotte

Wind

1430 hrs
Lawrence and Detroit badly damaged. Perry transfers to the Niagara

Hunter
Somers
Trippe
Porcupine
Tigress
Queen Charlotte
Caledonia
Little Belt
Lawrence
Chippewa
Detroit
Niagara
Lady Prevost
Ariel
Scorpion

1500 hrs
British surrender

Wind

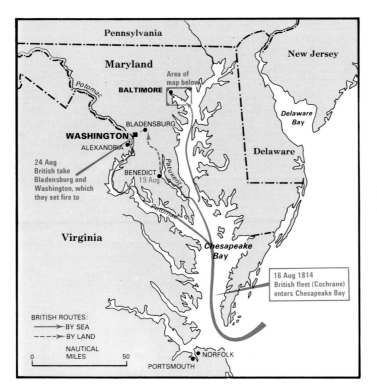

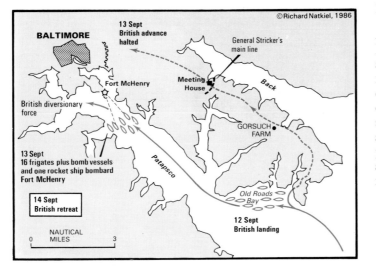

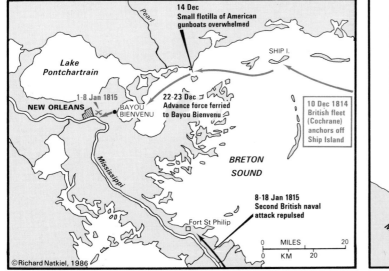

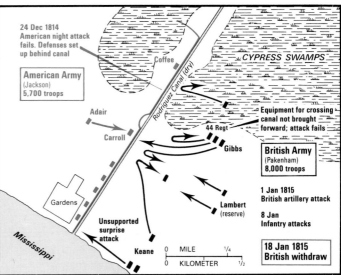

MAP left: The British advance on Washington. Having superiority on the water, and finding the capital virtually undefended, the British soon occupied the city, set fire to some of the public buildings, and then returned to their ships.

MAP below left: The British assault on Baltimore. Fresh from their success at Washington, the British staged a second amphibious advance on Baltimore, but earthworks constructed by a local militia, and the strength of Fort McHenry, guarding the harbor, persuaded them to retire.

MAPS, bottom: Two stages of the British attack on New Orleans. The river and the swamps, together with the fortifications built by the American commander, Andrew Jackson, gave few options to the British, and they were shattered when they attempted a frontal assault. In fact the attack was particularly futile since peace terms had already been agreed but news of this had not arrived.

Expansion
and Civil War

General Ulysses S Grant, narrowly escaping complete disaster at the Battle of Shiloh, leads a counter-attack against the Confederates.

The process of expansion manifested by the Louisiana Purchase, the War of 1812, and the Adams-Onis Treaty of 1819 led directly into more expansion, the annexation of Texas and the Mexican War. The result was the American Civil War. This war of 1861-5, the greatest conflict in the Western world between Waterloo and World War I, arose from rapid expansion and the creation of new states. The American South wanted to keep a balance of slave and free states in the Senate, whatever the number of free-state representatives in the Lower House. Southerners believed that the Union had been created in 1787 as a wondrous balance between the country's sections – South and North, slave and free states. These sections must not be permitted to overreach, to interfere in each other's institutions, the most important of which in the South was the 'peculiar institution' of black slavery.

The initial compromise between slave and free had taken place in the Philadelphia Convention of 1787. There the capital of Washington was placed between South and North; the Senate was created to represent states rather than populations; representatives to the Lower House were appointed according to the three-fifths rule whereby slaves were counted as three-fifths of a person; and the slave trade was allowed for 20 years after ratification of the document, which meant until 1808. After the expansions of 1803 and 1819, it became apparent that slavery might be allowed by some constitutions of new states and not by others, and that a national law should address that problem rather than states' rights (a strange point of view for Southerners) . The result was the Compromise of 1820, allowing for admission of Missouri and Maine, slave and free, evenhandedly adding to the momentary balance of 22 states – 11 slave and 11 free. The slave states were Virginia, Maryland, Delaware, Kentucky, Tennessee, North Carolina, South Carolina, Georgia, Alabama, Mississippi, and Louisiana. Free states were Massachusetts, Connecticut, Rhode Island, Vermont, New Hampshire, New York, New Jersey, Pennsylvania, Ohio, Indiana and Illinois. By the Compromise of 1820 the line of 36°30' – excepting the new slave state of Missouri – would constitute the northern boundary of slavery in states created from the Louisiana Purchase.

The arrangement of 1820 lasted for 30 years, until the Compromise of 1850 following the Mexican War. But at the outset it seemed likely to last much longer, if only because slavery as an institution showed signs of dwindling away. The Compromise of 1820 was a palliative until the day when slavery would disappear of itself. At that time it was not really economical, and people doubted that it would be able to compete with free labor. No one suspected that about a decade later (around 1830) the opening of virgin lands to cotton culture, and the apparently insatiable demands of English and then French mills for raw cotton, would give slavery a new lease of life.

The cotton economy soon fastened itself upon the South, especially in the new states of Alabama, Mississippi, Louisiana, and after 1845, Texas. 'Cotton is king!' was the cry. The South that began the Civil War in 1861 had been roughly 30 years in developing – its cotton culture had arisen within the memory of most middle-aged inhabitants.

Meanwhile the economy of the Northeast and Middle West, and the newer states created from the Northwest Territory, was coalescing. A road network developed, followed by a series of canals linking rivers of the two regions. A few years later came the railroads, dependent not upon natural pathways, or connecting waterways, but upon the ingenuity of their entrepreneurs backed by pressure for regional development.

It was natural that the agriculture of the Middle West should support the increasing industrialism of the Northeast with its sizable towns and cities. First came the roads, including the Cumberland Road – more commonly known as the National Road or Turnpike – from Cumberland, Maryland, to Wheeling on the Ohio River. It was begun after the War of 1812 and interrupted by the Panic of 1819 that paralyzed the economy after the war. Vetoed by Monroe, supported by President Jackson in 1830, the road crept slowly toward the Wheeling terminus. Although he supported the Cumberland Road, Jackson in effect passed roadbuilding back to the states when he vetoed the proposed Maysville Road between the Kentucky town of Maysville, Washington, Paris, and Lexington. The president from Tennessee held that a road within a state was that state's responsibility, not the Federal Government's.

In the 1820s began the great era of canal construction, providing alternative routes for the heavy loads that traveled so laboriously over the roadways. The advantage of canals was obvious, whether barges were drawn by mules or propelled by paddle wheels powered by steam engines. The Chesapeake and Ohio Canal (1828-50) linked Georgetown (next to Washington, DC) with Cumberland, Maryland. In the Middle West, in states organized from the Northwest Territory, Ohio boasted a canal connecting Portsmouth and Cleveland (1825-32), the Miami Canal linking Cincinnati and Toledo (1825-45), the Louisville and Portland Canal around the falls of the Ohio River (1826-31), and the Wabash and Erie Canal linking Toledo with Evansville, Indiana. The latter, the longest canal in the United States, was built between 1832 and 1856. Other states vied for construction of these magical waterways.

Of all the connections between Middle West and Northeast, the railroads proved the most important. By the time of the Civil War, they united what had been two disparate sections. Perhaps more than anything else, they made possible the solid – in fact, flourishing – economy that contributed to Northern military success when Constitutional law proved unavailing in preserving the Union.

The first railroad appeared in England in 1825, and the Americans soon emulated it with construction of the Mowhawk and Hudson Railroad. Chartered in 1826, built in 1830, it operated between Albany and Schenectady by 1831. The Baltimore and Ohio Railroad, the first passenger railway in the United States, was chartered in 1827, but it took until 1853 to complete a line from Baltimore to Wheeling. Other lines followed, with incessant incorporation of smaller into larger: by 1840 the United States boasted a total of 3328 miles of railroad. In all of Europe there were only 1818. Between 1840 and 1860 an additional 28,000 miles were added, at capital expenditure of close to $1 billion – a huge sum in those days. By 1855 a continuous line of rails connected New York and Chicago. However, there was no direct connection along the East Coast between Washington, Charleston, and Savannah. The westernmost extension of railroads by 1860 was to St Joseph, Missouri; on the Pacific Coast near Sacramento a short road had been built; the remaining gap, east-west, would of course close after the Civil War.

Rates for transportation varied remarkably by 1860. Per ton-mile they averaged fifteen cents for turnpikes, three-fourths to one cent for canals, and two cents for railroads. In the West, the trails of the pre-Civil War period hardly equalled the network of roads, canals, and railroads east of the Mississippi. But in binding together an isolated section of the country, the Far West (including after the 1840s the Pacific Coast) they proved almost equally important. Principal trails until 1860 began at Independence, Missouri, whence ran the trail to Santa Fe and the Oregon Trail that passed through Utah and over the Rockies. The former trail opened in 1821-2; the one to Oregon was not heavily used until the 1840s.

It was during the 1840s that the nation's Northeast and Northwest boundaries were permanently defined. In both cases, much diplomacy and not a little bluster were involved, perhaps inevitably, as the young nation asserted itself against the former Mother Country, Great Britain. In the Northeast an argument had sputtered since the Treaty of Paris of 1783 over what constituted Maine's northern boundary and the US border from Maine to the Lake of the Woods. A veritable battle of maps ensued, in which one confusion led to another. The argument over Maine's borders took on more serious proportions after the organization of the state in 1820. Massachusetts insisted upon taking interest in the problem, as Maine had broken away from the older state. Presumably a definition of the Maine border that resulted in loss of territory to Canada would require compensation of the people of Massachusetts. In the late 1830s the Aroostook War, as it was called, over construction of a railroad into the disputed northern area, focused attention on the unsettled boundary. In 1841 the new administration of President William Henry Harrison brought Daniel Webster into the issue as secretary of state. Webster may have intimated that British money might resolve everything, including his own insistent needs for financial support. The British Government, apparently sensing a fortunate moment, sent Lord Ashburton as minister. The resultant Webster-Ashburton Treaty of 9 August 1842 gave the United States a little more than half of the 12,000 square miles of disputed land and paid off Maine and Massachusetts equally with $150,000 of federal funds. Unknown to either principal,

the arrangement from Lake Superior to the Lake of the Woods gave the United States the Mesabi iron ore range.

The division of the Oregon Territory, comprising everything north of California's upper border to Alaska, was set out in the Oregon Treaty of 15 June 1846, in which the signatories ran the line of the 49th parallel westward to the Pacific Coast from the Rockies. To some Americans of the time it appeared grossly unfair, for they were asking for a line of 54°40′: there was talk of 'Fifty-Four-Forty or Fight.' President James K Polk, at one juncture in the treaty discussion, opined that the best way to treat John Bull was to look him straight in the eye. When the treaty came into final form, it testified against that principle: Polk surrendered (so his enemies said) and fell victim to the Forty-Nines. But if one remembers the sparseness of American settlement north of the Columbia River (in 1844 only five Americans lived in the area), the wonder was that Britain did not insist upon the river line rather than giving up the present-day state of Washington. By the 1840s, perhaps, the once-imperial Britons had tired of empire. There was talk of retreat at that time, a feeling that the huge expansion of British commerce attendant upon the Industrial Revolution would benefit British citizens far more than overseas territory. The British Government also appears to have discovered suddenly that the Columbia River, unlike the Thames, was not at all navigable – that it was in no sense another St Lawrence, opening huge inland territories to settlement. For these reasons and others, the British gave in to Polk, not he to them, as 'Fifty-Four-Forty' proponents had charged.

Polk may have moved rapidly to settle the Oregon boundary

Below: Dred Scott and his wife. In 1857 the Supreme Court ruled in the Dred Scott Case that the Missouri Compromise was unconstitutional.

Above: *The capture of Monterey by General Zachary Taylor's army in 1846, one of the earlier American victories in the Mexican War.*

because of the imminence of war with Mexico over Texas. The Texas issue had begun a decade before the Mexican War. The huge northern province of Mexico, which consisted of present-day Texas and parts of New Mexico, Colorado, and Kansas, had declared its independence of faraway Mexico City in its own war of 1835-6. This conflict was supported by American volunteers and fought almost entirely by nominal Mexicans of American descent. Maintaining a precarious independence, Texans looked longingly to the Republic from which they had come, and at last President John Tyler, on 1 March 1845, signed the joint resolution of annexation. He argued that the election of his successor, Polk, showed the victory of expansionist sentiment, that he was only anticipating what Polk would have done anyway, and that the friction between Texas and Mexico weakened both powers and created opportunities for such hostile foreign powers as Great Britain. The Mexican Government warned that annexation might well bring war. The incoming president, Polk, took the opportunity to incite the Mexicans by sending United States troops not merely into Texas, but into a disputed area between the Nueces River and the Rio Grande. Mexican troops attacked on 25 April 1846, and the United States declared war on 13 May.

If ever there was a one-sided contest, it was the Mexican War of 1846-8. The troops of the government in Mexico City seldom showed any fight, and those of the United States displayed all the zeal of what John O'Sullivan had described as

his country's 'manifest destiny,' which was to extend its territory in every possible way. Many years earlier Henry Clay, who was secretary of state in 1825, had suggested to the Mexicans that they would benefit by giving their northern territories, far from their capital of Mexico City, to the United States. Unmoved by this proposal, the Mexicans chose to keep what was theirs, but they lacked the force to hold on to it. The Battle of Palo Alto on 8-9 May 1846 brought victory to General Zachary Taylor, who raked a Mexican force of 6000 with artillery fire. Taylor took Monterrey on 24 September. That same year Americans took all of California, partly by use of US Navy ships. The conquest of California was no large task, because the province contained only a few thousand Mexicans of Spanish descent who were squabbling among themselves and almost incapable of uniting against the local and incoming Americans.

General Taylor's greatest victory was the Battle of Buena Vista on 22-3 February 1847. The American leader had only 4800 men, mostly volunteer infantry, but he entrenched them along deep gullies and ravines to await the ill-trained troops of the Mexican general, Antonio Lopez de Santa Anna – some 15,000 men. Taylor defeated the Mexicans thoroughly, and Santa Anna returned to Mexico City.

A major feat of American arms followed – the expedition of General Winfield Scott from Vera Cruz to Mexico City. Scott landed with 10,000 men, on 9 March 1847, and marched inland, fighting along the way. By mid-May he was 50 miles from Mexico City, reduced to 7000 men by the expiration of short-term enlistments. Gradually he rebuilt his force to 13,000, and by 8 September was attacking the capital itself, which he took six days later. After considerable turmoil within the Mexican Government, which had abandoned its capital to Scott, the Americans signed the Treaty of Guadalupe Hidalgo on 2 February 1848. It was the result of unauthorized negotiation between the American commissioner accompanying Scott's army, Nicholas Trist, and Mexican commissioners. At first Polk was furious over this arrangement, which he interpreted as a maneuver by Scott, who belonged to the Whig Party rather than Polk's party, the Democrats. But when he understood what Trist had obtained – cession of everything that Mexico had claimed north of the Rio Grande – he sent the treaty to the Senate, which consented to its terms. Thereby Polk accomplished as much as his Democratic predecessor Jefferson, doubling again the territory of the erstwhile Thirteen Colonies. The newly acquired area included parts of the later states of New Mexico, Colorado, and Wyoming; all of Nevada, Arizona, and Utah; and of course California. In return for the territory, the United States paid Mexico $15 million and assumed claims of its citizens against Mexico for an additional $3,250,000.

Several years later, on 30 December 1853, James Gadsden of South Carolina negotiated a $10-million settlement with Mexico for a rectangular strip of territory in the Mesilla Valley, south of the Gila River. The strip acquired by the Gadsden Purchase was wanted for a southern railroad to the Pacific.

By this time a second adjustment of the rapidly developing slavery controversy had proved necessary. In the Compromise of 1850, California was admitted as a free state, New Mexico and Utah were organized as territories without restriction on slavery, a Fugitive Slave Act gave Southerners better protection for their property, and slavery was abolished in the District of Columbia.

Meanwhile, agriculture and industry, South and North, developed concurrently. The two great sections of the country (the Middle West and the Northeast were now closely linked) faced one another with whatever economic force they could muster. Southern production of cotton had increased by leaps and bounds, from 731,000 bales in 1830 to 2.1 million in 1850 to 5.3 million in 1859. In order of production, the leading states were Mississippi, Alabama, Louisiana, and Georgia. Only 18 percent of Southern farms could be described as plantations in 1850; small planters and yeomen farmers owned three-fourths of the landed wealth. Rice production in the South remained stable in the early and mid-nineteenth century. Sugar production rose to 270,000 tons in 1861, almost all of it grown in Louisiana. Tobacco production increased slowly, reaching 160,000 hogsheads on the eve of the Civil War. Corn amounted to 274 million bushels, about a third of the United States total.

In the North the top-ranking wheat states by 1860 were Illinois, Indiana and Wisconsin. Production in the Northeast in 1850-60 was about 30 million bushels, but in the Middle West it increased from 43.8 million to 95 million. Corn production occupied a belt directly below the wheat area, and doubled from 222 million bushels in 1850 to 406 million in 1860; corn comprised about half of the total national crop. Leading corn states in 1860 were Illinois, Ohio, Missouri, and Indiana. Hog raising, closely related to corn production, was also on the rise, with Cincinnati the center of meat-packing until 1860, when Chicago replaced it. In the North agricultural machinery was making a major difference in production. The cradle replaced the sickle for reaping between 1820 and 1840, the cast-iron plow replaced the wooden moldboard plow during the same years, the steel plow appeared in the 1830s. Mechanical reapers began to take over in the 1840s. Mowing,

threshing, and haying machines, seed drills, and cultivators were adopted.

Southern industry lagged far behind that of the North. In 1860 manufacturing establishments numbered 20,000, capital nearly $100 million, laborers about 100,000, and value of products $150 million. New England alone did better than that, with an equal number of establishments, two and a half times the capital invested, four times the laborers, nearly three times the annual value of products. Pennsylvania and New York boasted 50,000 establishments, $450 million in capital, half a million laborers, $800 million in annual value of products. The Middle Western states could show 36,000 establishments, nearly $200 million in capital invested, 200,000 laborers, nearly $400 million in annual value of products. It was a time of textile factories, iron manufacture, machinery, and paper. Household manufactures were declining, steam engines and steam power rapidly increasing.

The election of 1860 heightened Southern fears that President Abraham Lincoln would destroy the Southern way of life by refusing to protect the institution of slavery. Cotton production would collapse, reducing the South to a position of vassalage. Without waiting to see what Lincoln's Administration might do, Southern leaders promptly took their states out of the Union. South Carolina was the first to go, on 20 December 1860, followed by the other ten states that would form the Confederate States of America. During 1861 they seceded one after another: Mississippi, 9 January; Florida, 10 January; Alabama, 11 January; Georgia, 19 January; Louisiana, 26 January; Texas, 1 February, followed by the border states – Virginia, 17 April; Arkansas, 6 May; Tennessee, 7 May; North Carolina, 20 May. The deed, effectively, was done. When the Civil War was finally over, the government in Washington would contend that the Southern States had never left the Union, but only believed they had done so. In any case, the Southerners declared secession and acted in every way as if they were independent of the Lincoln Administration in the District of Columbia.

The causes of the Civil War were hotly debated after the war came to an end in April 1865: ever since then, historians, political leaders, and others have remained uncertain of what actually drove the Southern States to rebellion. Terminology, perhaps, has confused the debate. The root cause of Southern dissatisfaction was surely the burden of slavery – the cargo brought to the New World by the unknown Dutch ship in 1619. Southern society proved unable to deal with the presence of large numbers of blacks in its midst short of enslaving them. By the early years of the nineteenth century slavery was virtually an uneconomic arrangement – the care and feeding of slave dependents was fastening itself around the necks of white Southerners in a manifestly burdensome way. But then the rapidly increasing demand for cotton – in the North, in Britain and on the Continent – which began about 1830, gave slavery a new impetus. The simultaneous opening of virgin cotton soil in the Deep South provided a new sphere of operation. The constitutional arrangements of earlier years did not suffice, and by 1860 economic interest and popular feeling had consolidated into rebellion. Later historians pointed variously to a difference in economic systems, disagreement on constitutional law, or a failure of leadership in both sections. These theories ignored the root cause of it all: slavery.

The American Civil War began with South Carolina's attack on the federal fort in Charleston's harbor – Fort Sumter – and effectively ended when General Robert E Lee surrendered to General Ulysses S Grant at Appomattox Court House in

Virginia early in 1865. Other bodies of Southern troops capitulated soon afterwards. The war lasted four long years, a tragic waste in view of the fact that it was decided halfway through – in the first days of July 1863, when Union forces won at Vicksburg and Gettysburg. From then on Southern armies struggled in the ever-lengthening shadow of defeat. The involvement of civilian populations and the war's prolongation fueled antagonism on both sides, making Reconstruction an ordeal rather than a simple process.

After Fort Sumter's surrender (13 April 1861) the Lincoln Administration called for volunteers. For both North and South, it was too late to turn back. In the war's first year, 1861, the North resorted to an initial attack at Bull Run in Virginia (21 July), and lost when Confederate forces under General Thomas J (Stonewall) Jackson rallied from a near-rout. Northern troops began to retreat, ever more rapidly as they approached Washington. General George B McClellan took over Northern troops and began to train them for a long war rather than a few gallant rushes against the foe. The North rapidly increased its navy, buying up anything it thought would float, including some things that would not. Ships appeared off Southern ports, to cut off supplies from Europe. In 1862 Union forces under McClellan in the East, in what became the war's principal theater, northern Virginia, moved again toward the Confederates and met another repulse. The Confederates caught McClellan's army of 70,000 near Sharpsburg, Maryland, and with a much smaller army of 40,000, on 17 September 1862, Lee defeated his opposite in the bloodiest day of the war. Union casualties included 2108 killed; Confederate, 2700. By some measures Sharpsburg (also known as Antietam) was a draw, and Lee pulled back, but a draw was small consolation when McClellan had nearly twice as many men. For the Union, this kind of stalemate offered no resolution to the problem of Southern secession.

In 1863, the war's real year of decision, a change was apparent on 1 January when President Lincoln enlarged the war's purpose from preservation of the Union to an attack on the institution of slavery. The Emancipation Proclamation of this date did not actually free any slaves; in fact, it went no further than Congress had gone already. It freed Southern slaves only nominally – in areas over which the Lincoln Administration had no control. The four loyal slave states and areas of the South under Federal occupation were exempted. By the beginning of 1863, despite defeats in the field, the Union's superior manpower and financial/industrial strength were showing. Union enlistments totaled 1.5 million; Confederate, 1 million. In financing the Union effort, the Lincoln Administration established a banking system that required national banks to invest a third of their capital in United States bonds and authorized them to issue notes – really currency – up to 90 percent of such bond holdings. The Confederacy, without any banking structure worthy of the name, resorted to inflation – its paper money eventually totalled $1 billion and depreciated to the value of souvenirs by the war's end. With the advantage of far better financing, and more importantly, a much larger industrial and agricultural base, the North, over the long run, was unbeatable. This was the base of the Northern victory that became inevitable in the summer of 1863.

In order to split the South, it was necessary to capture the fortified city of Vicksburg on the Mississippi River. This would open the great river to Union shipping and cut off the Confederacy's Western states. General Grant moved against the city with 20,000 men and took it under siege. When the Confederates surrendered on 4 July, the North took over 30,000 prisoners. Meanwhile, General Lee had moved boldly to invade Pennsylvania, hoping to encourage Northern dissension and perhaps win foreign recognition from Britain and France. (Pro-South sentiment abroad was encouraged by mill owners who desired Southern cotton.) The Confederates advanced until they met Union troops near the little town of Gettysburg, where what started as a series of small skirmishes turned into the war's major and decisive battle. Troops poured in from both armies, took and fortified positions, and moved into massive attacks that suddenly turned into Confederate defeat. In four days the Confederacy poured out its life's blood, notably in the vain attack launched on 3 July at 1:00 PM, when 15,000 men converged on Cemetery Ridge. Union forces under General George G Meade, a thorough soldier, had fortified the ridge with artillery and riflemen, and Meade's troops mowed down the Confederate lines. Less than half a company managed to reach the crest of the ridge, only to be killed or taken prisoner. It was the high-water mark for the Union, and the end for the Confederacy. The next day Lee retreated back into Virginia, and the creaking wagons of his train, carrying wounded men who screamed in pain as the wagons jolted them back to the Southland, symbolized the defeat of a dream of Southern independence. Meade's army was about twice the size of Lee's, 60,000 to 30,000. Casualties were 3155 Union men killed, 3903 Confederates. Lee could ill afford the losses, and had been outmaneuvered tactically by Meade. His hopes at the outset of the Pennsylvania campaign had come to nothing.

The remainder of the war would be anticlimactic, but some of the fiercest fighting of the entire conflict occurred in 1864. Grant was shifted from the West to take command of all Union forces as lieutenant general, a new rank superseding that of major general. He did not station himself in Washington, like his predecessor General John Halleck, but with the major Union force, the Army of the Potomac, under Meade's command. Thus the principal theater in 1864 was northern Virginia, where Lee confronted both Grant and Meade. Union tactics were to move upon Lee frontally and smash his army by incessant battering. These tactics meant heavy casualties on both sides, but Grant looked forward to victory when he began a battle in the tangled terrain known as the Wilderness in the summer of 1864. In one month, ending 12 June, Grant's losses amounted to nearly 60,000, equal to Lee's total strength. Confederate casualties were only half that number. But Lee could not take such losses and survive. Meanwhile, Grant turned the indomitable General William T Sherman loose upon the Lower South, where he marched through Georgia to the sea. Atlanta and Savannah fell to Sherman at the year's end: his army of 60,000 was virtually unopposed. On December 15-16, in the Battle of Nashville, Union forces all but destroyed Confederate troops in Tennessee.

The last days of the Confederacy were played out in early 1865, when Sherman unleashed his divisions in the Carolinas and Lee abandoned Petersburg and the Confederate capital at Richmond (2 April). He surrendered his 54,000 men to Grant (who by this time possessed an overwhelming army of 115,000) on 9 April at Appomattox Court House. The trauma of Lincoln's assassination followed on 14 April and Confederates everywhere capitulated between 26 April and 26 May.

Losses on both sides were huge, in part from battle action, in greater part from disease. Casualties from all causes totaled between 33 and 40 percent of all forces engaged. Union dead totaled 359,528, including 110,070 killed outright or dying

Above: *The long but inconclusive struggle in Hampton Roads between the Union turret ship* Monitor *and the Confederate ironclad* Merrimack, *a landmark in naval history.*

later of wounds. Confederate dead reached 248,000, with 94,000 killed in battle or dying of wounds. These losses were too devastating for either North or South to forget, and the bitterness endured for generations. Black civil rights was another source of interregional discord that would smolder for over a century.

Diplomacy steered an uncertain course throughout the Civil War. The Lincoln Administration sought to avoid intervention on behalf of the South by the governments in London and Paris. Such intervention might have broken the North's blockade and supplied the Confederacy with the munitions it so desperately needed, in exchange for Southern cotton, which was now without a market. As events turned out, the British and French Governments waited out the military campaigns of the war to see how the Confederacy might fare. As Southern armies proved unavailing against increasing Northern strength and prowess, the European Governments displayed ever more prudence. The military decisions of 1863 were crucial abroad as well as within the New World. By 1865 the governments in both London and Paris had accepted the inevitable: that there would be a Northern victory.

Non-neutral behavior, and especially the depredations of such Confederate raiders as the *Alabama*, produced a series of claims by the United States. Estimates of Northern shipping sunk by raiders, including cargoes, reached 100,000 tons. The Treaty of Washington (8 May 1871) established a series of rules of 'due diligence' for neutrals, in this case Britain. The following August an arbitral tribunal (with representatives from Italy, Switzerland, Brazil, and the interested parties) decided that Britain had been non-neutral and awarded the United States $15.5 million. Senator Charles Sumner of Massachusetts had audaciously asked for indirect damages as well – he cited the prolongation of the war from 1863 until 1865 – and totaled those damages at $1 billion, which, he explained, might be paid by cession of Canada. The tribunal of 1872 did not find it necessary to address these indirect claims, which subsequently lapsed.

American expansion continued with the purchase of Alaska from Russia in 1867 at a cost of two cents per acre. Secretary of State William H Seward was the moving force behind this acquisition. Critics referred to the unpopulated region as 'a large lump of ice,' and 'Seward's Folly,' although the territory was rich in fish and furs. Greatly increased settlement quickly followed upon the discovery of gold in the Klondike region in 1896.

The purchase of Alaska would prove to be the only foreign-policy triumph of Andrew Johnson's Administration, which succeeded that of Abraham Lincoln after his assassination in April 1865. Russia wanted to relinquish the territory as an economic liability, and her minister in Washington bargained with Seward for a price of $7.2 million. Reportedly, the extra $200,000 was for bribery in the House of Representatives, where it was necessary to dispel members' doubts about voting for the appropriation. Alaska was transferred to the United States on 18 October 1867, and the appropriation passed the House on 14 July 1868. In 1903 a dispute with Britain over Canada's border along the Alaskan panhandle (the Alexander Archipelago) led to an arbitration by which the Americans received what they claimed was theirs. The dispute had arisen after the Klondike Gold Rush of 1896, when the Canadians asserted control of panhandle harbors.

The rapid expansion of US territory before and after the War of 1812, and the ensuing North-South conflict concerning the addition of new states to the Union, had finally severed that Union in the appalling war of 1861-5. After the Civil War, Americans sought, with limited success in terms of black rights, to bind up the wounds of conflict and to turn attention to national economic growth. By the end of the century the memories of the Civil War were slipping into history. Then suddenly a war blew up over the actions of Spain in Cuba – and in 1898 the American nation turned to expansion far from its existing borders, in the Caribbean, Central America, and the Far East.

New States and Slavery

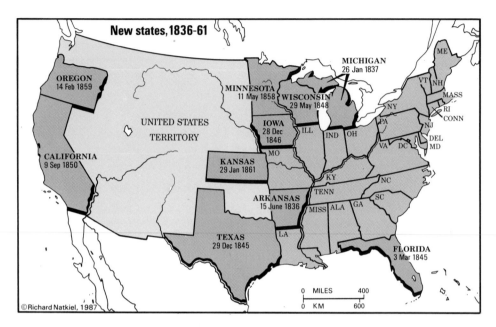

New states, 1836-61

OREGON
14 Feb 1859

MICHIGAN
26 Jan 1837

MINNESOTA
11 May 1858

WISCONSIN
29 May 1848

UNITED STATES
TERRITORY

IOWA
28 Dec
1846

CALIFORNIA
9 Sep 1850

KANSAS
29 Jan 1861

ARKANSAS
15 June 1836

TEXAS
29 Dec 1845

FLORIDA
3 Mar 1845

ME
VT NH
MASS
RI
CONN
NY
PA
NJ
DEL
MD
VA DC
ILL IND OH
MO
KY
NC
TENN
MISS ALA GA
SC
LA

0 MILES 400
0 KM 600

©Richard Natkiel, 1987

MAP left: The new states admitted in the last pre-Civil War decades. The Middle West is now being organized, but further west huge expanses await their new populations and meantime are classified as US Territory.

MAPS right: The increase of free, or non-slave, states after the four crucial decisions of the 1820 Missouri Compromise, the 1850 Compromise, the Kansas-Nebraska Act, and the Dred Scott Case.

Left: *Henry Clay, who successfully proposed the Compromise of 1850. This superseded the failing Missouri Compromise, so far as new states were concerned, and ensured that slavery would not be introduced in California, New Mexico and Utah, although the laws against fugitive slaves would be tightened.*

Right: *An 1893 painting showing the pre-Civil War 'Underground Railroad,' which was a secret network of routes and helpers organized by fervent Abolitionists to help escaped slaves pass to free states or to Canada.*

Far right: *Advertisement for the Pony Express, which in its short life (1860-61) showed that the overland mail could be carried from St Joseph in Missouri to Sacramento in California with a two-week transit.*

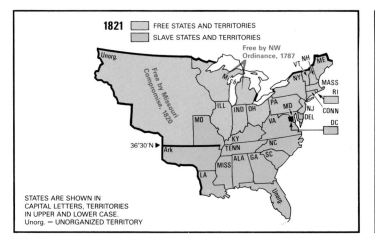

1821 · FREE STATES AND TERRITORIES · SLAVE STATES AND TERRITORIES

STATES ARE SHOWN IN CAPITAL LETTERS, TERRITORIES IN UPPER AND LOWER CASE. Unorg. = UNORGANIZED TERRITORY

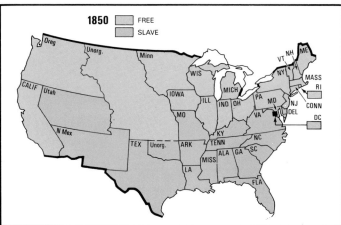

1850 · FREE · SLAVE

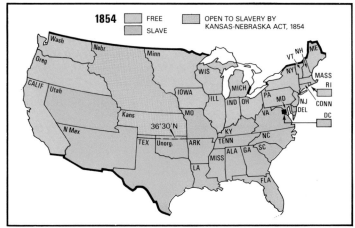

1854 · FREE · SLAVE · OPEN TO SLAVERY BY KANSAS-NEBRASKA ACT, 1854

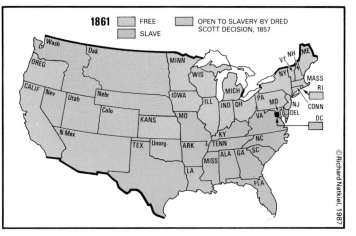

1861 · FREE · SLAVE · OPEN TO SLAVERY BY DRED SCOTT DECISION, 1857

© Richard Natkiel, 1987

PONY EXPRESS!

CHANGE OF TIME! · REDUCED RATES!

10 Days to San Francisco!

LETTERS

WILL BE RECEIVED AT THE

OFFICE, 84 BROADWAY,

NEW YORK,

Up to 4 P. M. every TUESDAY,

AND

Up to 2½ P. M. every SATURDAY,

Which will be forwarded to connect with the PONY EXPRESS leaving ST. JOSEPH, Missouri,

Every WEDNESDAY and SATURDAY at 11 P. M.

TELEGRAMS

Sent to Fort Kearney on the mornings of MONDAY and FRIDAY, will connect with PONY leaving St. Joseph, WEDNESDAYS and SATURDAYS.

EXPRESS CHARGES.

LETTERS weighing half ounce or under............$1 00
For every additional half ounce or fraction of an ounce 1 00
In all cases to be enclosed in 10 cent Government Stamped Envelopes,
And all Express CHARGES Pre-paid.

☞ PONY EXPRESS ENVELOPES For Sale at our Office.

WELLS, FARGO & CO., Ag'ts.

New York, July 1, 1861.

SLOTE & JANES, STATIONERS AND PRINTERS, 92 FULTON STREET, NEW YORK.

Exploring the West

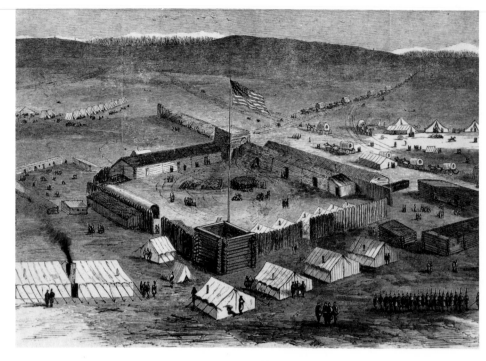

MAP below: Exploration of the
continent. Hitherto, exploration of the
interior had typically been the work of
private individuals in search of furs or
other resources, but in the early years of
the 19th century this changed.
Thereafter expeditions were often
officially sponsored and given surveying
and mapping tasks.

Right: *A stockade fort. Such structures were a
common feature on the western frontier.*

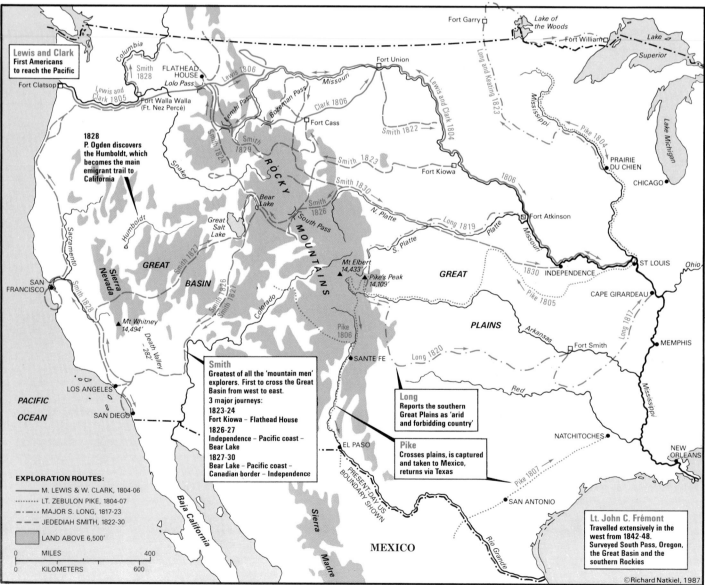

Lewis and Clark
First Americans
to reach the Pacific

1828
**P. Ogden discovers
the Humboldt, which
becomes the main
emigrant trail to
California**

Smith
Greatest of all the 'mountain men'
explorers. First to cross the Great
Basin from west to east.
3 major journeys:
1823-24
Fort Kiowa – Flathead House
1826-27
Independence – Pacific coast –
Bear Lake
1827-30
Bear Lake – Pacific coast –
Canadian border – Independence

Long
Reports the southern
Great Plains as 'arid
and forbidding country'

Pike
Crosses plains, is captured
and taken to Mexico,
returns via Texas

Lt. John C. Frémont
Travelled extensively in the
west from 1842-48.
Surveyed South Pass, Oregon,
the Great Basin and the
southern Rockies

EXPLORATION ROUTES:
——— M. LEWIS & W. CLARK, 1804-06
··········· LT. ZEBULON PIKE, 1804-07
–·–·– MAJOR S. LONG, 1817-23
– – – JEDEDIAH SMITH, 1822-30

LAND ABOVE 6,500'

0 — MILES — 400
0 — KILOMETERS — 600

PACIFIC
OCEAN

MEXICO

©Richard Natkiel, 1987

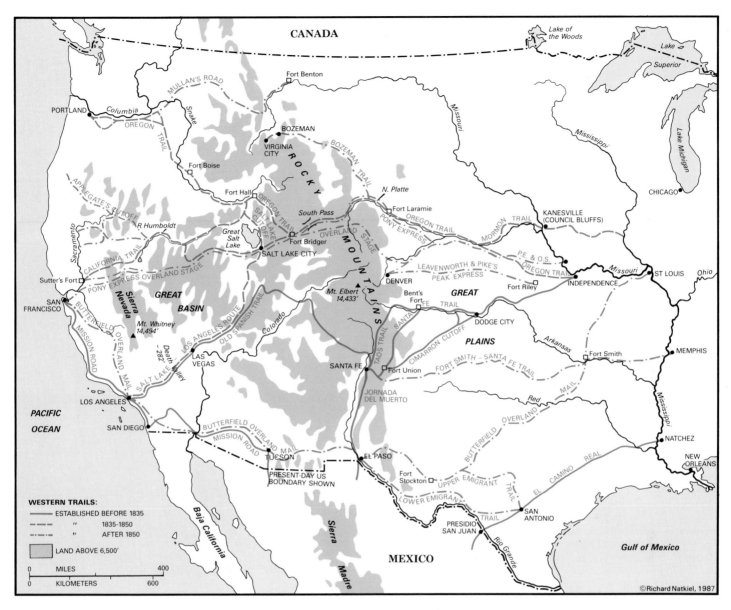

MAP above: The great trails to the West. The discovery of practical overland routes to the West was one of the aims of the early explorers, who were soon followed by the first intrepid settlers.

Right: *An emigrant train settling in for the night. Emigrating settler families often preferred to travel in groups, for security and self-help.*

The Seminole Wars

MAP below: The Second Seminole War. The First War had occurred in 1816-18, and had been started when US troops blew up a Seminole strongpoint while searching for escaped slaves. The Second War began when Osceola and many Seminoles refused to move out of Florida, in accordance with an 1832 treaty, signed under coercion, under which they had promised to move west of the Mississippi. Over the next decade they were hunted down by the Army and, for the most part, killed off.

Right: *Osceola, leader of the Seminole Indians.*

Below right: *'Old Rough and Ready,' General Zachary Taylor, who acquired the nickname during his campaign against the Seminoles. He later led US forces in the Mexican War, as shown in this illustration.*

GEORGIA

30 Jan 1838
Osceola dies in dungeon

● Fort Marion

28 Dec 1835
Fort King

Only 3 soldiers survive the 'Dade massacre'

28 Dec 1835
Withlacoochee

FLORIDA

ATLANTIC OCEAN

25 Dec 1837
Okeechobee

Lake Okeechobee

Gulf of Mexico

EVERGLADES

BAHAMA IS.
(Brit.)

After 1841 Some Seminoles remain hidden in the Everglades

© Richard Natkiel, 1986

0   MILES   100
0   KILOMETERS   150

1832 Treaty of Payne's Landing
Seminoles required to leave Florida within 3 years

Apr 1835
Osceola organises resistance movement

1836-37
Many unsuccessful American expeditions. Seminoles retreat into Everglades

Spring 1841
Gen. Worth begins a 'scorched-earth' policy. Seminoles begin to surrender

Texas' Fight for Independence

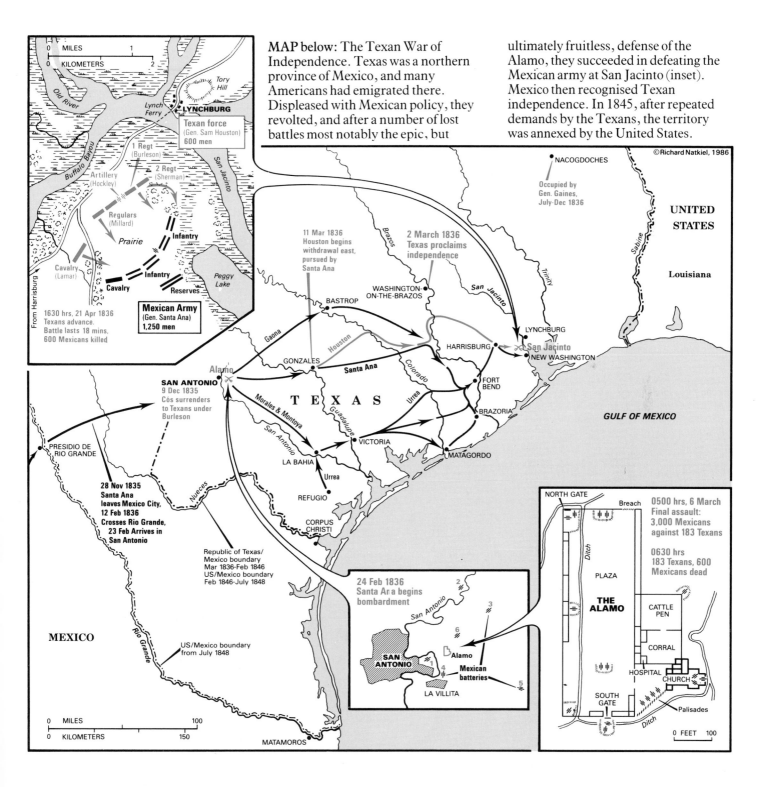

MAP below: The Texan War of Independence. Texas was a northern province of Mexico, and many Americans had emigrated there. Displeased with Mexican policy, they revolted, and after a number of lost battles most notably the epic, but ultimately fruitless, defense of the Alamo, they succeeded in defeating the Mexican army at San Jacinto (inset). Mexico then recognised Texan independence. In 1845, after repeated demands by the Texans, the territory was annexed by the United States.

©Richard Natkiel, 1986

MILES 0 ... 1
KILOMETERS 0 ... 2

Old River

Buffalo Bayou

San Jacinto

Lynch Ferry
LYNCHBURG
Tory Hill

Texan force
(Gen. Sam Houston)
600 men

1 Regt (Burleson)

Artillery (Hockley)

2 Regt (Sherman)

Regulars (Millard)

Prairie

Infantry

Cavalry (Lamar)

Infantry

Cavalry

Reserves

Peggy Lake

From Harrisburg

1630 hrs, 21 Apr 1836
Texans advance.
Battle lasts 18 mins,
600 Mexicans killed

Mexican Army
(Gen. Santa Ana)
1,250 men

NACOGDOCHES

Occupied by
Gen. Gaines,
July-Dec 1836

UNITED STATES

Louisiana

Sabine

Brazos

Trinity

11 Mar 1836
Houston begins
withdrawal east,
pursued by
Santa Ana

2 March 1836
Texas proclaims
independence

WASHINGTON-
ON-THE-BRAZOS

San Jacinto

BASTROP

Gaona

Houston

GONZALES

Santa Ana

Colorado

HARRISBURG

LYNCHBURG
San Jacinto
NEW WASHINGTON

Alamo

SAN ANTONIO
9 Dec 1835
Cós surrenders
to Texans under
Burleson

Morales & Montoya

T E X A S

Guadalupe

Urrea

FORT BEND

BRAZORIA

GULF OF MEXICO

San Antonio

VICTORIA

LA BAHIA

Urrea

MATAGORDO

PRESIDIO DE
RIO GRANDE

Nueces

28 Nov 1835
Santa Ana
leaves Mexico City,
12 Feb 1836
Crosses Rio Grande,
23 Feb Arrives in
San Antonio

REFUGIO

CORPUS
CHRISTI

Republic of Texas/
Mexico boundary
Mar 1836-Feb 1846
US/Mexico boundary
Feb 1846-July 1848

MEXICO

Rio Grande

US/Mexico boundary
from July 1848

0 MILES 100
0 KILOMETERS 150

MATAMOROS

24 Feb 1836
Santa Ana begins
bombardment

San Antonio

2

3

6

**SAN
ANTONIO**

1

4
Alamo

**Mexican
batteries**

5

LA VILLITA

NORTH GATE

Breach

0500 hrs, 6 March
Final assault:
3,000 Mexicans
against 183 Texans

0630 hrs
183 Texans, 600
Mexicans dead

Ditch

PLAZA

**THE
ALAMO**

CATTLE PEN

CORRAL

HOSPITAL

CHURCH

SOUTH GATE

Palisades

Ditch

0 FEET 100

The Maine and Oregon Frontiers

MAPS right: The evolution of the north-eastern frontier. Frontier delineation between the United States and British North America, especially in the extreme north-east and north-west, was frequently disputed, but peaceful agreements were eventually reached.

MAP below: The settlement of the Oregon boundary dispute. This was a long-standing dispute and the compromise finally adopted in 1846 was a continuation of the 49th Parallel frontier line westward to the Pacific, the part of Oregon lying north of that line becoming, in due course, the Canadian province of British Columbia.

Right: *American sailors and marines land in Mexico.*

Below right: *President Polk. An expansionist president, Polk secured the annexation of Texas, welcomed the Mexican War, and took an initially hard line in the Oregon dispute.*

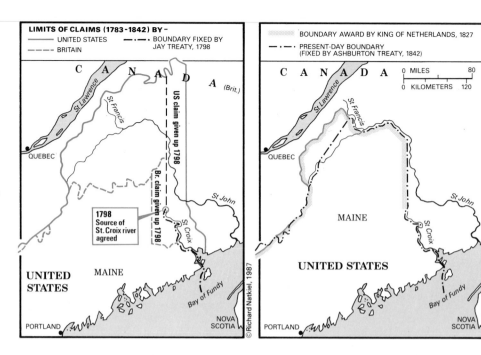

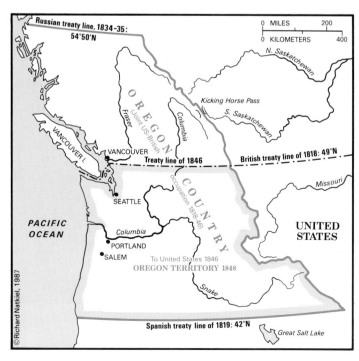

The Mexican War

MAP below: The course of the Mexican War. The first big battle, at Palo Alto, resulted in a Mexican defeat, and the war was virtually over within a year, even though peace was not made until 1848. Then and later, this war was denounced by many Americans as an aggression aimed at acquiring new states which would, by the Missouri Compromise, become slave states. Abraham Lincoln voted against the declaration of war.

Right: *The Battle of Buena Vista, the biggest of several Mexican defeats leading to the capture of Mexico City by the US Army.*

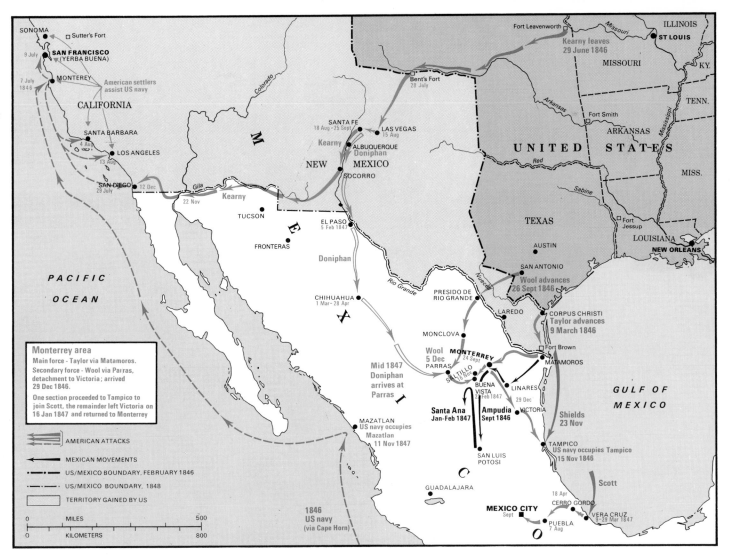

The Frontier with Mexico

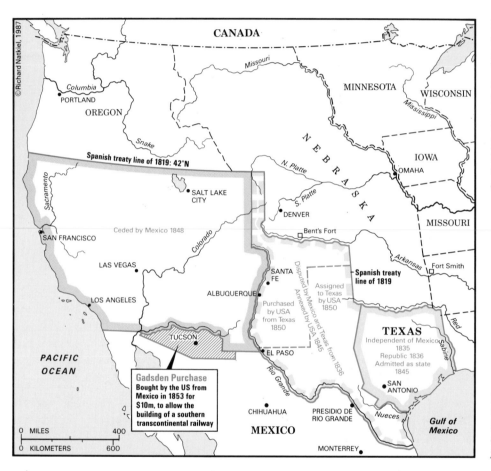

MAP left: United States expansion at the expense of Mexico. Most of the acquisitions emerged from the Mexican War, but the Gadsden Purchase, negotiated by a railroad promoter with the aim of securing a route for a transcontinental railroad controlled by the southern, slaveholding, states, was a peaceful acquisition. Ratified in 1854 by the Senate, this Purchase proved to be the final boundary adjustment of the continental USA.

Below: *A southern cotton plantation. Typical of innumerable such plantations, this employs slave labor but is dependent on steam for processing the crop and (far distance) for shipping its production to markets.*

Slavery and Secession

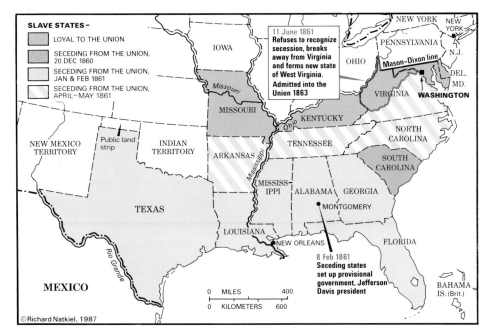

MAP right: The secession of the southern states. Secession was a three-stage process. The nucleus of Confederate states were those which voted for secession after the election of Lincoln in December 1860. These were followed by others in February 1861 when the Confederate Constitution was drafted. Four other slave states joined the Confederacy after the opening of hostilities with the bombardment of Fort Sumter in April, but four others, the northernmost tier, remained in the Union.

MAP below: Areas of preponderant slave population on the eve of the Civil War. In effect, these were the areas where slavery was most strongly regarded by the slaveowners as an economic necessity.

MAP below right: Main cotton-growing areas. Comparison with the adjacent map confirms that the most important cotton-growing areas were those with the highest proportion of slaves in the population.

Right: *A poster supporting Lincoln for the presidency in the 1860 election.*

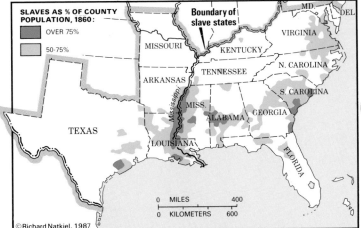

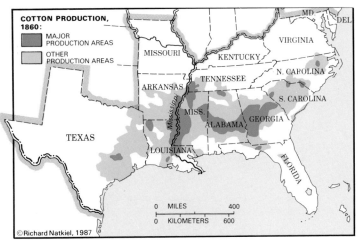

Battles of the Civil War

MAP below: The principal campaigns of the Civil War. The very wide area over which the war was fought, the frequent use of railroads to move troops, and the disproportionate involvement of Virginia and Tennessee, are very evident. This was the first war in which railroads became vital, but both sides, the South more than the North, mismanaged rail transport, allowing military officers to override experienced railroad administrations.

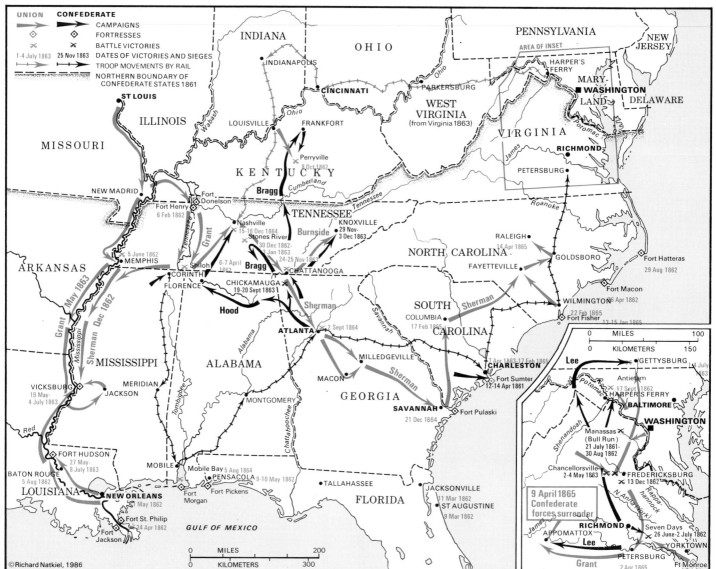

MAP right: The First Battle of Bull Run.
The Union Army commanded by
McDowell was intended to capture
Richmond but, finding the Confederates
under Beauregard well entrenched,
waited for three days before attacking.
Those three days enabled Confederate
reinforcements to be brought up, and the
result was a Union failure to capture the
position, followed by demoralization
and a retreat back to Washington.

MAP below: The prelude to the Battle of
Bull Run. The Confederates' use of the
railroad to bring up troops from
Piedmont Station was crucial to their
success here, for the reinforcements
arrived fresh as well as fast.

Bottom right: *General Sheridan. An Irish
immigrant, Sheridan led the cavalry of the
Union's Army of the Potomac.*

Above left: *A 13-inch rail-mounted mortar used
in the siege of Petersburg.*

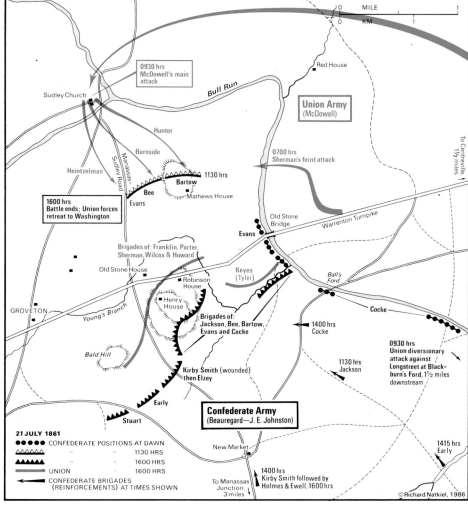

21 JULY 1861
●●●●● CONFEDERATE POSITIONS AT DAWN
△△△△△ " " 1130 HRS
▲▲▲▲▲ " " 1600 HRS
━━━━━ UNION " 1600 HRS
➤ CONFEDERATE BRIGADES
(REINFORCEMENTS) AT TIMES SHOWN

© Richard Natkiel, 1986

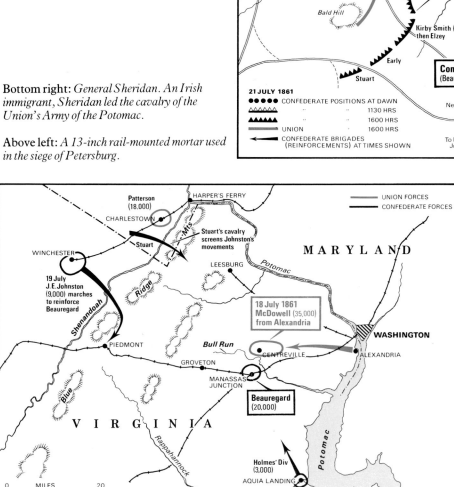

UNION FORCES
CONFEDERATE FORCES

© Richard Natkiel, 1986

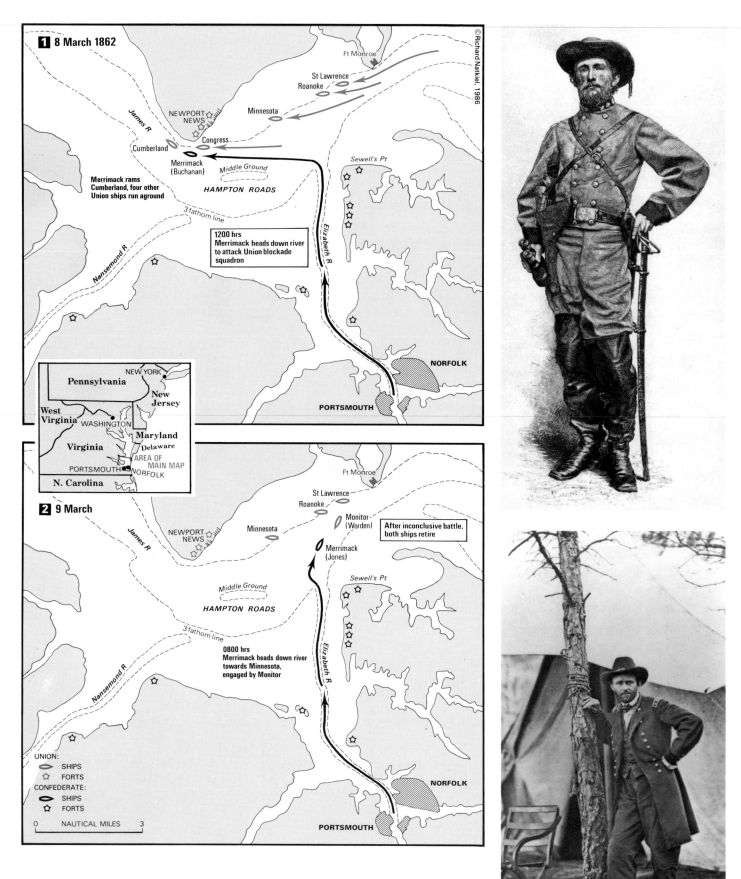

1 **8 March 1862**

Ft Monroe

St Lawrence
Roanoke

Minnesota

James R

NEWPORT NEWS

Congress
Cumberland

Merrimack (Buchanan)

Middle Ground

HAMPTON ROADS

Sewell's Pt

Merrimack rams Cumberland, four other Union ships run aground

3 fathom line

Nansemond R

Elizabeth R

1200 hrs Merrimack heads down river to attack Union blockade squadron

NORFOLK

PORTSMOUTH

©Richard Natkiel, 1986

NEW YORK

Pennsylvania

New Jersey

West Virginia
WASHINGTON

Maryland
Delaware

Virginia

AREA OF MAIN MAP

PORTSMOUTH NORFOLK

N. Carolina

2 **9 March**

Ft Monroe

St Lawrence
Roanoke

Monitor (Worden)

Minnesota

James R

NEWPORT NEWS

Merrimack (Jones)

After inconclusive battle, both ships retire

Middle Ground

HAMPTON ROADS

Sewell's Pt

3 fathom line

Nansemond R

Elizabeth R

0800 hrs Merrimack heads down river towards Minnesota, engaged by Monitor

NORFOLK

PORTSMOUTH

UNION:
SHIPS
FORTS
CONFEDERATE:
SHIPS
FORTS

0   NAUTICAL MILES   3

MAPS left: The Battle of Hampton Roads. This was the first major naval engagement and also a landmark in naval technology. The Confederates built the *Merrimack* into a massive, powerfully-armed ironclad, and sent her out to break the Union blockade. She did this very successfully, but then was confronted by the novel turret ship USS *Monitor*. Neither ship was sunk, but the *Merrimack* retired and the Union blockade of Hampton Roads was reimposed.

MAP right: Farragut's ships force their way up the Mississippi. This was the essential prelude to the capture of New Orleans from the Confederates.

Above left: *John S Mosby, a lawyer who formed 'Mosby's Rangers,' a mounted, fast-moving, partisan band which harried the Union forces.*

Below left: *General Ulysses S Grant, veteran of the Mexican War, Union victor at Vicksburg and Chattanooga, commander in chief of the Union armies, and subsequently US President.*

Below: *The famous contest between the* Merrimack *and the low-lying* Monitor.

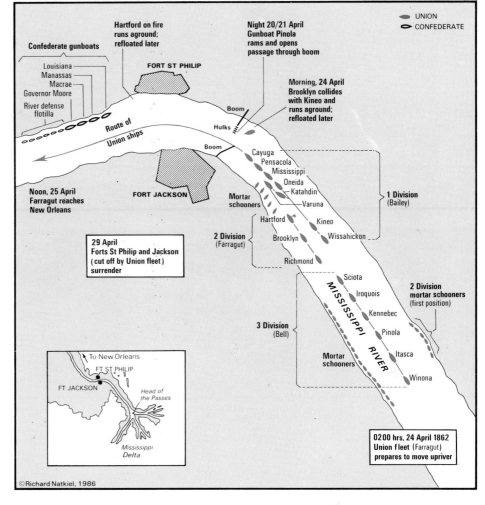

UNION
CONFEDERATE

Confederate gunboats
Louisiana
Manassas
Macrae
Governor Moore
River defense flotilla

FORT ST PHILIP

Hartford on fire runs aground; refloated later

Route of Union ships

Boom

Hulks

Boom

Night 20/21 April Gunboat Pinola rams and opens passage through boom

Morning, 24 April Brooklyn collides with Kineo and runs aground; refloated later

Cayuga
Pensacola
Mississippi
Oneida
Katahdin
Varuna

1 Division (Bailey)

Noon, 25 April Farragut reaches New Orleans

FORT JACKSON

Mortar schooners

Hartford

Kineo

2 Division (Farragut)

Brooklyn

Wissahickon

29 April Forts St Philip and Jackson (cut off by Union fleet) surrender

Richmond

Sciota

Iroquois

2 Division mortar schooners (first position)

Kennebec

3 Division (Bell)

Pinola

Mortar schooners

Itasca

Winona

MISSISSIPPI RIVER

To New Orleans
FT ST PHILIP
FT JACKSON
Head of the Passes
Mississippi Delta

0200 hrs, 24 April 1862 Union fleet (Farragut) prepares to move upriver

© Richard Natkiel, 1986

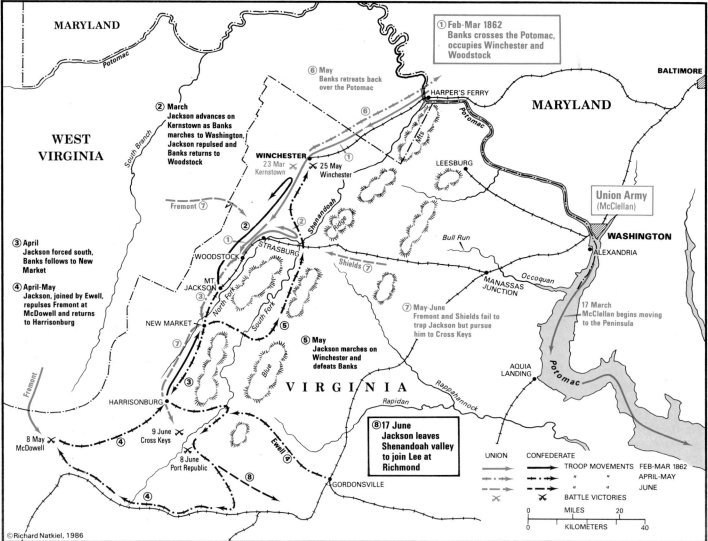

MARYLAND

WEST
VIRGINIA

① Feb-Mar 1862
Banks crosses the Potomac,
occupies Winchester and
Woodstock

⑥ May
Banks retreats back
over the Potomac

BALTIMORE

HARPER'S FERRY

MARYLAND

② March
Jackson advances on
Kernstown as Banks
marches to Washington,
Jackson repulsed and
Banks returns to
Woodstock

WINCHESTER
23 Mar
Kernstown

25 May
Winchester

LEESBURG

Potomac

Fremont ⑦

Union Army
(McClellan)

③ April
Jackson forced south,
Banks follows to New
Market

STRASBURG

WOODSTOCK

Bull Run

WASHINGTON

ALEXANDRIA

④ April-May
Jackson, joined by Ewell,
repulses Fremont at
McDowell and returns
to Harrisonburg

MT.
JACKSON

Shields ⑦

MANASSAS
JUNCTION

Occoquan

17 March
McClellan begins moving
to the Peninsula

NEW MARKET

⑤ May
Jackson marches on
Winchester and
defeats Banks

⑦ May-June
Fremont and Shields fail to
trap Jackson but pursue
him to Cross Keys

VIRGINIA

Rappahannock

AQUIA
LANDING

Potomac

Fremont

HARRISONBURG

Rapidan

8 May
McDowell

9 June
Cross Keys

Ewell ④

⑧ 17 June
Jackson leaves
Shenandoah valley
to join Lee at
Richmond

8 June
Port Republic

⑧

④

GORDONSVILLE

UNION   CONFEDERATE

TROOP MOVEMENTS   FEB-MAR 1862
"   "   APRIL-MAY
"   "   JUNE
BATTLE VICTORIES

0   MILES   20
0   KILOMETERS   40

© Richard Natkiel, 1986

MAP below left: Jackson's Valley Campaign of 1862. General 'Stonewall' Jackson, in a skilled delaying action, frustrated a Union attempt to capture Richmond by an advance along the Shenandoah Valley. Several Union armies tried to trap Jackson but he defeated them in succession before withdrawing to join Lee at Richmond.

MAP right: The Seven Days Battle. This was a series of counterattacks by General Lee against the faltering Union army of McClellan, which had been advancing toward Richmond, and resulted in the retirement of the Northerners. McClellan's army was completely withdrawn in August.

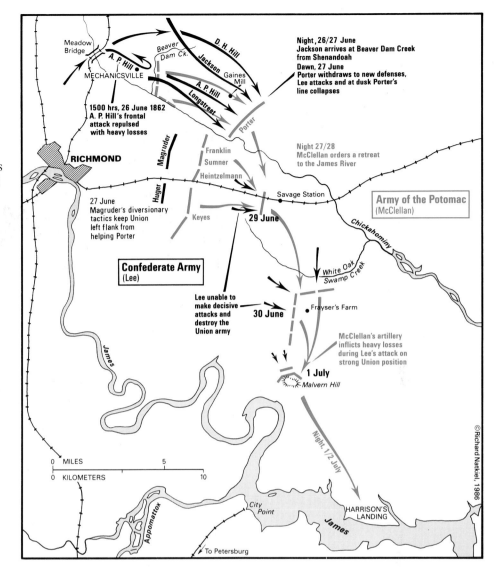

Night, 26/27 June
Jackson arrives at Beaver Dam Creek from Shenandoah
Dawn, 27 June
Porter withdraws to new defenses, Lee attacks and at dusk Porter's line collapses

1500 hrs, 26 June 1862
A. P. Hill's frontal attack repulsed with heavy losses

Night 27/28
McClellan orders a retreat to the James River

Army of the Potomac (McClellan)

27 June
Magruder's diversionary tactics keep Union left flank from helping Porter

Confederate Army (Lee)

Lee unable to make decisive attacks and destroy the Union army

McClellan's artillery inflicts heavy losses during Lee's attack on strong Union position

29 June

30 June

1 July

Night, 1/2 July

©Richard Natkiel, 1986

Above left: *The 1st Connecticut Heavy Artillery. This was one of the prime regiments serving in the Union Army.*

Below: *A pontoon bridge at Jericho Mills.*

Below right: *Fort Sumter, just after the bombardment that began the Civil War.*

66

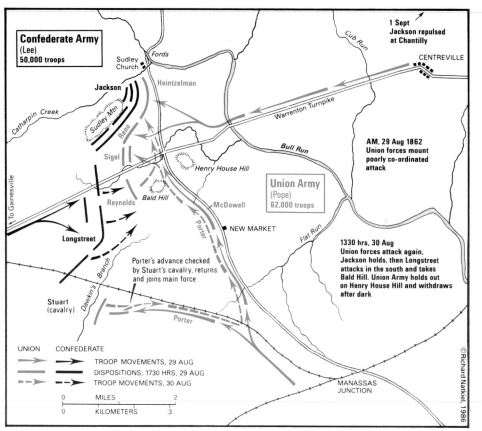

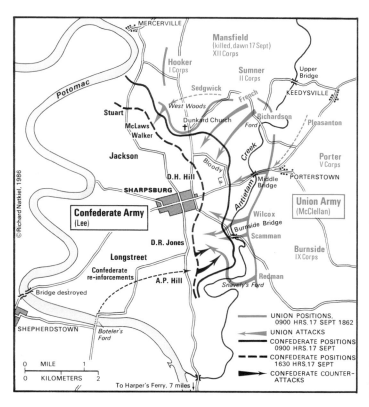

MAP left: The Second Battle of Bull Run. Sometimes known as Second Manassas, this was very much a repetition of the previous year's battle, with Northern forces, descending from Washington to capture Richmond, being thrown back.

MAP below left: Battle of Sharpsburg (Antietam). Taking advantage of the victory of Second Bull Run, Lee advanced into Maryland but was overhauled by McClellan with a stronger force. The Union attempt to turn Lee's flanks was unsuccessful. There were more than 20,000 casualties but the battle was indecisive, although the casualty list persuaded Lee to end his offensive.

Below: *The Union Army's infantry; two privates and a lieutenant from Michigan.*

MAP below: The Battle of Chancellorsville. Hooker's Union Army, attempting to capture Fredericksburg in a two-pronged advance, found its right wing attacked by Lee's Confederates at Chancellorsville. There were about 30,000 casualties in this battle, which resulted in Hooker's retreat.

Left: The carnage of the Civil War, casualties at Fredericksburg. Despite the relatively small population, American deaths in the Civil War exceeded those of World War II.

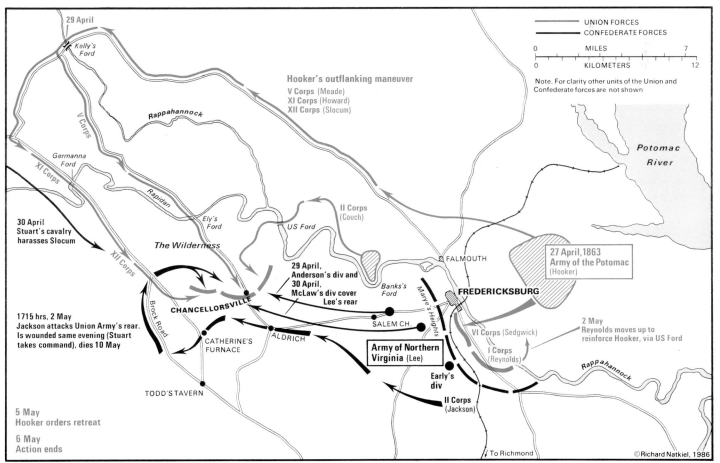

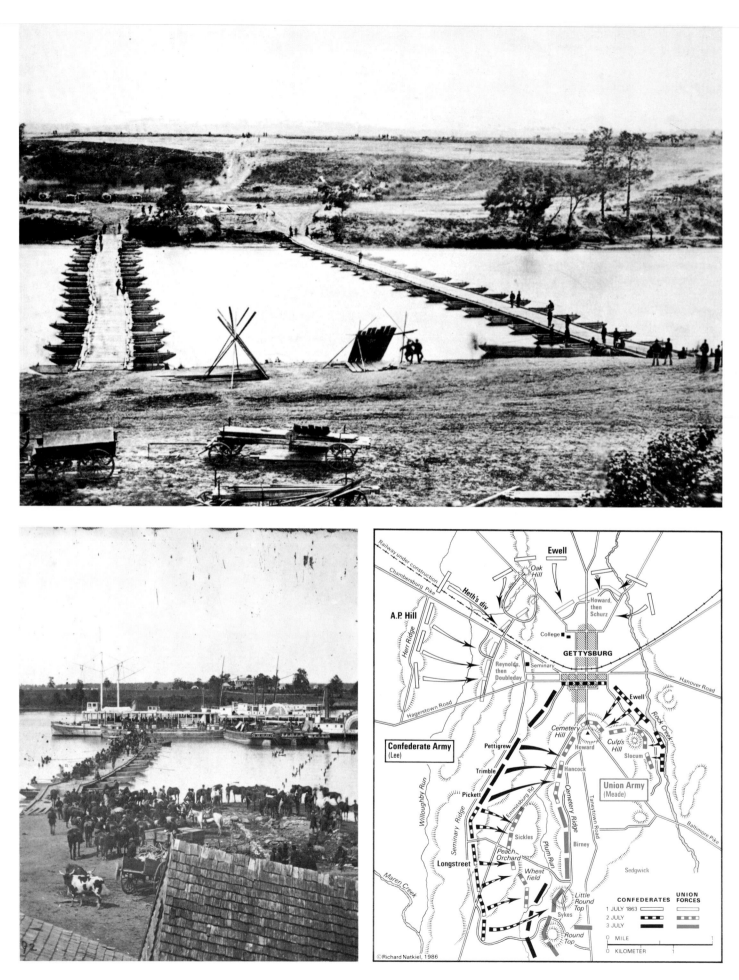

MAP below left: Gettysburg, the decisive battle. General Lee's Confederates, after roaming through southern Pennsylvania virtually unopposed by the shaken Union forces, concentrated at Gettysburg before assaulting that town. Favored by their elevated positions, the Union defenders inflicted heavy casualties and after a final unsuccessful assault on Cemetery Hill the Confederates retired to Virginia.

MAP below: The Union's capture of Vicksburg. By 1863 Vicksburg was the Confederacy's one remaining strongpoint on the Mississippi. General Grant finally succeeded in capturing it when he adopted a plan that involved the preliminary capture of Jackson and then a westward advance.

Left: *Bridgework by the Union Army's engineers across the Rappahannock.*

Bottom left: *A troop movement by steamboat.*

Right: *One of the several thousand dead at Gettysburg; a Confederate soldier killed in the heights north of the town.*

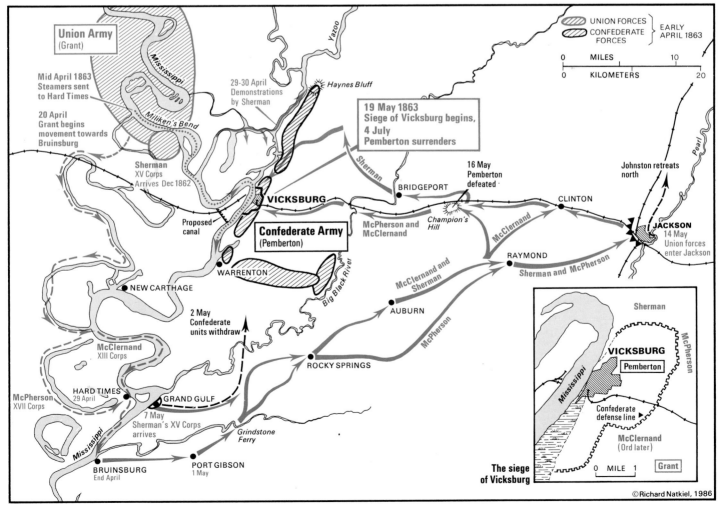

UNION FORCES
CONFEDERATE FORCES
} EARLY APRIL 1863

Union Army (Grant)

Mid April 1863 Steamers sent to Hard Times

20 April Grant begins movement towards Bruinsburg

29-30 April Demonstrations by Sherman

Haynes Bluff

19 May 1863 Siege of Vicksburg begins, 4 July Pemberton surrenders

Sherman XV Corps Arrives Dec 1862

Proposed canal

VICKSBURG

Confederate Army (Pemberton)

WARRENTON

NEW CARTHAGE

2 May Confederate units withdraw

McClernand XIII Corps

HARD TIMES 29 April

McPherson XVII Corps

GRAND GULF

7 May Sherman's XV Corps arrives

Grindstone Ferry

BRUINSBURG End April

PORT GIBSON 1 May

ROCKY SPRINGS

AUBURN

Big Black River

McClernand and Sherman

McPherson

16 May Pemberton defeated

BRIDGEPORT

McPherson and McClernand

Champion's Hill

RAYMOND

McClernand

Sherman and McPherson

CLINTON

Johnston retreats north

JACKSON 14 May Union forces enter Jackson

Pearl

The siege of Vicksburg

Sherman

VICKSBURG

Pemberton

McPherson

Confederate defense line

McClernand (Ord later)

Grant

0   MILE   1

© Richard Natkiel, 1986

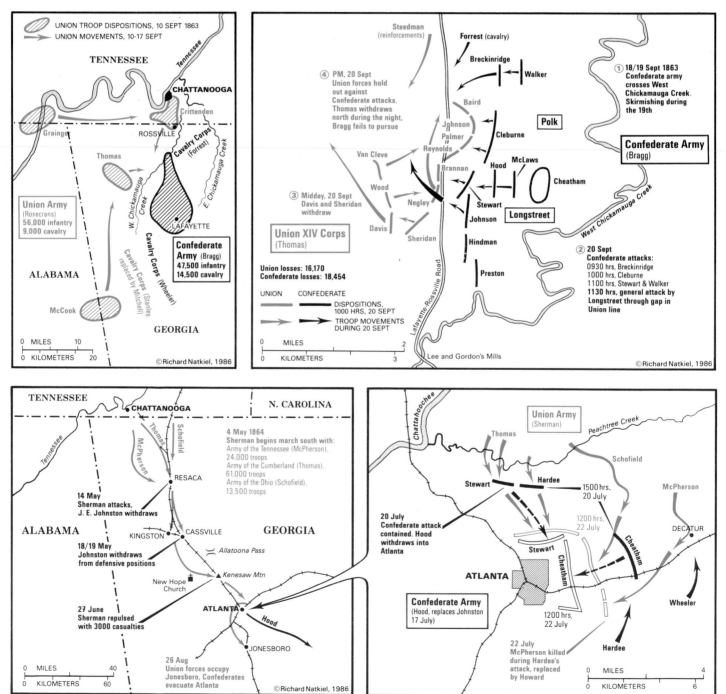

UNION TROOP DISPOSITIONS, 10 SEPT 1863

UNION MOVEMENTS, 10-17 SEPT

TENNESSEE

Tennessee

CHATTANOOGA

Crittenden

Grainger

ROSSVILLE

Thomas

Cavalry Corps
(Forrest)

W. Chickamauga Creek

E. Chickamauga Creek

Union Army
(Rosecrans)
56,000 infantry
9,000 cavalry

LAFAYETTE

Cavalry Corps
(Stanley,
replaced by Mitchell)

Confederate Army (Bragg)
47,500 infantry
14,500 cavalry

ALABAMA

McCook

GEORGIA

0 MILES 10
0 KILOMETERS 20

©Richard Natkiel, 1986

Steedman
(reinforcements)

Forrest (cavalry)

Breckinridge

Walker

④ PM, 20 Sept
Union forces hold
out against
Confederate attacks.
Thomas withdraws
north during the night,
Bragg fails to pursue

Baird

Johnson

Palmer

Reynolds

Van Cleve

Brannan

Wood

Negley

③ Midday, 20 Sept
Davis and Sheridan
withdraw

Davis

Sheridan

Union XIV Corps
(Thomas)

Union losses: 16,170
Confederate losses: 18,454

UNION   CONFEDERATE

DISPOSITIONS,
1000 HRS, 20 SEPT

TROOP MOVEMENTS
DURING 20 SEPT

0 MILES 2
0 KILOMETERS 3

Polk

Cleburne

Hood   McLaws

Cheatham

Stewart

Longstreet

Johnson

Hindman

Preston

① 18/19 Sept 1863
Confederate army
crosses West
Chickamauga Creek.
Skirmishing during
the 19th

Confederate Army
(Bragg)

West Chickamauga Creek

② 20 Sept
Confederate attacks:
0930 hrs, Breckinridge
1000 hrs, Cleburne
1100 hrs, Stewart & Walker
1130 hrs, general attack by
Longstreet through gap in
Union line

Lafayette-Rossville Road

Lee and Gordon's Mills

©Richard Natkiel, 1986

TENNESSEE

CHATTANOOGA

N. CAROLINA

Thomas

Schofield

McPherson

RESACA

4 May 1864
Sherman begins march south with:
Army of the Tennessee (McPherson),
24,000 troops
Army of the Cumberland (Thomas),
61,000 troops
Army of the Ohio (Schofield),
13,500 troops

14 May
Sherman attacks,
J. E. Johnston withdraws

ALABAMA

KINGSTON   CASSVILLE

GEORGIA

18/19 May
Johnston withdraws
from defensive positions

Allatoona Pass

New Hope
Church

Kenesaw Mtn

27 June
Sherman repulsed
with 3000 casualties

ATLANTA

Hood

JONESBORO

26 Aug
Union forces occupy
Jonesboro, Confederates
evacuate Atlanta

0 MILES 40
0 KILOMETERS 60

©Richard Natkiel, 1986

Chattahoochee

Union Army
(Sherman)

Thomas

Peachtree Creek

Schofield

Stewart   Hardee

1500 hrs,
20 July

McPherson

20 July
Confederate attack
contained. Hood
withdraws into
Atlanta

Stewart

1200 hrs,
22 July

Cheatham

DECATUR

ATLANTA

Cheatham

Confederate Army
(Hood, replaces Johnston
17 July)

1200 hrs,
22 July

Wheeler

22 July
McPherson killed
during Hardee's
attack, replaced
by Howard

Hardee

0 MILES 4
0 KILOMETERS 6

MAP right: The Battle of Mobile Bay. Admiral Farragut took his US Navy ships under the guns of Fort Morgan, through minefields, and up to the powerful Confederate ironclad *Tennessee*, which was eventually defeated. This action closed Mobile to the Confederacy.

MAPS opposite, center left and center right: The Battle of Chickamauga. After the capture of Vicksburg the next major Union goal in the west was Chattanooga. But the Confederates brought up reinforcements from the east in a well-organized railroad operation. In the resulting battle of Chickamauga Creek the Union forces were badly mauled, and took refuge in Chattanooga.

MAPS bottom left: Sherman's Union troops capture Atlanta. In 1864, having secured Chattanooga, the Union Army could envision an advance from there along the railroad into Georgia. This was led by General Sherman, who captured Atlanta after a series of costly engagements with the retreating but robust Confederate army of General Johnston.

Above left: *Abraham Lincoln visits his generals.*

Below: *Troopers of the Union's 3rd Pennsylvania Cavalry photographed at Brandy Station, Virginia, in 1864.*

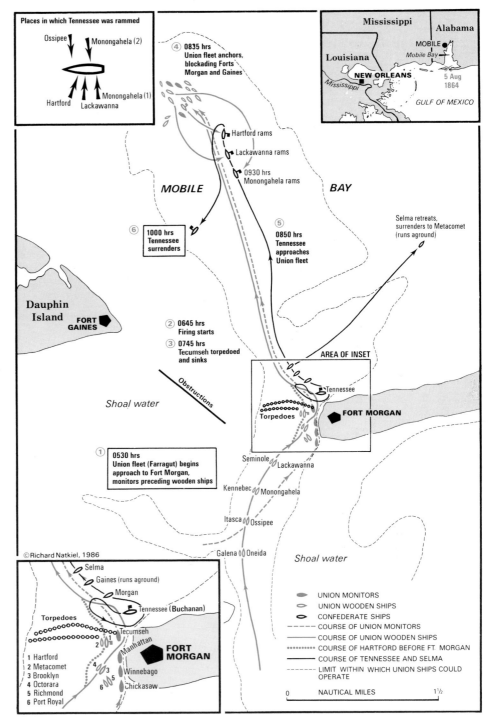

Places in which Tennessee was rammed

Ossipee   Monongahela (2)

Hartford   Lackawanna   Monongahela (1)

Mississippi   Alabama

Louisiana   MOBILE
             Mobile Bay

Mississippi   NEW ORLEANS   5 Aug 1864

GULF OF MEXICO

④ 0835 hrs Union fleet anchors, blockading Forts Morgan and Gaines

Hartford rams

Lackawanna rams

0930 hrs Monongahela rams

MOBILE   BAY

Selma retreats, surrenders to Metacomet (runs aground)

⑥ 1000 hrs Tennessee surrenders

⑤ 0850 hrs Tennessee approaches Union fleet

Dauphin Island   FORT GAINES

② 0645 hrs Firing starts

③ 0745 hrs Tecumseh torpedoed and sinks

AREA OF INSET

Tennessee

Obstructions

Shoal water   Torpedoes   FORT MORGAN

① 0530 hrs Union fleet (Farragut) begins approach to Fort Morgan, monitors preceding wooden ships

Seminole   Lackawanna

Kennebec   Monongahela

Itasca   Ossipee

©Richard Natkiel, 1986   Galena   Oneida   Shoal water

Selma

Gaines (runs aground)

Morgan

Torpedoes   Tennessee (Buchanan)

Tecumseh

Manhattan   FORT MORGAN

1 Hartford
2 Metacomet   Winnebago
3 Brooklyn
4 Octorara   Chickasaw
5 Richmond
6 Port Royal

UNION MONITORS
UNION WOODEN SHIPS
CONFEDERATE SHIPS
COURSE OF UNION MONITORS
COURSE OF UNION WOODEN SHIPS
COURSE OF HARTFORD BEFORE FT. MORGAN
COURSE OF TENNESSEE AND SELMA
LIMIT WITHIN WHICH UNION SHIPS COULD OPERATE

0   NAUTICAL MILES   1½

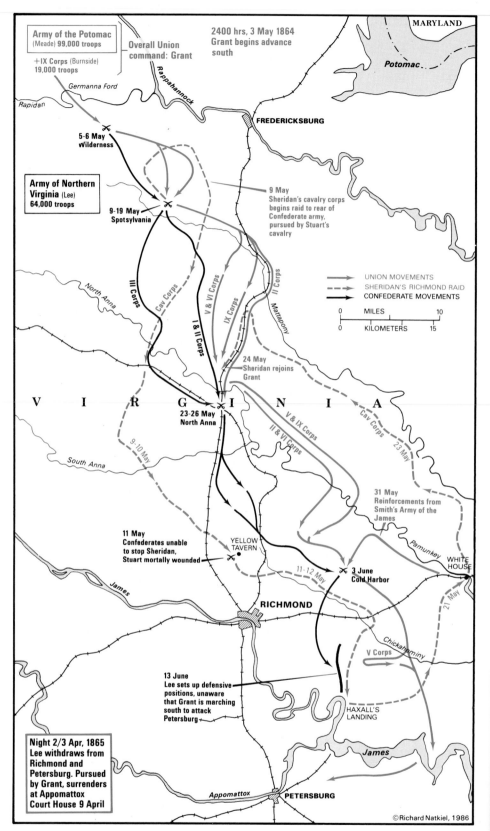

Army of the Potomac (Meade) 99,000 troops

+IX Corps (Burnside) 19,000 troops

Germanna Ford

Rapidan

Overall Union command: Grant

2400 hrs, 3 May 1864 Grant begins advance south

MARYLAND

Potomac

Rappahannock

FREDERICKSBURG

5-6 May Wilderness

Army of Northern Virginia (Lee) 64,000 troops

9-19 May Spotsylvania

9 May Sheridan's cavalry corps begins raid to rear of Confederate army, pursued by Stuart's cavalry

North Anna

III Corps

Cav Corps

V & VI Corps

IX Corps

I & II Corps

II Corps

Mattapony

24 May Sheridan rejoins Grant

V I R G I N I A

23-26 May North Anna

V & IX Corps

II & VI Corps

Cav Corps 23 May

South Anna

9-10 May

31 May Reinforcements from Smith's Army of the James

11 May Confederates unable to stop Sheridan, Stuart mortally wounded

YELLOW TAVERN

Pamunkey

WHITE HOUSE

3 June Cold Harbor

11-12 May

James

RICHMOND

21 May

V Corps

Chickahominy

13 June Lee sets up defensive positions, unaware that Grant is marching south to attack Petersburg

HAXALL'S LANDING

James

Night 2/3 Apr, 1865 Lee withdraws from Richmond and Petersburg. Pursued by Grant, surrenders at Appomattox Court House 9 April

Appomattox

PETERSBURG

UNION MOVEMENTS
SHERIDAN'S RICHMOND RAID
CONFEDERATE MOVEMENTS

MILES 0 — 10
KILOMETERS 0 — 15

©Richard Natkiel, 1986

MAP left: General Grant's 1864 advance on Richmond, the Confederate capital. While, in the west, Sherman was advancing on Atlanta, the Union's Army of the Potomac was moving south from Washington toward Richmond. Almost 100,000 strong, it suffered heavy casualties from Lee's delaying actions before it stealthily crossed the James River and, unknown to Lee, marched on Petersburg.

MAP right: Sherman's celebrated march through Georgia. Meeting little opposition, Sherman's Union Army took the opportunity to pillage and burn as much as possible during this excursion, ostensibly to weaken Southern morale.

MAP opposite, bottom left: The siege of Petersburg. Although Lee held off the Union besiegers, the approach of Sherman from the south and Sheridan from the north to support Grant made his long-term situation untenable.

MAP opposite, bottom right: Lee's breakout from Petersburg. This breakout was thwarted when, at the Battle of Five Forks, Lee's flank was turned by Sheridan. Grant followed this with an attack on the Confederate line and then occupied Richmond. A week later Lee surrendered the Confederate army at Appomattox Court House.

Right: *The Battle of Antietam.*

Far right: *The Battle of Lookout Hill, one of many small engagements in 1863.*

Below: *Defensive earthworks of the Civil War.*

73

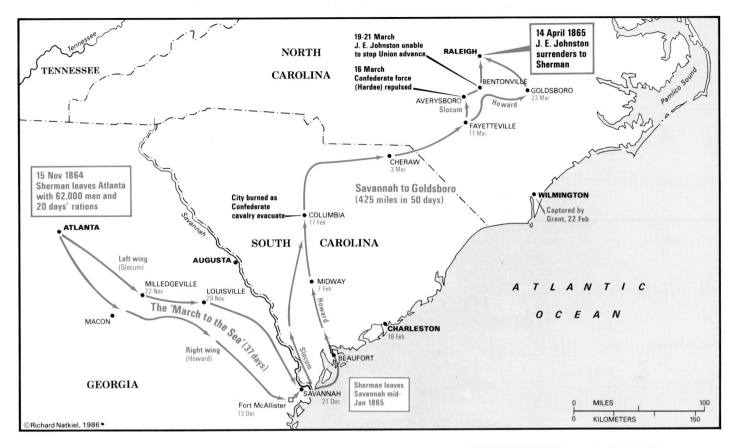

NORTH CAROLINA

19-21 March
J. E. Johnston unable
to stop Union advance

14 April 1865
J. E. Johnston
surrenders to
Sherman

16 March
Confederate force
(Hardee) repulsed

RALEIGH

BENTONVILLE

AVERYSBORO · GOLDSBORO 23 Mar
Slocum · *Howard*

FAYETTEVILLE
11 Mar

15 Nov 1864
Sherman leaves Atlanta
with 62,000 men and
20 days' rations

CHERAW
3 Mar

Savannah to Goldsboro
(425 miles in 50 days)

WILMINGTON
Captured by
Grant, 22 Feb

City burned as
Confederate
cavalry evacuate

COLUMBIA
17 Feb

TENNESSEE

ATLANTA

Left wing
(Slocum)

AUGUSTA

SOUTH CAROLINA

MILLEDGEVILLE
22 Nov

LOUISVILLE
29 Nov

MIDWAY
7 Feb

MACON

The 'March to the Sea' (37 days)

Right wing
(Howard)

Howard

Slocum

GEORGIA

Savannah

CHARLESTON
18 Feb

BEAUFORT

A T L A N T I C

O C E A N

Fort McAllister
13 Dec

SAVANNAH
21 Dec

Sherman leaves
Savannah mid-
Jan 1865

© Richard Natkiel, 1986

MILES 0 — 100
KILOMETERS 0 — 150

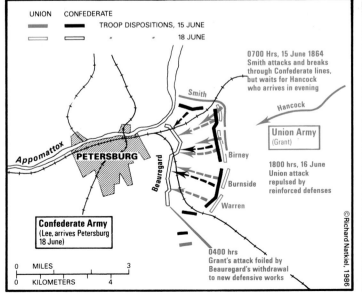

UNION CONFEDERATE
——— ——— TROOP DISPOSITIONS, 15 JUNE
▭ ▬ " " " 18 JUNE

0700 Hrs, 15 June 1864
Smith attacks and breaks
through Confederate lines,
but waits for Hancock
who arrives in evening

Smith · Hancock

Union Army
(Grant)

Birney

1800 hrs, 16 June
Union attack
repulsed by
reinforced defenses

Burnside

Warren

PETERSBURG

Appomattox

Beauregard

Confederate Army
(Lee, arrives Petersburg
18 June)

0400 hrs
Grant's attack foiled by
Beauregard's withdrawal
to new defensive works

MILES 0 — 3
KILOMETERS 0 — 4

© Richard Natkiel, 1986

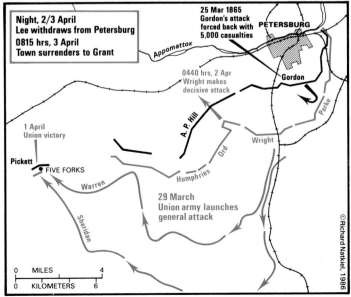

Night, 2/3 April
Lee withdraws from Petersburg
0815 hrs, 3 April
Town surrenders to Grant

25 Mar 1865
Gordon's attack
forced back with
5,000 casualties

PETERSBURG

Appomattox

Gordon

0440 hrs, 2 Apr
Wright makes
decisive attack

A. P. Hill

Parke

1 April
Union victory

Pickett

FIVE FORKS

Warren

Ord

Wright

Humphries

29 March
Union army launches
general attack

Sheridan

MILES 0 — 4
KILOMETERS 0 — 6

© Richard Natkiel, 1986

US troops ordered out, rather unnecessarily, to protect railway property in Chicago during the Pullman strike of 1894.

Imperial Democracy

During the years immediately after the Civil War, the government's greatest political concern was Reconstruction of the Southern states. This task seemed simple at the outset, but eventually it bogged down irretrievably in the complexities surrounding the election of 1876.

The initial feeling that Reconstruction would be a simple matter stemmed from the abject condition of the South at the end of the war – its economy in ruins, many of its towns and cities shattered, the aura of defeat everywhere. Southerners appeared eager to begin again, despite vivid memories of the ordeal through which they had passed. Northerners, too, had borne a huge human cost during the war, but for them those years had fostered prosperity rather than poverty, as war orders poured into their factories. For the most part Northern farmlands, towns, and cities were untouched by the war. The people of the North looked forward to continued national growth for every part of the nation, including the defeated South.

It was an unfortunate combination of national politics and a Northern perception of Southern intransigence that resulted in the harsh measures of Reconstruction. Military occupation of Southern States was never foreseen at the outset. But President Andrew Johnson assumed that he had the right, as chief executive, to reconstruct the South – the Constitution was silent on this novel subject. He may also have been courted by Southerners who hoped for a mild Federal policy, especially in view of Johnson's Tennessee background and known racism. The President was promptly opposed by leading Congressmen who believed that Reconstruction was a Congressional prerogative. When Johnson arranged to admit Southern representatives and senators to Congress, his effort at presidential Reconstruction came to naught: Congress refused them admission on the basis of its right to choose its membership. Early in 1866 the increasing dissension between Johnson and Congress came into the open, and so-called Radical Republicans seized control of Reconstruction. The First Reconstruction Act of 1867, passed over Johnson's veto, divided the South into five military districts subject to martial law. It mandated new state conventions, with delegates chosen by universal manhood suffrage, and establishment of state governments guaranteeing black suffrage and ratifying the Fourteenth Amendment, which defined citizenship. Supplementary Reconstruction Acts followed, forcing action on the part of dilatory Southerners.

Early in 1868 President Johnson violated the Tenure of Office Act, which required Congressional consent for removal of cabinet officers and other officials appointed with consent of Congress; the president rightly believed the act to be unconstitutional. With this excuse Congress filed articles of impeachment against Johnson. He was tried by the Senate and acquitted on 16 May 1868 – the only president so arraigned. Congressional Reconstruction continued into the 1870s, with increasing resistance by Southerners and decreasing concern among Northerners. Then the presidential election of 1876 proved impossible to resolve short of an electoral commission, because of disputes over electors chosen by Southern States and by Oregon. The eventual choice of the Republican candidate, Rutherford B Hayes, involved an implicit agreement in favor of the South by consenting to withdrawal of Federal troops from Southern States. Actually, by this time conservatives had won control in Georgia, North Carolina, Tennessee, and Virginia (1869-71); and then in Alabama, Arkansas, Mississippi, and Texas (1874-5). By the year of the disputed national election, only Florida, Louisiana, and South Carolina remained in Radical Republican hands. In January 1877, so-called carpetbag rule (by Republicans) ended in Florida. Radicals also lost out in the two remaining states of the South, and Federal troops withdrew from South Carolina on 10 April and from Louisiana on 24 April.

In subsequent years the post-Civil War rush of settlers into the Far West (beyond the Mississippi) led to new states, notably in the Omnibus Bill of 22 February 1889. It provided for admission of North Dakota, South Dakota, Montana, and Washington. Oklahoma, settled under bedlam conditions in 1889 after the opening of what had been Indian Territory, became a state in 1907.

As the Civil War's end encouraged settlers to move into the Far West, railroad builders were motivated to span the continent. The years after 1865 might well be entitled the Railroad Age. The country's economy needed binding together to a much greater degree than in prewar times, for industry now anticipated a continental market based on transportation by rail.

The secession of the Southern States during the Civil War improved the climate for industry in the North. The Southerners had seen any Federal assistance for industry as a boon only to Northern industry and had frequently voted against it. With their representatives gone, Civil War Congresses were free to encourage transportation and manufactures, the former with subsidies, the latter with tariffs. The Pacific Railroad Act of 1 July 1862, enacted before the war's outcome could be known, authorized the Union Pacific Railway to build a line from Nebraska to Utah, where it was to meet the Central Pacific inching east from California. The government made land grants of ten alternate sections per mile on both sides of the projected railway. When the two railroads joined at Promontory Point in Utah (10 May 1869) after astonishing feats of construction, it was one of the major acts of US transportation history. This transcontinental road was soon followed by other lines. Congress chartered a northern route in 1864, from Lake Superior to Portland, Oregon. Completed in 1883, the Northern Pacific rivaled the accomplishment of its predecessor of 1869. Another northern route begun in 1878 reached Seattle by 1893; it was accomplished without land grants by the promotion of farm settlement along the entire route, to create traffic. On the 35th parallel appeared the Atchison, Topeka and Santa Fe railroad, authorized by a Congressional land grant of 1863 – 3 million acres in alternate sections of Kansas. Twenty years later it reached Los Angeles. A southern route along the 32nd parallel went to El Paso by 1881, and the next year joined eastern lines to complete a route to New Orleans.

Meanwhile, railroads were also expanding into the South. The Chesapeake and Ohio reached Asheville, North Carolina, in 1892; the Norfolk and Western extended to the Ohio Valley in 1892. The principal north-south portion of the Southern Railway opened to Atlanta in 1873. Southern Florida was reached by the 1890s.

After the Civil War railroad consolidations were the order of the day in the East. The New York Central was organized in 1867, the Pennsylvania Railroad in 1870. The Erie expanded into a major line. Such men as Cornelius Vanderbilt, Daniel Drew, Jay Gould, James Fisk, and J P Morgan, Sr made large fortunes from consolidations.

An estimate of all public lands granted to railroads runs to 155 million acres – almost the area of Texas. The Northern Pacific took the lion's share, 44 million, with the Central Pacific (which controlled the Southern Pacific) next with 24 million. The Union Pacific obtained 20 million, the Santa Fe only 17 million. The Federal Government eventually took back 25 million acres for noncompletion of projected railroads, but this minor renegotiation of an unprecedented gift subtracted little from its munificence. Western States also granted railroads 49 million acres.

After the turn of the century, the nation's railroads continued to increase their trackage, which in 1860 totaled 30,000 miles and in 1900 reached 250,000. The decade from 1900 to 1910 saw another 100,000 miles of construction. Peak trackage occurred in 1930, with 429,883 miles, after which a decline set in that turned downward sharply after World War II.

Additions to trackage after the Civil War showed not merely the increasing industrialization of the country, but its rapidly rising population, which totaled 100 million by 1915, up from roughly 3 million in Revolutionary days. Most of the increase between 1775 and 1915 was caused by what nineteenth-century observers described as the American multiplication table, that is, the excess of births over deaths. The average family size in the nineteenth century was five, a number that began to drop only after 1900. Meanwhile, there was an enormous influx of immigrants, partly from Canada and Mexico but mainly from Western Europe. Immigrants numbered 26 million between 1865 and 1915. Throughout the post-Civil War years, population mounted inexorably, reaching (in millions) 5 by 1800, 9 in 1820, 17 in 1840, 31 in 1860, 40 in 1870, 50 in 1880, 63 in 1890, 76 in 1900, 92 (the result of huge immigration) in 1910. Of this increase, black Americans constituted a varying proportion: 1 million in 1800, 1.7 in 1820, 2.8 in 1840, 4.4 in 1860, 6.5 in 1880, 8.4 in 1900, 10 in 1910. Compared to black Americans, the number of Indians in the continental United States was minuscule. Until 1890 the statistics on Indians did not include people in Indian Territory or on reservations. Hence the figure for 1890 represented the first reliable calculation – 125,000. By 1900 it had fallen to 120,000, but it rose to 135,000 in 1915.

The enumeration of the Indians marked the end of an era, as did the last Indian war at the end of 1890, in which the Indians met defeat at the Battle of Wounded Knee. Their enumeration and conquest went hand in hand with the announcement that the frontier had ceased to exist. The director of the census in 1890 declared that the apparently endless American quest for land farther west had come to an end. The frontier, according to the historian Frederick J Turner, had been a place of renewal, where failures might find success again – a safety valve for the discontented. Now that place of renewal was gone forever.

When the era of free or nearly free land closed, another opened – what one might describe as the era of conservation. No longer could Americans spend their resources, especially their lands, as if they were inexhaustible. President Theodore Roosevelt, after the turn of the century, voiced the new need for conservation. Himself a homesteader and rancher during the 1880s, Roosevelt sensed deeply the need for conservation. At the outset of his administration in 1901, he said that conservation of forest and water resources was a problem of vital import. During his administration the Federal Government set aside nearly 150 million acres as national forest lands; 80 million acres of mineral lands were withdrawn from public sale, and 1.5 million acres of water-power sites. In later years many of the Roosevelt national forests became national parks,

Below: Opposition to the Freedman's Bureau, established by Congress after the Civil War to assist former slaves.

where urban Americans could reclaim their wilderness heritage for a while.

In foreign relations the Republic desired and accomplished little in the years after the Civil War. Only a generation later, in the 1890s, did the nation begin to look outward. As late as 1895, when revolution broke out in nearby Cuba, the people of the United States were unconcerned, perhaps because the mid-1890s found the country in the trough of economic depression. The depression seemed to begin with a panic in 1893 and continued until roughly 1897. The panic of the 1890s was worldwide, and played some part – a downturn in the price of Cuban sugar – in bringing revolution to the Ever Faithful Isle. But there was no easy or quick decision: rather a protracted conflict that apparently neither the Cubans nor the Spanish could win. Then a Spanish commander sought to separate revolutionaries from loyalists in the countryside by bringing Cubans of every persuasion into 'reconcentration camps' where his troops could watch them. American sentiment altered as disease began to afflict the camps and reports circulated that thousands of Cubans were dying. By the spring of 1898 the reports were confirmed by a visiting delegation of Americans that included a respected senator, Redfield Proctor. Meanwhile, the United States ship *Maine* exploded mysteriously in Havana Harbor on 15 February 1898. President William McKinley proposed that the Spanish relinquish Cuba, which they refused to do, and on 20 April the United States declared war on Spain.

If ever there was 'a splendid little war,' as Senator Henry Cabot Lodge predicted to his friend Theodore Roosevelt, it was the summer war of 1898, which began in April and ended in an armistice on 12 August. The United States marshaled 275,000 men, almost all volunteers, of whom 5500 died – though only 379 deaths were battle casualties, the rest being attributed to disease and other causes. The war's cost was a mere $250 million. Spanish forces in Cuba, Puerto Rico, and the Philippines suffered more casualties, but not many. They, too, soon realized that the contest between Spain, with its population of 19 million, and the United States, with its 75 million, was altogether unequal.

US strategy called for direct strikes on the enemy by land and sea. Three principal actions resulted, two of them naval engagements. Commodore George B Dewey, with a small squadron of half a dozen ships, was at Hong Kong when war broke out and departed from Mirs Bay, China, on 27 April. He entered Manila Bay three days later and on the morning of 1 May engaged a Spanish squadron of twice his size off Cavite. With the loss of one man, who died of a heart attack while the squadron was moving up the bay, Dewey destroyed or captured the Spanish ships. In response to his subsequent request for troops to take Manila and the Philippines, the War Department sent 10,000 men. After a token Spanish resistance, the Americans captured Manila on 13 August, almost at the same time as the armistice ending the war was being announced in Washington.

Meanwhile, Cuba had been invaded on 22 June by a force of 17,000 regulars and volunteers who besieged Santiago. The Spanish squadron that had taken refuge in the harbor attempted to escape to the open sea on the morning of 3 July, but the Americans destroyed it in a battle along the coast. One American was killed, as against several hundred Spaniards. Santiago and its garrison of 24,000 surrendered on 17 July.

Right: *Part of Pittsburgh, center of the US steel industry, in 1909. In the last years of the 19th century the US became the world's largest producer of steel.*

The importance of the Spanish-American War derived from its territorial results. Peace negotiations took place in Paris, where the belligerents signed a treaty on 10 December that awarded the United States the islands of Puerto Rico and Guam. The Spanish agreed to cede the Philippines to the United States for $20 million. Spain gave up Cuba, which after a brief American occupation became independent in 1902-04, although clauses incorporated into the Cuban constitution made this large Caribbean island an American protectorate. These clauses were not abandoned by the United States until 1934.

The war persuaded the McKinley Administration to annex the Hawaiian Islands, which had sheltered a republican government since an American-led revolution in 1893. Prior to that, the islands had been independent under a native dynasty. Annexation of the Hawaiians by joint resolution was not unprecedented, since Texas had joined the Union in 1845 by that arrangement. But both these accessions proved awkward in that the Senate refused its consent to a treaty. Sympathetic administrations had to resort to joint resolutions that required only a majority vote in Congress rather than a two-thirds vote in the Senate. Critics of the McKinley Administration pointed out that the Hawaiian Islands lay nearly 3000 miles west of the Pacific Coast, far into the Pacific Ocean, and were unsuitable for acquisition because they were noncontiguous. However, there was a precedent in the annexation of Wake Island as a US naval base in 1898. The Hawaiian Islands, if far larger, were 2130 miles closer. The real argument for taking Hawaii lay in the fact that it controlled access to the nation's Pacific Coast. It would have been dangerous to allow Hawaii independence after the turn of the twentieth century, for it might have been seized by Japan or even by Imperial Germany.

The only acquisition that really aroused American sentiment was that of the Philippine Islands, and in retrospect it may well have been a mistake to take them. They lay 8000 miles into the far Pacific – so close to Japan that Americans taking a ship for the Philippines in subsequent years were accustomed to sail to Japan and transship to the archipelago. The islands came into American possession largely because of the ardent nationalism excited by the Spanish-American War, which almost demanded that the United States acquire territory as a result of victory. Ignorance played a large part in their acquisition, for many Americans, including Mrs William McKinley, believed that the Philippines might become a field for American Protestant missionaries – not realizing that most Filipinos were Catholics. Another point of ignorance was belief that the islands might constitute a vestibule, so to speak, from which the United States could enter the China trade. Many saw possibilities of trading with the 400 million (as people guessed) Chinese, not understanding that while the Chinese desired to trade, they were very poor and could offer the Americans little, perhaps almost nothing, in exchange. The China trade proved largely ephemeral.

Acquisition of the Philippines conferred few benefits upon the United States and two remarkable disadvantages. For one, the Filipinos soon rebelled against their new imperial owners, in a costly insurrection that lasted until 1902. Further, US possession of the Philippines gave Japan a hostage for American good behavior. The time soon came when rising Japanese nationalism could exact concessions from the government of the United States, in return for Japan's nonaggression against the nearby and vulnerable Philippines. President Theodore Roosevelt, who possessed a sense of military strategy rare in holders of his office, wrote in 1908 that defense of the Philippines would require an army as large as the German Army and a navy as large as the British Navy. Thus the Philippines involved the United States in Far Eastern equations out of all proportion to their intrinsic importance.

The United States took an almost immediate interest in the trade and territorial integrity of China via notes by Secretary of State John Hay that announced the 'open door,' a time-worn phrase in international affairs. In the first open door note (1899) the American secretary of state sought to prevent the division of China into individual trading areas by the principal nations of Europe, to the exclusion of American commerce. The second note, of 1900, was occasioned when attacks by Chinese irregulars known as Boxers threatened the breakup of the Chinese nation through foreign invasion. Hay hoped to commit the Europeans not to take Chinese territory, even if they joined the Americans in a punitive expedition to protect US and European embassies in Peking.

In the 'American lake,' as US citizens viewed the Caribbean, and in its surrounding nations of Central America, American power pursued goals that effectively constituted an effort at hegemony during the years after 1898. Here Americans seemed to be displaying imperialism, or domination, with racial overtones – imposing their ideas, customs, and preferences upon peoples of Latin descent.

The War of 1898 inaugurated American imperialism in the Caribbean and Central America. Several motives were involved, including a desire to 'civilize' through introduction of American ways; to proselytize on behalf of Protestantism; and to arrange for an isthmian canal across Panama, a Colombian province, or Nicaragua. Americans settled on Panama. The site was obtained in 1903 by encouraging a revolution in the Colombian province, where an *opera bouffe* revolt on 3 November brought in a local government that pronounced itself a nation. It promptly gave the United States a canal zone ten miles wide, with a lease of 99 years, for an initial payment of $10 million and an annual fee of $250,000. The United States assigned construction to the US Army, which arranged for a canal with locks, one of the marvels of the world at the time it opened in 1914. Then came a succession of events in the Dominican Republic (1904-05), Nicaragua (1912), Haiti (1915), and Mexico (1914-17).

When the government of the Dominican Republic gave every evidence of fiscal incompetence, opening itself to forcible collection of its debts by European debtors, President Roosevelt announced what became known as the Roosevelt Corollary to the Monroe Doctrine (6 December 1904). This stated that any Latin American nation that could not manage its own affairs was liable to US intervention and, in the case of the Dominican Republic, to American supervision of its customs houses. The Senate refused to go along with Roosevelt until 1907, but meanwhile the president supervised Dominican customs by executive agreement.

Roosevelt's successor William Taft arranged on 14 August 1912 for the landing of a force of Marines in Nicaragua to protect American interests. A small detachment remained until 1925. When it left, a revolution broke out, and it returned to stay until 1933. Nicaragua's geography made construction of a canal possible by a combination of lakes and rivers, and the US was sensitive to this fact, even though it had chosen the Panamanian alternative some years before.

Intervention in Haiti in 1915, by President Woodrow Wilson, may well have been the least debatable act of American imperialism during the early twentieth century, for Haiti's government had virtually disintegrated. A group of Haitians

Above: *Opposition to monopolistic practices in the early twentieth century. Standard Oil was regarded by many as the most dangerous of the monopolies later to be limited by antitrust laws.*

ousted President Vibrun Guillaume Sam, who had presided over the murder of dozens of his political enemies, and pursued him into the French legation, whence they removed him and literally tore him to pieces. These trophies they paraded around the capital of Port-au-Prince. Early that afternoon of 29 July 1915, American Marines landed and began restoring order, after which Haiti became a protectorate, an arrangement that lasted until 1941.

The largest American intervention of these years was in Mexico, where one incident led to another, all related to the political turmoil surrounding the Mexican Revolution that broke out in 1910. The revolution continued into the 1920s, when its victors won control of the country.

Mexico's descent into revolution seemed unlikely at first to involve the United States. But factional leaders vied for power around Mexico City, and it was inevitable that some would appeal to or against the huge republic to the north. On 9 April 1914 a party from a small American ship, the *Dolphin*, stationed in Mexican waters, went ashore to secure supplies and mistakenly entered a restricted area of Tampico, where it was arrested and then released. US Admiral Henry Mayo demanded a twenty-one-gun salute to the American flag by way of apology. President Wilson backed him up, but Mexican dictator Victoriano Huerta refused to comply. On 21 April an American force bombarded and occupied the port city of Veracruz. The force withdrew in November, after several Latin American nations mediated the dispute.

A far more serious incident occurred in 1916, when a dissident Mexican general, Doroteo Arango (known as Pancho Villa), seeking to discredit the regime of President Venustiano Carranza, invaded Columbus, New Mexico, on 9 March and killed 17 Americans. Brigadier General John J Pershing crossed the border with a punitive expedition that eventually comprised 15,000 men, in what proved a vain hunt for Villa. Wilson called out the militia, 150,000 strong, and stationed it along the border. Only when war with Germany became imminent early in 1917 did the president withdraw the troops.

Thus much had changed in the United States since 1865, when it had seemed that the principal American problem was Reconstruction of the defeated Confederate states. During the next half century, the country grew mightily in population, agriculture, and industry and extended its railroads coast to coast to move people, produce, and industrial goods. The Spanish-American War of 1898 marked a surge in national sentiment, and offered opportunities to acquire territory beyond the continental United States. By far the most important result of the war of 1898 was the taking of the Philippines, which constituted a possession too close to Japan. After the turn of the century the United States constructed the Panama canal, coerced nearby countries, and did not hesitate to intervene in Mexico. But at this time the rivalries of Europe, which had been quiescent for many years, renewed themselves. British interests conflicted with German ambitions, and France (humbled by the Prussians in 1870-71 in an embarrassingly short war) plotted revenge. With these rivalries the distant United States had had almost nothing to do, but when war broke out again in Europe in August 1914 it soon involved the New World.

New States and Reconstruction

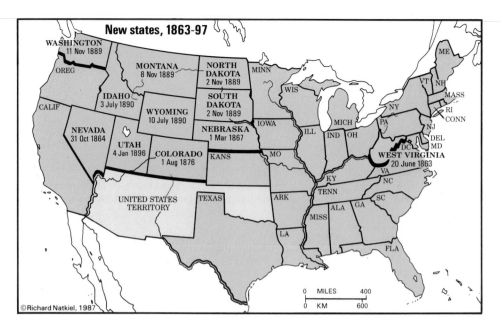

New states, 1863-97

WASHINGTON 11 Nov 1889

OREG

MONTANA 8 Nov 1889

NORTH DAKOTA 2 Nov 1889

MINN

ME

IDAHO 3 July 1890

CALIF

WYOMING 10 July 1890

SOUTH DAKOTA 2 Nov 1889

WIS

VT NH

MASS

NY

NEVADA 31 Oct 1864

UTAH 4 Jan 1896

COLORADO 1 Aug 1876

NEBRASKA 1 Mar 1867

IOWA

ILL IND

MICH OH

PA

RI CONN

NJ

DEL MD

KANS

MO

KY

DC

WEST VIRGINIA 20 June 1863

VA

NC

UNITED STATES TERRITORY

TEXAS

ARK

TENN

SC

ALA GA

MISS

LA

FLA

0 MILES 400

0 KM 600

©Richard Natkiel, 1987

MAP right: The creation of new states after the Civil War. The westward movement seemed to gain strength as soon as the War was over, encouraged by a government eager to populate the continent with its own people. By the end of the nineteenth century the map of the United States was virtually complete.

MAP bottom right: The Reconstruction period. The defeated southern states were gradually re-admitted to the Union, but north-south animosity led to Congress imposing military control over the south so as to enforce Reconstruction laws which the southerners regarded as unacceptable.

Right: *Steamboats on the Mississippi. These craft, despite the occasional boiler explosion or fire, provided a north-south trunk route which facilitated the economic development of a wide belt of territory.*

Below: *A western railroad entices settlers with easy terms for land purchase.*

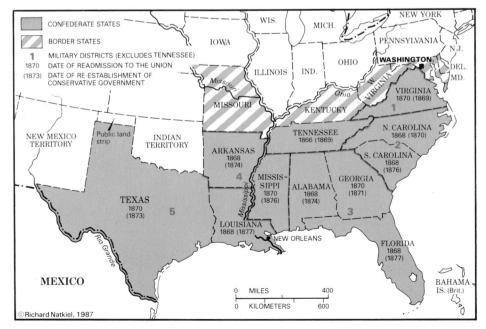

CONFEDERATE STATES

BORDER STATES

1 MILITARY DISTRICTS (EXCLUDES TENNESSEE)

1870 DATE OF READMISSION TO THE UNION

(1873) DATE OF RE-ESTABLISHMENT OF CONSERVATIVE GOVERNMENT

©Richard Natkiel, 1987

Communication Systems
in 1870

MAP below: Transportation after the
Civil War. Railroads are dominant in the
North-East, but thinner in the South,
and are just beginning to penetrate west
of the Mississippi. They are still
operated by a multiplicity of small
companies, and long-distance through
trains are rare. In the late 1860s,
however, railroads began to be
consolidated into larger companies and
the first moves toward gauge
standardization were made. Water
transport was still very important,
especially along the coasts and on the
Mississippi and Great Lakes.

Right: *Emigrants to the West halt for the night.
The covered wagon remained the chosen vehicle
of settlers using the overland trails up to and even
beyond the coming of the railroad.*

COMMUNICATIONS, 1870:
  RAILROADS
  OVERLAND MAIL ROUTES
  CANALS:
  Ⓐ ERIE CANAL
  Ⓑ CHESAPEAKE & OHIO CANAL

© Richard Natkiel, 1987

Railroads to the Pacific

MAP below: The coming of the transcontinental railroads. Government surveys of possible routes had been carried out in 1853, but decisions had been delayed by the lobbying of states anxious to have the first transcontinental running through their own territory. But the Pacific Railroad Bill, signed by Abraham Lincoln in 1862, awarded land grants and government assistance to the line proposed by the Union Pacific and Central Pacific companies, passing through Omaha and Sacramento. Several other transcontinentals were built subsequently. The last to be built the Milwaukee Railroad's line from St Paul to Seattle, would also be the first to close, seven decades later.

Right: Sioux Chief Red Cloud, who prevented the construction of Army forts along the Bozeman Trail and won a fairly favorable peace treaty.

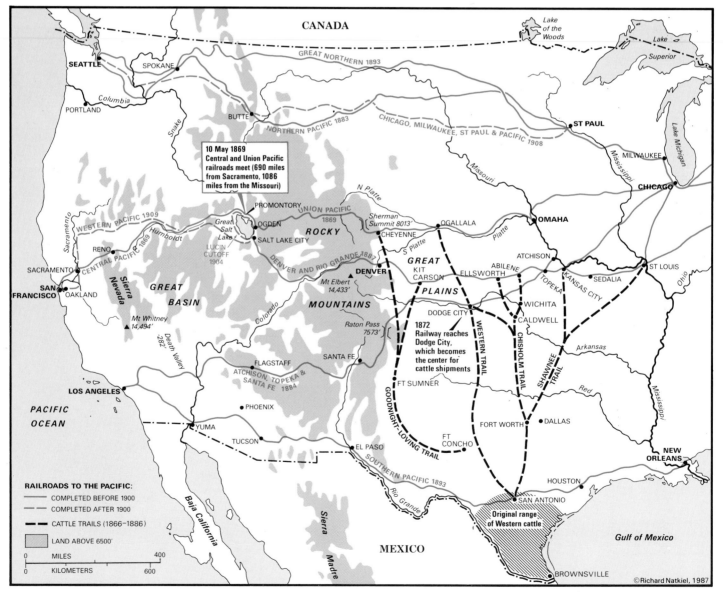

10 May 1869
Central and Union Pacific railroads meet (690 miles from Sacramento, 1086 miles from the Missouri)

1872 Railway reaches Dodge City, which becomes the center for cattle shipments

RAILROADS TO THE PACIFIC:
— COMPLETED BEFORE 1900
-- COMPLETED AFTER 1900
■■ CATTLE TRAILS (1866–1886)
▨ LAND ABOVE 6500'

© Richard Natkiel, 1987

Indian Wars

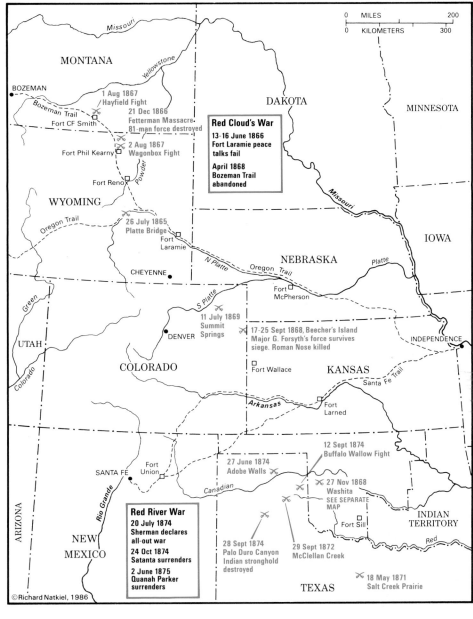

MAP right: The Battles of the Great Plains. The Indian Wars, which lasted from about 1865 to 1880, and resulted in the eviction and defeat of most of the Indian inhabitants of the West, were especially hard-fought in the Great Plains, where the populous Sioux and Cheyenne tribes lived. The availability of the Union Army after the Civil War brought extra weight to bear on the Indians, who resisted, among other things, the construction of the Army's forts. By 1880 the region was subdued, but there was a fresh outbreak of violence in 1890, when at the so-called Battle of Wounded Knee the Army massacred about 150 Sioux.

Below: *An emigrant family of the mid-1880s poses by their wagon, a photograph taken in the Loup Valley area of Nebraska.*

MAP right: The Indian Campaign of 1868-69. The high (or low) point of this campaign was the massacre, by cavalry under the command of Colonel George Custer, of Southern Cheyenne Indians whose chief was in favor of peaceful relations with the white man. This took place while the Indians were encamped at Washita, and Custer escaped before other Indians could retaliate.

Below: *Chief Sitting Bull, leader of the Dakota Sioux in their resistance against removal to reservations, who defeated Custer at the Little Bighorn, escaped to Canada, appeared in Buffalo Bill's Wild West Show, and was finally killed in the prelude to the massacre at Wounded Knee.*

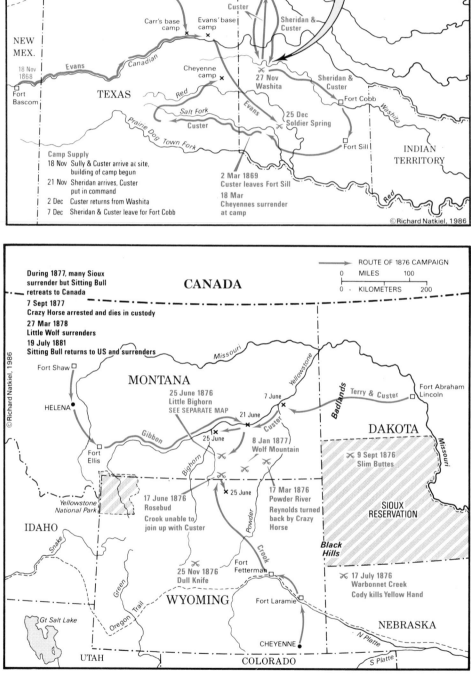

MAP below left: The Sioux Campaign of 1876. This began with Indian revolts against the influx of gold-seeking white men into their sacred Black Hills. The Army sent three columns to converge on the Indians' main concentration at Little Bighorn, but when one of these columns was blocked at the Battle of the Rosebud, Colonel Custer was sent ahead to contain the Indians in the Bighorn Valley, where he was killed.

MAP right: Battle of the Little Bighorn. Despite the unexpected size of the Indian concentration, Colonel Custer decided to attack. His faith in the superiority of his own force was further shown by his decision to divide it into three groups. Custer's group of five troops was wiped out, and the other two groups retreated with heavy losses. Paradoxically Custer, whose record in the Indian Wars was exciting but counter-productive, became a national hero, and a monument was erected at the scene of his 'Last Stand.'

Below: *Sioux Indians in their reservation.*

25 June 1876
Battle of Little Bighorn

1600-1700 hrs
Custer's command wiped out, 215 dead

Northern Cheyenne

Crazy Horse, 1600 hrs

C&F Troops

I Troop

E Troop

Brule

Oglala

L Troop

Fort Abraham Lincoln 300 miles

Yankton

Shoulderblade Creek

Great Lodge of the Annual Council

Gall, 1600 hrs

Santee Sioux

Custer (according to Lt. E Godfrey)

Blackfoot Sioux

Minneconjou

Custer

Sans Arc

Little Bighorn

Medicine Tail Coulee

Hunkpapa Sioux

Gall, 1500 hrs

Capt. Weir unable to join up with Custer

1500 hrs

Major Reno (A, G & M Troops)

1600 hrs

26 June
Indians lay siege to Reno and Benteen's position but withdraw in evening. Troops fall back to Fort Abraham Lincoln

7 Cavalry Bde (Custer), consisting of 12 troops

Capt. Benteen (D, H & K Troops) 1630 hrs

B Troop brings up the rear with the pack train

©Richard Natkiel, 1986

MAP right: The Apache Wars. These were the longest and often the bitterest of the Indian campaigns, lasting from 1861 to 1886. The Apache, who were a fierce, marauding, tribe, did most of their raiding in Mexico, but from 1861 began to terrorize Arizona and New Mexico. After the attacks began to subside, they were revived in 1871 by a raid of vigilantes on a peaceful Indian settlement near Camp Grant. The US Army then imposed an uneasy peace which lasted until the government tried to move the Apache into reservations. The Indian leader, Victorio, was killed in 1880, but his successor Geronimo was even more determined.

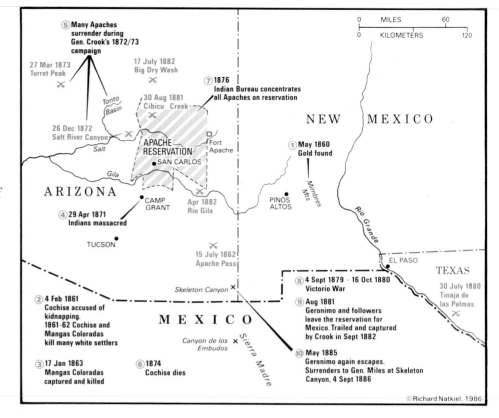

MAP right: The contraction of the Indian lands in the West. The removal of Indians to reservations freed vast expanses for new white settlement. The policy of Indian removal, from which reservations originated, was formally adopted as early as 1786, and eventually 200 reservations were established. Unable, for the most part, to practise their old way of life, the Indians tended to languish on these lands, although many left them in the 20th century. Arizona had the largest concentration, followed by Oklahoma. The Indian Territory of Oklahoma was reserved for the so-called Five Civilized Tribes in 1834, but by 1900 other tribes had been admitted. The land was then divided into Indian Territory and Oklahoma Territory, which subsequently joined to become the state of Oklahoma. Today the Indian population of the United States is approaching 1.5 million. The state with the largest Indian population is California and the largest remaining Indian reservation is the Navaho reservation in Arizona.

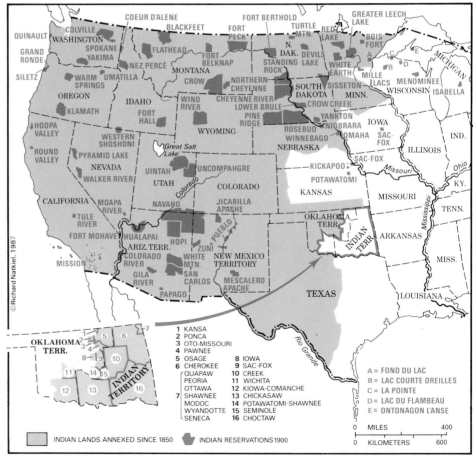

Immigration to the USA

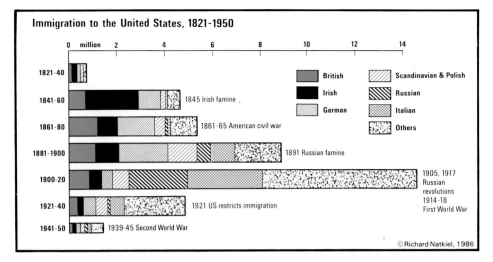

Immigration to the United States, 1821-1950

Legend: British, Irish, German, Scandinavian & Polish, Russian, Italian, Others

- 1821-40
- 1841-60 — 1845 Irish famine
- 1861-80 — 1861-65 American civil war
- 1881-1900 — 1891 Russian famine
- 1900-20 — 1905, 1917 Russian revolutions / 1914-18 First World War
- 1921-40 — 1921 US restricts immigration
- 1941-50 — 1939-45 Second World War

©Richard Natkiel, 1986

CHART right: Immigration into the USA. The 'Old Immigration' began about 1820 and lasted into the 1880s, and was predominantly German, Scandinavian and Irish. It was then overtaken by the 'New Immigration' from eastern and southern Europe. The Irish, who were mainly poverty-stricken peasants, provided much of the manual labor required for railroad-building and industrialization. Scandinavians tended to move to frontier farmsteads, while the Germans often stayed together in their own newly-founded communities, of which Milwaukee was the most striking example. Chinese arrived on the Pacific coast under contract to build railroads, but were subsequently limited by the Chinese Exclusion and other acts. When the 'New Immigration' began, cities were fast developing, and these absorbed the bulk of the newcomers. In the peak period for immigration, the early years of the twentieth century, Poles and Jews, escaping persecution in the Russian Empire, formed a high proportion.

MAP below: The main immigration flows. This division between the 'old' and 'new' immigration should be taken as a generalization expressing a trend, rather than a clear-cut transformation.

Right: *An immigrant ship arrives at New York in 1906.*

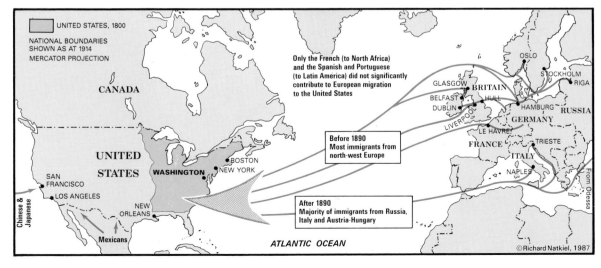

UNITED STATES, 1800

NATIONAL BOUNDARIES SHOWN AS AT 1914
MERCATOR PROJECTION

Only the French (to North Africa) and the Spanish and Portuguese (to Latin America) did not significantly contribute to European migration to the United States

Before 1890 Most immigrants from north-west Europe

After 1890 Majority of immigrants from Russia, Italy and Austria-Hungary

CANADA

UNITED STATES — WASHINGTON, BOSTON, NEW YORK, NEW ORLEANS, SAN FRANCISCO, LOS ANGELES

Chinese & Japanese

Mexicans

OSLO, STOCKHOLM, RIGA, GLASGOW, BRITAIN, BELFAST, HULL, DUBLIN, LIVERPOOL, HAMBURG, RUSSIA, GERMANY, LE HAVRE, FRANCE, TRIESTE, ITALY, NAPLES, From Odessa

ATLANTIC OCEAN

©Richard Natkiel, 1987

The Spanish American War

MAP below: The prelude to the Battle of Manila Bay. The Navy Secretary, Theodore Roosevelt, had forewarned Commodore Dewey, who kept his squadron ready and, immediately war was declared, attacked the Spanish fleet.

MAP below right: The Battle of Manila Bay. The engagement was a long-drawn-out gunnery duel, interrupted for a few hours when Commodore Dewey retired to look after his casualties and, discovering they were negligible, returned to finish the battle.

Right: Insurgents under guard in Manila. The Filipino insurgents, who had been fighting against their Spanish oppressors, turned against their American allies when the latter began to behave as conquerors rather than liberators.

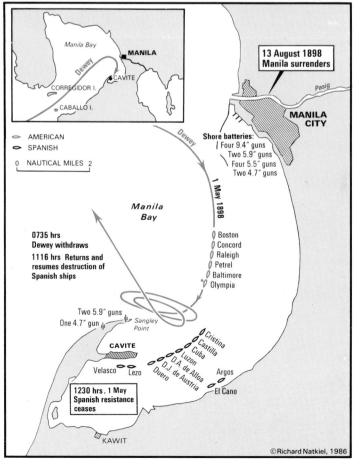

MAP right: First moves in the Cuban campaign. The US Army, quite unprepared for the invasion of Cuba demanded by press and public, managed to land a small force in June which, aided by Theodore Roosevelt's Rough Rider volunteers, succeeded in capturing the heights commanding Santiago.

MAP below right: The Battle of Santiago. The American threat to Santiago encouraged the Spanish Admiral Cervera to remove his cruiser squadron from that port. In the Bay he was confronted by a much stronger US force which, after a gun duel lasting less than four hours, completely destroyed the Spanish squadron. As elsewhere in this war, American casualties were negligible. In the war as a whole, less than 400 Americans were killed in action, although about 5000 died from other causes (mainly tropical diseases, for which the US Army was ill-prepared).

Below: *Theodore Roosevelt in a favorite, and symbolic, pose.*

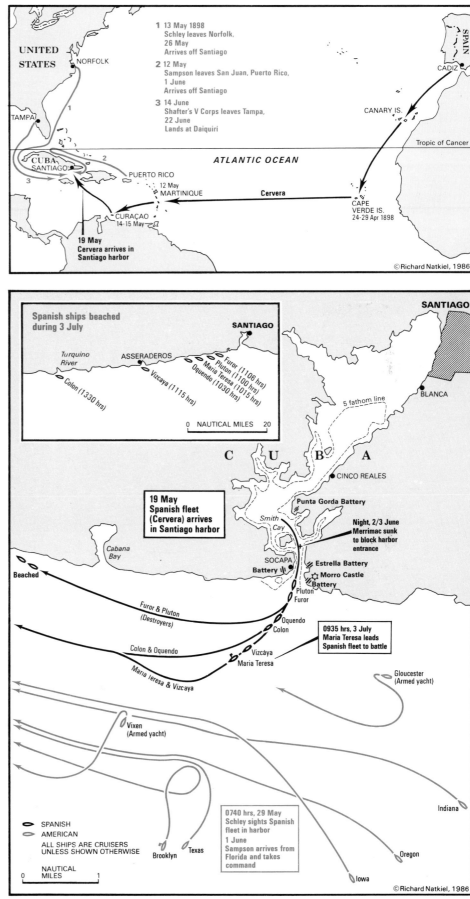

MAP below: The advance on Santiago (inset) and the Battle of San Juan. After their unopposed landing the American troops pushed on toward the main Spanish defenses on the San Juan Heights. Their plan was for a frontal attack supported by a left flanking assault, with a diversionary attack on El Caney which would develop into a thrust from the north. In the event, the artillery was unable to protect the attackers from strong defensive fire and the battle was finally won by the storming of Kettle Hill by US cavalry, with the volunteer Rough Riders in support.

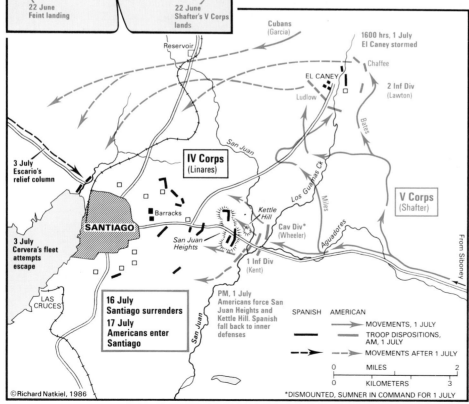

AREA OF MAIN MAP

EL CANEY

SANTIAGO

0 MILES 5

0 KM 8

24 June
Las Guasimas
Wheeler's cavalry
held by Spanish

Shafter

CABANAS

AGUADORES

SIBONEY
23 June

DAIQUIRI

22 June
Feint landing

22 June
Shafter's V Corps
lands

Cubans
(Garcia)

1600 hrs, 1 July
El Caney stormed

Reservoir

Chaffee

EL CANEY

2 Inf Div
(Lawton)

Ludlow

Bates

San Juan

Los Guamas Ck

IV Corps
(Linares)

Miles

V Corps
(Shafter)

3 July
Escario's
relief column

Barracks

Kettle
Hill

Cav Div*
(Wheeler)

Aguadores

SANTIAGO

San Juan
Heights

3 July
Cervera's fleet
attempts
escape

1 Inf Div
(Kent)

From Siboney

LAS
CRUCES

16 July
Santiago surrenders

17 July
Americans enter
Santiago

San Juan

PM, 1 July
Americans force San
Juan Heights and
Kettle Hill. Spanish
fall back to inner
defenses

SPANISH AMERICAN

MOVEMENTS, 1 JULY

TROOP DISPOSITIONS,
AM, 1 JULY

MOVEMENTS AFTER 1 JULY

0 MILES 2

0 KILOMETERS 3

©Richard Natkiel, 1986

*DISMOUNTED, SUMNER IN COMMAND FOR 1 JULY

Alaska and Panama

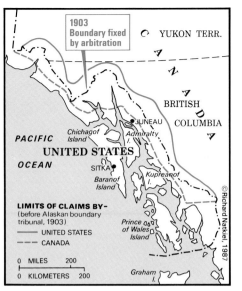

MAP above: The Alaska boundary dispute. Alaska had been bought by the USA in 1867 from the Russian government, which was anxious to raise funds for railroad construction at home. An imprecision in the fixing of the Alaska/Canada frontier was unimportant until gold was discovered in the Klondike in 1896. Confusion, then acrimony, and finally a hotly-argued controversy ended when a boundary arbitration commission of two Americans, two Canadians and one Briton reached a compromise which, on balance, favored the American position.

Above left: *An impression of the hoisting of the US flag over Santiago. The artist has accorded due prominence to Roosevelt's Rough Riders, in the foreground.*

Below left: *Theodore Roosevelt photographed with his Rough Riders atop Kettle Hill. Roosevelt skilfully extracted maximum publicity from his role in Cuba.*

Above right: *Construction of the Panama Canal. A French company failed to build the Canal, and its rights were purchased by the US government. Planning began in 1904, and construction ceased in 1914. The Canal was a dollar-earner for the Panamanian economy, a strategic gain for the US Navy, which could henceforth rapidly transfer ships between its Pacific and Atlantic squadrons, and an economic benefit for US and international shipping.*

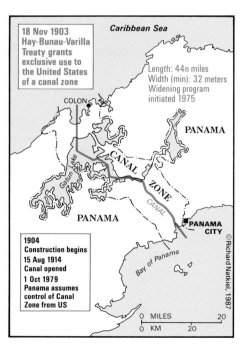

MAP left: The Panama Canal Zone. This was leased by Panama in perpetuity to the US government from 1904, against an annual rent. It provided the territory in which to construct the Panama Canal together with a belt sufficiently wide for security purposes. It extended five miles on each side of the Canal, although Panama City and Colon were excluded. It was under the jurisdiction of the US Army Department, and its main administrative units were the Canal Zone Government, headed by a governor appointed by the US President, and the Panama Railroad Company, which was responsible for operations (ships were towed through the locks by locomotives). In 1979, following years of Panamanian agitation and protest, a revised treaty transferred control to the government of Panama.

The Pacific and Caribbean

MAP right: The USA and the Pacific Basin. While turning its back on European affairs, the USA developed commercial and political interest in the Far East. China was a particular object of attention, as it promised great opportunities for trade. In opposition to other powers, who were carving up China into 'spheres of influence,' the USA adopted an 'Open Door' policy, which implied unimpeded access of all nations to the Chinese market. Despite this disagreement the US joined the major European powers in suppressing the Boxer Rebellion in China in 1900. The Boxer movement was largely inspired by Chinese hostility to foreign influence. In the same period, a strong US Pacific fleet was established: Theodore Roosevelt emphasized this by despatching 'The Great White Fleet' around the world in 1907-09.

MAP below right: The USA and the Caribbean. The US government was very sensitive to events in the Caribbean, and especially wary of possible foreign intrusion in this region. At the same time, it expected free entry for US trade and attention to US requirements. It therefore tended to intervene, usually peacefully, in the political affairs of the region and sometimes, when things seemed to go wrong, resorted to armed intervention. Theodore Roosevelt's advocacy of the 'Big Stick' implied that might was right and America was mighty.

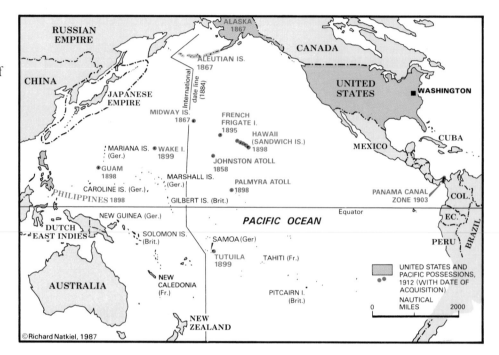

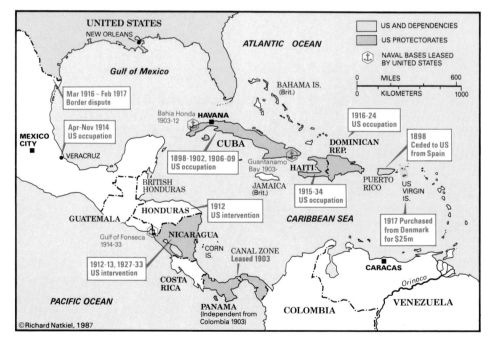

Intervention in Mexico

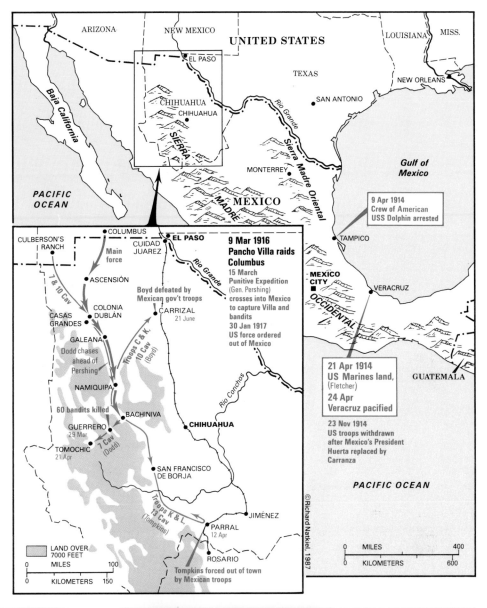

MAP right: Mexico 1914-17. In 1911 the pro-American Mexican dictator Diaz was overthrown, and was succeeded by a series of short-lived and chaotic regimes. Frontier incidents with the USA occurred, and the US government began to send punitive expeditions to Mexico in response. In 1914 Veracruz was occupied following an 'insult to the flag' and in 1916, following a cross-border raid by the bandit-revolutionary Pancho Villa, the US sent a large force into Mexico. A new Mexican constitution in 1917 marked the end of US armed interventions.

9 Apr 1914
Crew of American
USS Dolphin arrested

21 Apr 1914
US Marines land,
(Fletcher)

24 Apr
Veracruz pacified

23 Nov 1914
US troops withdrawn
after Mexico's President
Huerta replaced by
Carranza

9 Mar 1916
Pancho Villa raids
Columbus
15 March
Punitive Expedition
(Gen. Pershing)
crosses into Mexico
to capture Villa and
bandits
30 Jan 1917
US force ordered
out of Mexico

Boyd defeated by
Mexican gov't troops
CARRIZAL
21 June

60 bandits killed

Dodd chases
ahead of
Pershing

Tompkins forced out of town
by Mexican troops

©Richard Natkiel, 1987

Below: *General Pershing, soon to win fame in World War I, leading the US Army in Mexico.*

America becomes a world power: US tanks at war in France, 1918.

The Two World Wars

When World War I began in Europe during the first days of August 1914, President Wilson hastily declared American neutrality. In subsequent months, almost down to April 1917, he told his countrymen that the United States could have no interest in the war's obscure causes. In a similar vein, he asked the belligerents for a peace without victory. Wilson imagined that a neutral United States would be able to hold a balance of conscience against violence; as he saw it, the Europeans had lost their reason and hence the US must retain its intelligence and understanding. All the while he maintained that Americans understood all peoples because they comprised all peoples.

Slowly, inexorably, the web of American commercial connections entrapped the nation. Wilson allowed it because he believed in the necessity – despite his pacifist protests – of an Anglo-French victory for democracy against German autocracy. But ultimately it was Germany's use of submarine warfare against US ships that tipped the balance. Early in 1915 and again the following year, the Germans had attempted to loose submarines against all commerce around the British Isles. Their third effort precipitated a break in relations that brought America into the war on 6 August 1917.

When the United States declared war, neither the president nor the people knew precisely what they would do to help the Allies, and for several months confusion reigned. Without much idea of how it would use them, the administration asked Congress for permission to draft American males of military age into the services.

Eventually 4.7 million men would serve in the army and navy, of whom 2.8 million were drafted. Not until the late spring of 1918, when the British and French were in dire straits on the Western Front, did the Allies find shipping to help bring American troops to France. But once such transport began, it turned into a gigantic pipeline, delivering 2 million American soldiers overseas in less than a year's time, most of them in the war's last months. This development persuaded Germany and its allies to ask for an armistice, which was signed on 11 November 1918.

The American Expeditionary Force was commanded by General John J Pershing, the navy in European waters by Admiral William S Sims. The army, of course, had the most arduous task – fighting veteran German troops in the several theaters assigned to them by the Allied High Command. In early summer of 1918, inexperienced American troops entered the front in division strength at Belleau Wood (6 June through 1 July) and fought gallantly, if sometimes recklessly. They halted a German offensive that threatened Paris. On 18 July an American force of 85,000 attacked along the Aisne Salient, three days after a massive German incursion, and forced a withdrawal. It was more than a victory, quite possibly it was the turning point on the Western Front. The German chancellor at the time later wrote that 'The fate of the war was played out in three days.' The Germans had expected to break through to Paris. American participation in the Aisne-Marne offensive lasted until 6 August and ultimately involved 270,000 US troops. On 12-16 September the AEF under Pershing engaged in its first distinct offensive – both planning and attack were entirely American. Pershing's troops moved out, 550,000 strong, against a salient that the Germans had held for nearly four years and eliminated it, capturing 16,000 prisoners in a battle that became known as the St Mihiel Offensive.

The last major American battle of World War I, the Meuse-Argonne, was the costliest fight in US military annals, but it was of notable assistance in bringing World War I to an end.

Pershing's troops fought through a hilly area, cleft by ravines, with the Meuse River to the right and the Argonne Forest to the left. They began on a narrow front, and gradually expanded it – the deployment formed an inverted pyramid. Eventually the battle, which began on 26 September 1918 and lasted until the November armistice, involved 1.2 million American troops. US deaths mounted to 26,000, with perhaps 100,000 men wounded. But by early November, American troops had driven to the outskirts of Sedan, where their artillery brought the vital Sedan-Mezieres railroad under fire. The German line from Switzerland to the Channel became untenable with the loss of this single front-line supply railroad. The British and French Armies were also on the offensive by this time, and the Germans gradually retreated everywhere along the line. November's victory was properly an Allied achievement, not that of US forces alone.

In subsequent months the Allies assembled in Paris for the peace conference that signed the German treaty at Versailles on 28 June 1919. However, the US Senate had been antagonized by what it considered offhand treatment from President Wilson. It became the scene of partisan bickering by the president's political adversaries, the Republicans, and ultimately refused its consent to the German treaty in votes on 19 November 1919 and 21 March 1920. The United States made a separate treaty with Germany – the Treaty of Berlin – ratified 18 October 1921. The treaty reserved to the United States all the rights of the Allies in the Treaty of Versailles, but the American Government did not avail itself of many of those rights. The small American occupation force that had assumed supervision of a bridgehead in Germany was withdrawn with other American troops in 1923.

During American participation in World War I, two amendments to the Constitution, the Eighteenth and Nineteenth, were proposed. National Prohibition had received growing support even before the war removed numerous American males from the scene. This made its passage easier, but it probably would have passed even without World War I. Its instrument of enforcement, the Volstead Act, passed over Wilson's veto on 28 October 1919 to go into effect on 16 January 1920. The Nineteenth Amendment, guaranteeing female suffrage, was ratified on 26 August 1920, just in time to permit women to exercise their new right to vote in that year's presidential election.

The decade that followed, the 1920s, was perhaps the last unclouded era in the history of the United States in that young men and women had no apparent reason to fear the intrusion of war into their lives. In this sense the 1920s recalled the nineteenth century, with its widespread belief that the European balance of power would ensure peace. The presidents of the era – Harding, Coolidge, Hoover – concerned themselves with domestic issues. The country appeared to have expanded enough to ensure domestic tranquility. A great continental market lay at hand, ready for exploitation, and it seemed that life would improve from year to year. Many Americans now had more money than their daily needs absorbed, and the option of investing it in stocks and bonds. New York brokers opened offices far from the East Coast, and new entrepreneurs joined them in asserting that investment in the stock market was investment in America. Then a catastrophic downturn in the market brought a new era that dashed these hopes.

The greatest calamity in the history of the United States, apart from the Civil War, was the Great Depression. Its origin was the collapse of the stock market in 1929 and it lasted until the nation's entry into World War II on 7 December 1941. In

Above: *US field artillery in action in France during 1918. The gun in use is a French 75mm design. Much of the US Army's equipment in WWI was foreign-made or designed – a token of America's lack of preparedness.*

the country's effort to extract itself from this economic morass, the most promising approach was offered by Franklin D Roosevelt, whose New Deal was embodied in a series of Congressional enactments.

When he came to office in 1933, Roosevelt made numerous legislative proposals that Congress promptly passed, establishing a new order, first of all for agriculture. Until that time the nation's farmers had managed against market ups and downs as best they could; their tradition for production and prices was boom and bust. World War I was a boom time, and the years thereafter a bust. During the 1920s agriculture remained in trouble. Beginning with the Great Depression, which produced a collapse of foreign trade, agricultural prices reached new lows. The response was the Agricultural Adjustment Act of May 1933, which established the Agricultural Adjustment Administration, known as the AAA. It sought to raise prices by eliminating farm surpluses; in return for reducing acreage or crops, the farmers received subsidies. In varied form, the subsidy principle became a fixture of American agricultural policy from that time onward, even after the AAA was declared unconstitutional by the Supreme Court in 1936.

World War II raised prices of farm commodities. Again, farmers flourished momentarily. Afterward came renewed trouble. A forward-looking postwar secretary of agriculture, Charles F Brannan, proposed in 1948 to support all farm products, not just a few. But farmers would receive only so many units – 1800 in all – of support, eliminating the advantage of the large farmer. The Brannan Plan proposed direct subsidies rather than the prevailing complex arrangement of government loans and purchase agreements, but this arrangement was too open and it failed.

F D Roosevelt, like his distant cousin Theodore, made efforts at conservation, largely to stimulate the economy. One was a make-work scheme, the Civilian Conservation Corps, by which young men under army supervision worked at forestation and other environmental projects. But most of the New Deal's conservation effort went into the huge project known as the Tennessee Valley Authority, one of the most successful undertakings of its kind in American history. Here the problem was the rural backwater of the Tennessee Valley, seemingly impervious to change, where for generations mountaineers and poor farmers had eked out their livings. Roosevelt envisioned the entire Tennessee River as a drainage basin, and established an independent public corporation, the Tennessee Valley Authority (TVA), to construct dams and power plants and develop the valley economically and socially. Between 1933 and 1944, nine large dams and many smaller ones changed the entire area. Wartime construction of a huge atom bomb plant at Oak Ridge, Tennessee, underlined the TVA's importance and manifested the area's progress into the twentieth century.

The New Deal devoted perhaps its principal effort to raising the productivity of American industry, which proved more of a public-relations job than a real success. The initial New Deal program for industry involved creation of virtual cartels under the National Industrial Recovery Act (NIRA). Each major industry, represented by workers as well as businessmen, drew fair-competition codes, approved by the president and enforceable by law. The codes were exempt from operation of the antitrust laws, and courts could issue injunctions against violators. The Supreme Court held the NIRA unconstitutional in 1935. One of its lasting results, however, was Section 7a of

Above: *A view over the US Pacific Fleet anchorage at Pearl Harbor, a few weeks before the Japanese attack. The layout of the naval base and the line of ships in 'Battleship Row' can be clearly seen.*

the original enactment, which guaranteed labor's right 'to organize and bargain collectively through representatives of their own choosing.' This proviso became the basis for organization of many industrial unions during the 1930s and thereafter.

Apart from NIRA, designed as the centerpiece of the New Deal's industrial revival, the Roosevelt Administration took many emergency measures, the most notable being the Reconstruction Finance Corporation. This agency was actually created during the preceding Hoover Administration, but its capital and operations were much strengthened by the new Democratic Administration. Other New Deal efforts to bolster the economy included the Public Works Administration (PWA), which spent $4.2 billion on 34,000 public projects. A similar effort to reinforce the economy was the New Deal's banking legislation, enacted to prevent runs on banks deemed unsafe for depositors. Here the principal measure was the Federal Deposit Insurance Corporation (FDIC). The New Deal also guaranteed principal and interest for $2 billion in bonds to refinance home mortgages in the Home Owners Loan Corporation (HOLC).

During Roosevelt's first term, economic troubles in Germany produced the new regime of Adolf Hitler, who came to power in Berlin in January 1933. Hitler pulled Germany out of the Great Depression through rearmament during his early years in power. In 1936, Anglo-French inaction during Italy's effort to conquer Ethiopia gave Hitler an opening for actions aimed at the domination of Europe and Russia. The deeds of

Hitler's Germany began to ring like hammer blows: reoccupation of the Rhineland (1936); absorption of Austria and Czechoslovakia (1938-9); demands upon Poland and the invasion that ignited World War II (1939).

In the interim between the outbreak of war in Europe and US involvement (December 1941), the Roosevelt Administration moved carefully to engage US economic and naval support on behalf of the Allies. (The touchstone commitment, the Army, was not involved.) The president arranged for amendment of the neutrality acts to allow for cash-and-carry shipment of munitions to the Allies via the Atlantic sea lanes. In 1940, after the Nazi onslaught upon the Netherlands, Belgium and France, Roosevelt made an executive agreement transferring 50 World War I destroyers to Britain in exchange for British bases in the New World. When it became evident in 1941 that the British Government could no longer afford to purchase munitions from the United States, Roosevelt produced a formula that opened the US Treasury: the Lend-Lease Act. Under this arrangement, any anti-German government could borrow for what it could not pay. Ultimately, Lend-Lease would cost over $50 billion. German submarines threatened US shipments in the summer of 1941, and the Roosevelt Administration countered with a convoy system to prevent the sinking of supplies bound for Britain. The President told his critics that the US Navy was not convoying, only engaging in patrols. The result was a shooting war in the Atlantic, but Germany made no declaration of war against the United States. The German Army had attacked Soviet Russia in the summer of 1941, and it was no time for Hitler to challenge the Americans openly.

It was the Japanese Government that assumed the role of belligerent against the US. Japanese predations against the

British Empire in the Far East led to US sanctions designed to inhibit Japan's expansionist policy. At first the Japanese moved indirectly, taking over French Indochina and threatening the Dutch East Indies. But when the Roosevelt Administration cut off all oil exports to Japan in the summer of 1941, the outcome was Pearl Harbor – a pre-emptive strike by Japanese militarists against the major hostile force in the area, the US Pacific Fleet, on 7 December 1941.

When American participation in World War II began, Japan seemed unbeatable in the Pacific: one Allied defeat after another marked the early months of the great struggle in that theater. Japanese forces took the Dutch East Indies and British Malaya. A more serious blow to the US was the loss of the Philippines. Soon thereafter – in a three-pronged attack – Japanese forces reached toward Australia, threatening Port Moresby, a small town on the archipelago's northern rim. The Americans rallied, barring Japanese progress in New Guinea. In June 1942 Japan's main fleet was engaged and defeated off Midway Island where US Navy planes sank four carriers in a matter of hours. Midway, as time was to reveal, marked the high-water mark of Japanese expansion, after which the Allies, mainly American forces, began a two-part advance toward the home islands. The US Navy moved westward through the flanking island groups, including the Marianas and the Carolines. A fleet train was created to supply US warships far from their bases during the 'island-hopping' campaign. The island of Tarawa proved a costly testing ground for this strategy in November 1943, when 3000 US Marines were casualties and only 17 of 4000 Japanese defenders were captured. However, thorough analysis of this battle helped the Americans to avoid similar mistakes in subsequent operations. Tarawa made it clear that determined Japanese soldiers would have to be dislodged from their bunkers and caves by close combat, including hand-to-hand fighting utilizing flame-throwers and grenades.

In the southwest Pacific, American and Australian forces under General Douglas MacArthur made steady progress toward Japan with heavy support from land-based aircraft. The Australians were determined allies, since a Japanese attack on their homeland was inevitable should it be cut off from US support.

The pressures of the moment favored a strategy of beating Japan first, but US policymakers realized that the greater threat lay in Europe, where the free world's future would be decided. The strategy chosen was that of Europe first.

In 1942, America's first year in the war, the US suffered from its lack of preparedness in the period since 1939. The joint landing with British troops in North Africa pointed up serious deficiencies in the US Army, despite the fact that it faced limited opposition. General Dwight D Eisenhower reinforced his Allied force in subsequent months, and by spring 1943 had captured all Italian and German forces. These included the troops of the 'Desert Fox,' General Erwin Rommel, who had been driven west into Tripoli and Algiers by British forces under General Bernard L Montgomery.

In 1943 the US was still unable to mount a cross-Channel offensive against German troops. But the conquest of French North Africa encouraged an assault on nearby Italy, in which the Allies landed first on Sicily, then on the Italian peninsula. German reinforcements offset the surrender of most Italian forces, and Allied progress up the Italian boot was vigorously opposed for most of the war's duration.

After the invasion of Italy, the United States was able to reinforce its divisions in the British Isles for invasion of the Continent through German-occupied France. The result was the pivotal Western Allied move of World War II – D-Day, 6 June 1944. This spearhead assault was launched against Normandy by 176,000 troops, 4000 invasion craft, 600 warships, and an air cover of 11,000, preceded by parachute and glider-troop landings. The initial invasion force was soon reinforced so strongly that the Allies broke out of Normandy and rolled up the weak German forces. Between 25 August and 11 September all of France was liberated, together with Belgium and Luxembourg. US troops entered Germany on 12 September, sought to gain a Rhine bridgehead with an airborne landing in Holland, but failed to take all objectives. Meanwhile, the Germans resisted in the sea approaches to Antwerp – a port essential for supplying the huge Allied armies – and thereby ensured that the war would continue through the winter. In a sudden offensive of 15-26 December, the so-called Battle of the Bulge, the Germans made a last-ditch effort to stop the invasion of their country from the west. The Allies held, and in early spring began their drive on Germany. The chance capture of a Rhine bridge was soon followed by enlargement of the bridgehead into enemy territory and the end of German resistance in the West.

The Soviet Union played a vital part in the defeat of Germany: without its assistance, the war might have lasted years longer. Soviet armies had suffered defeat in the summer of 1941, when the German invasion sent them reeling back into the depths of Russia. Not until December did they make a stand, in the suburbs of Moscow itself, even as Japanese forces moved against the United States. In 1942 the Soviet Union was still hard pressed by Germany's battering assault. But the following year it gained the initiative with the recapture of Stalingrad, where the Russians had isolated an entire German army. From that point on, it was an inexorable counter-offensive that drove Nazi troops all the way back into German territory. By early 1945 the Russians were threatening Berlin; their capture of Germany's devastated capital in April precipitated Hitler's suicide and the Third Reich's surrender.

By Victory in Europe (V-E) Day, 8 May 1945, Japanese forces were seriously depleted, although the Allies did not know this and sought to enlist Soviet assistance against Japan. The Big Three – leaders of the United States, the Soviet Union, and Britain – held three major wartime conferences: at Tehran (1943), at Yalta (February 1945), and again at Potsdam after the European war (July-August 1945). At Potsdam the US was represented by President Harry S Truman, who had succeeded Roosevelt upon the latter's death in office. During this conference, the Soviets pledged to enter the Japanese war in mid-August, a decision apparently influenced by the successful US test of a plutonium bomb device in Alamagordo, New Mexico, on 16 July. Ten days later, from Potsdam, the US and Britain issued a veiled ultimatum to Japan that mentioned neither the existence of nuclear weapons nor a time limit. When unconditional surrender was not forthcoming, the United States Air Force dropped the first nuclear bomb, a uranium weapon, on Hiroshima on 6 August. The Soviet rushed into the Far Eastern war two days later, a week ahead of time. Next day, 9 August, the second nuclear bomb, a plutonium weapon, was dropped on Nagasaki. (The United States had possessed only enough uranium for the bomb against Hiroshima.) The Japanese asked for an armistice on 10 August and obtained one on 15 August, V-J Day. A formal surrender was signed aboard the USS *Missouri* in Tokyo Bay on 2 September 1945, ending the most catastrophic war in world history.

World War I

MAP below: The Europe that was at war with itself in 1914. To Americans, viewing the war from afar, it seemed an unnecessary and irrelevant struggle. Having turned their back on the old empires, being emigrants or descendants of emigrants from the old European order, most Americans could regard the war as an interesting, if sad, spectacle which did not really concern them. But when American ships and American commerce began to suffer it was seen that a policy of isolation, however virtuous it might be, had its drawbacks. Allied propaganda also was very successful in portraying the operations of the German U-Boats as barbarous and anti-American. Equally the Allies made extensive capital of tales, mostly false; of German atrocities, particularly in the early months of the war when the Germans advanced into France and Belgium.

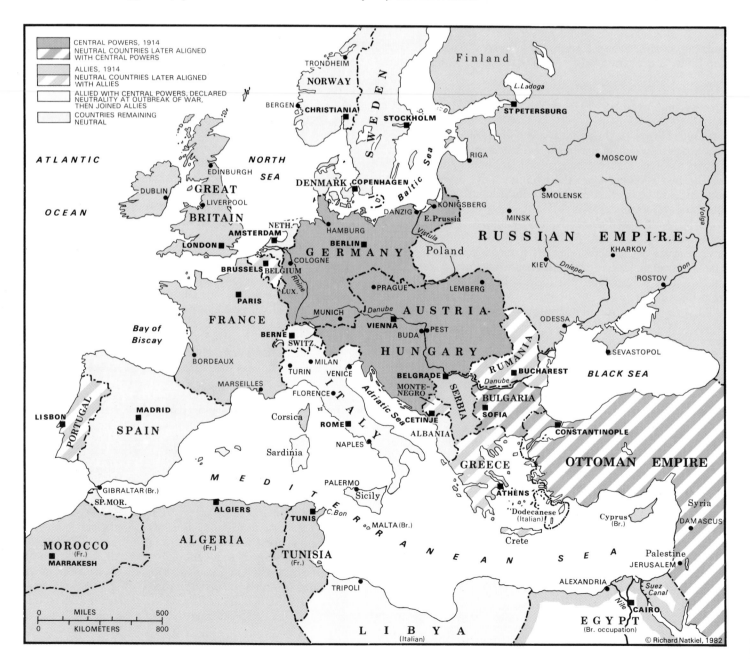

CENTRAL POWERS, 1914
NEUTRAL COUNTRIES LATER ALIGNED WITH CENTRAL POWERS

ALLIES, 1914
NEUTRAL COUNTRIES LATER ALIGNED WITH ALLIES

ALLIED WITH CENTRAL POWERS, DECLARED NEUTRALITY AT OUTBREAK OF WAR, THEN JOINED ALLIES

COUNTRIES REMAINING NEUTRAL

© Richard Natkiel, 1982

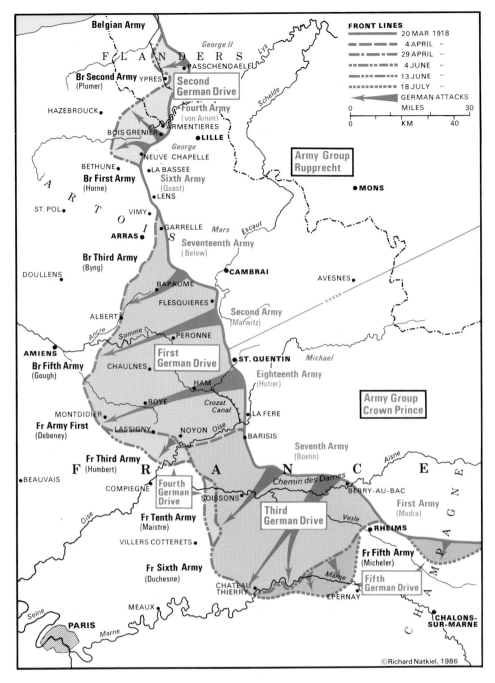

FRONT LINES

	20 MAR 1918
	4 APRIL "
	29 APRIL "
	4 JUNE "
	13 JUNE "
	18 JULY "
	GERMAN ATTACKS

0 MILES 30

0 KM 40

©Richard Natkiel, 1986

MAP left: The German offensives on the Western Front in 1918. With Russia out of the war, the Germans were able to mount strong offensives in France which, in their later stages, encountered newly-arrived US units. For Britain and France, America's entry into the war was timely compensation for Russia's exit, even though the first substantial US units went into action only in April 1918, a year after the American declaration of war. Transport and organizational problems, but especially the need to train US troops up to the standards of modern warfare, caused this delay.

Below: *Cartoon, one of many showing the Kaiser shedding neutral American blood and which helped to persuade Americans that they could no longer stay out of the war.*

Bottom left: *President Wilson announces the American declaration of war in April 1917.*

Bottom right: *A US government appeal.*

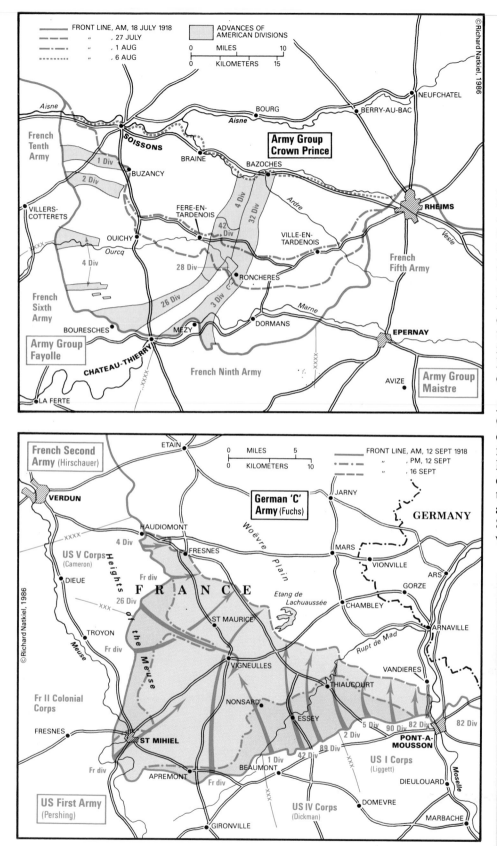

MAP left: The Aisne and Marne Offensive. By late July 1918 the American troops in France were strong enough to play a meaningful role. This map shows how they helped the French push back the German salient near Rheims. The main US defensive position was around Chateau-Thierry. At Belleau Wood, nearby, fighting was especially fierce, but the Americans held their ground and then, on 18 July, joined in the counter-offensive. Casualties were heavy, but the German salient was eliminated.

MAP below left: The St Mihiel Offensive. This operation, aimed at eliminating a German salient, was the first in which Americans played the leading role, in both planning and execution. Helped by tanks and over one thousand aircraft, the American infantry and artillery began work on 12 September and completed the operation within four days.

Right: *Douglas MacArthur, who took part in the Aisne and Marne Offensive.*

MAP below: The final Allied offensive. This offensive, which began in late September, continued up to the final German defeat. As previously, the American effort was concentrated in the south.

Left: *Newly-arrived US troops shortly after disembarking at Havre.*

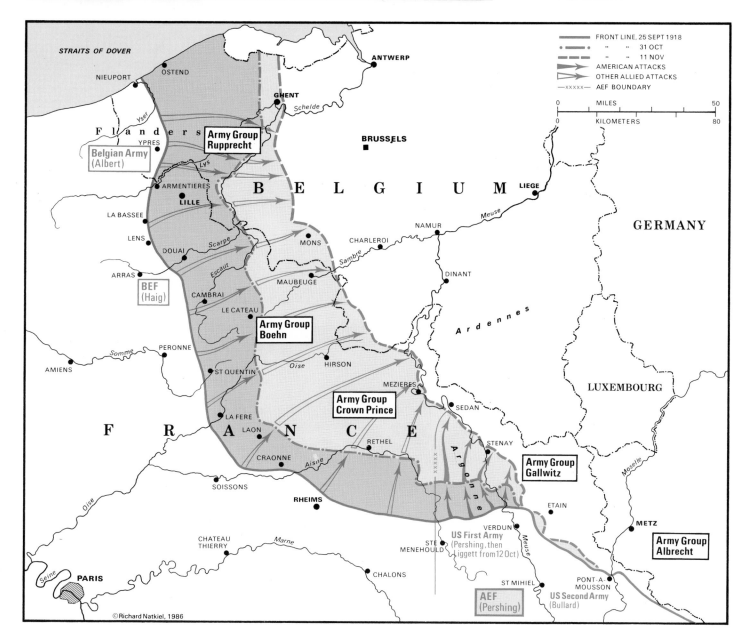

	FRONT LINE, 25 SEPT 1918
	" " 31 OCT
	" " 11 NOV
	AMERICAN ATTACKS
	OTHER ALLIED ATTACKS
xxxxx	AEF BOUNDARY

MILES 50
KILOMETERS 80

STRAITS OF DOVER

NIEUPORT
OSTEND
ANTWERP
GHENT
Schelde
F l a n d e r s
YPRES
BRUSSELS
Army Group Rupprecht
Belgian Army (Albert)
B E L G I U M
LIEGE
Lys
ARMENTIERES
LILLE
Meuse
LA BASSEE
NAMUR
GERMANY
LENS
Scarpe
MONS
CHARLEROI
DOUAI
Sambre
DINANT
ARRAS
Escaut
MAUBEUGE
BEF (Haig)
CAMBRAI
LE CATEAU
A r d e n n e s
Army Group Boehn
Somme
PERONNE
Oise
HIRSON
AMIENS
ST QUENTIN
MEZIERES
LUXEMBOURG
F   R   A   N   C   E
LA FERE
Army Group Crown Prince
SEDAN
LAON
RETHEL
STENAY
CRAONNE
Aisne
A r g o n n e
Army Group Gallwitz
SOISSONS
Moselle
RHEIMS
ETAIN
CHATEAU THIERRY
Marne
VERDUN
Army Group Albrecht
METZ
US First Army (Pershing, then Liggett from 12 Oct)
Seine
PARIS
STE MENEHOULD
CHALONS
ST MIHIEL
PONT-A-MOUSSON
AEF (Pershing)
US Second Army (Bullard)
Oise
Yser

©Richard Natkiel, 1986

MAP right: The American sector of the final Allied offensive against Germany. By this time the American Expeditionary Force, commanded by General Pershing, comprised two self-contained armies, and these co-operated with the French in the Meuse-Argonne Offensive which gained momentum until it was halted at Sedan by the Armistice.

MAP bottom right: The not-entirely-sweet fruits of victory in the Pacific. Japan, least active of the victorious Allies, received, as a trustee under League of Nations Mandate, the right to administer most of the former German possessions in the Far East. This extension of Japanese authority into the Pacific, and especially over the island of Yap, where there was a US cable station, aroused considerable misgiving in the United States.

Top right: *US infantry resting between actions during the Argonne Offensive in October 1918.*

Below: *US troops in the final stage of the war in France.*

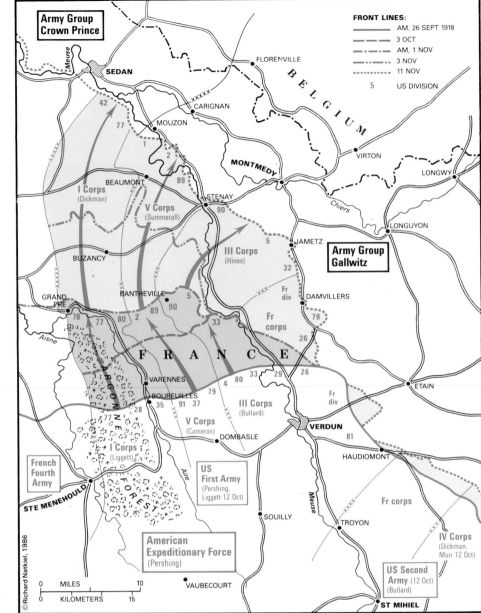

FRONT LINES:
AM, 26 SEPT 1918
3 OCT
AM, 1 NOV
3 NOV
11 NOV
5 US DIVISION

Army Group Crown Prince

Army Group Gallwitz

I Corps (Dickman)
V Corps (Summerall)
III Corps (Hines)
V Corps (Cameron)
III Corps (Bullard)
I Corps (Liggett)

French Fourth Army

American Expeditionary Force (Pershing)

US First Army (Pershing, Liggett 12 Oct)

US Second Army (12 Oct) (Bullard)

IV Corps (Dickman, Muir 12 Oct)

B E L G I U M

F R A N C E

SEDAN, CARIGNAN, MOUZON, FLORENVILLE, VIRTON, MONTMEDY, LONGWY, BEAUMONT, STENAY, LONGUYON, BUZANCY, JAMETZ, BANTHEVILLE, DAMVILLERS, GRAND PRE, VARENNES, BOUREUILLES, DOMBASLE, VERDUN, ETAIN, HAUDIOMONT, STE MENEHOULD, SOUILLY, TROYON, VAUBECOURT, ST MIHIEL

© Richard Natkiel, 1986

0 MILES 10
0 KILOMETERS 15

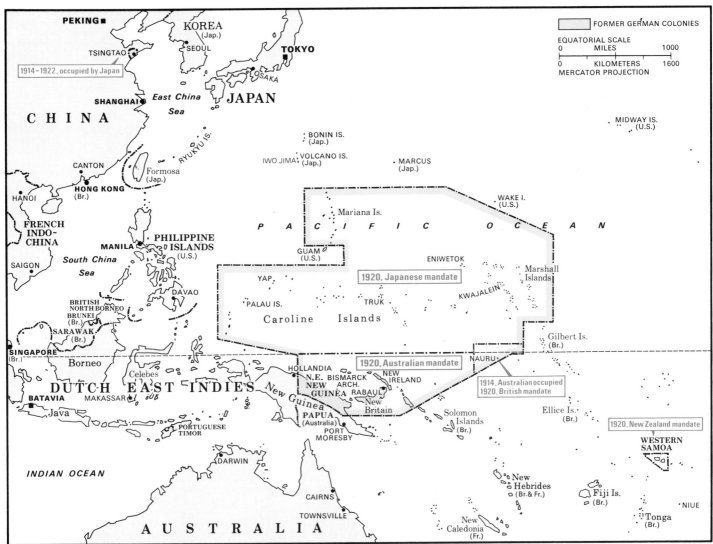

FORMER GERMAN COLONIES

EQUATORIAL SCALE

MERCATOR PROJECTION

PEKING

KOREA (Jap.)

TSINGTAO

SEOUL

TOKYO

1914-1922, occupied by Japan

OSAKA

East China Sea

JAPAN

SHANGHAI

CHINA

MIDWAY IS. (U.S.)

BONIN IS. (Jap.)

CANTON

IWO JIMA

VOLCANO IS. (Jap.)

MARCUS (Jap.)

Formosa (Jap.)

RYUKYU IS.

HONG KONG (Br.)

WAKE I. (U.S.)

HANOI

Mariana Is.

PACIFIC OCEAN

FRENCH INDO-CHINA

PHILIPPINE ISLANDS (U.S.)

MANILA

GUAM (U.S.)

ENIWETOK

Marshall Islands

SAIGON

South China Sea

YAP

1920, Japanese mandate

KWAJALEIN

DAVAO

PALAU IS.

TRUK

BRITISH NORTH BORNEO

Caroline Islands

Gilbert Is. (Br.)

BRUNEI (Br.)

SARAWAK (Br.)

SINGAPORE (Br.)

1920, Australian mandate

NAURU

Borneo

HOLLANDIA

Celebes

N.E. BISMARCK

NEW IRELAND

DUTCH EAST INDIES

New Guinea

NEW GUINEA

ARCH.

RABAUL

1914, Australian occupied
1920, British mandate

BATAVIA

MAKASSAR

New Britain

Ellice Is. (Br.)

Java

PAPUA (Australia)

Solomon Islands (Br.)

1920, New Zealand mandate

PORTUGUESE TIMOR

PORT MORESBY

WESTERN SAMOA

DARWIN

INDIAN OCEAN

New Hebrides (Br.& Fr.)

Fiji Is. (Br.)

NIUE

CAIRNS

New Caledonia (Fr.)

Tonga (Br.)

TOWNSVILLE

AUSTRALIA

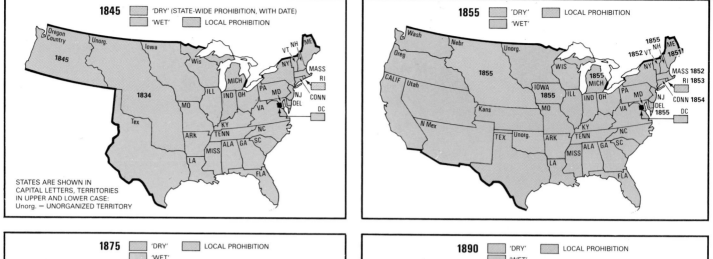

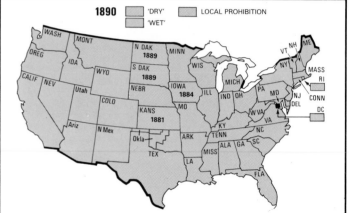
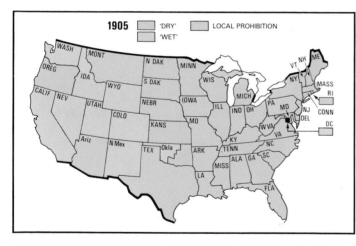
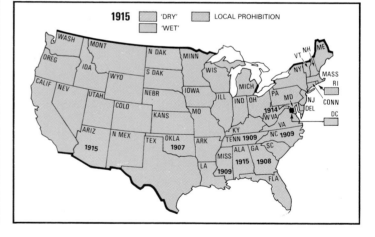
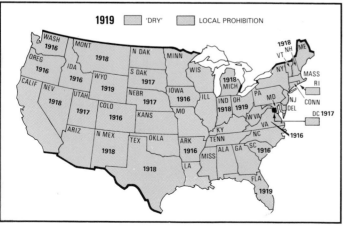
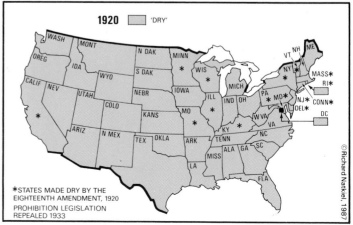

© Richard Natkiel, 1987

Prohibition and Female Suffrage

MAPS left: Prohibition in the USA. Although the 'Prohibition Era' was 1920-33, the banning of alcoholic beverages was by no means a new phenomenon, as individual states, or townships within those states, could declare themselves 'dry.' Nationwide prohibition was ended by the 21st Amendment in 1933, but several states chose to remain 'dry.'

MAPS below: The spread of female suffrage. Wyoming, while still a territory, had introduced votes for women as early as 1869, but only a few other states followed this example until, around 1910, female suffrage became a live political issue.

Right: *The Suffrage Movement in action.*

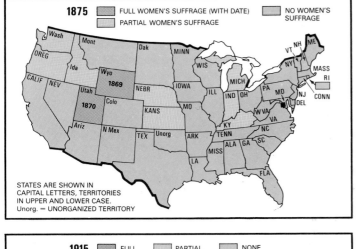

1875 · FULL WOMEN'S SUFFRAGE (WITH DATE) · PARTIAL WOMEN'S SUFFRAGE · NO WOMEN'S SUFFRAGE

STATES ARE SHOWN IN CAPITAL LETTERS, TERRITORIES IN UPPER AND LOWER CASE.
Unorg. = UNORGANIZED TERRITORY

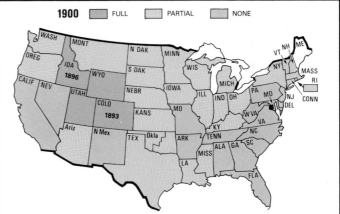

1900 · FULL · PARTIAL · NONE

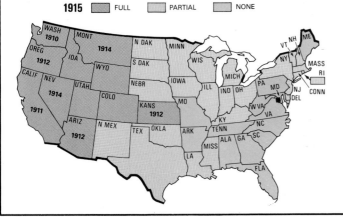

1915 · FULL · PARTIAL · NONE

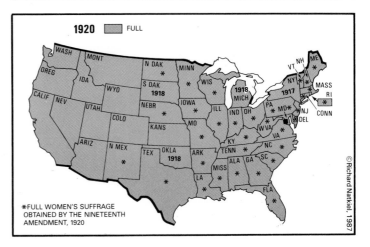

1920 · FULL

*FULL WOMEN'S SUFFRAGE OBTAINED BY THE NINETEENTH AMENDMENT, 1920

The Great Depression

MAP below: The intensity of unemployment. The farming states of the western plains were badly hit, whereas some areas of the East were comparatively unaffected (it should be remembered that 'full employment' in fact meant an unemployment rate of 5 per cent when account was taken of workers in the course of changing jobs). New industries, such as those producing automobiles, aircraft and radios, were relatively unscathed.

Right: *A WPA truck at work in Louisville. The WPA (Works Projects Administration), a New Deal agency, increased employment mainly by financing public construction works, especially road-building.*

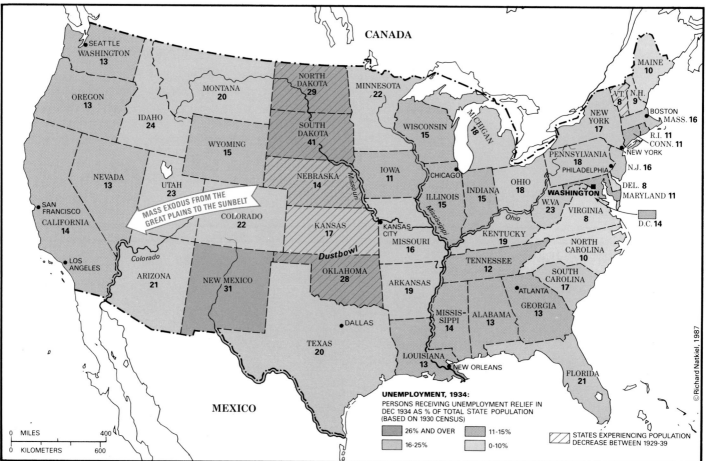

MASS EXODUS FROM THE GREAT PLAINS TO THE SUNBELT

UNEMPLOYMENT, 1934:
PERSONS RECEIVING UNEMPLOYMENT RELIEF IN DEC 1934 AS % OF TOTAL STATE POPULATION (BASED ON 1930 CENSUS)

26% AND OVER
16-25%
11-15%
0-10%

STATES EXPERIENCING POPULATION DECREASE BETWEEN 1929-39

© Richard Natkiel, 1987

0 MILES 400
0 KILOMETERS 600

MAP right: The Tennessee Valley Hydraulic Project. Better known as the Tennessee Valley Authority (TVA), this project had been studied for several years before the Depression, but the latter misfortune gave it impetus as a project which could not only transform the economies of seven states but also serve as a channel through which government expenditure could reduce unemployment. Attempts to declare the project unconstitutional were rejected by the Supreme Court. The TVA structure, as an independent corporate agency, was copied for river works elsewhere. As a long-term project, not confined to the Depression years, it was involved in the wartime atomic bomb project, eliminated malaria from its area of operation, and in the 1960s was supplying six percent of US electricity output.

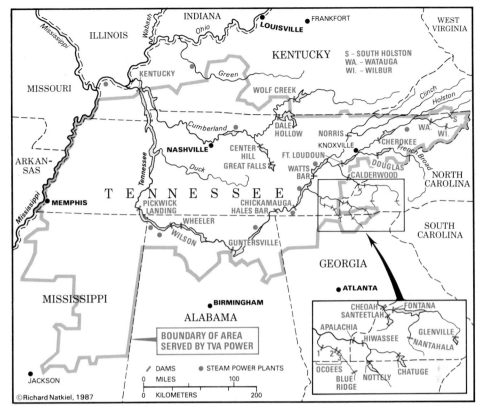

Below: *Building the TVA Fort London Dam in Tennessee in 1942.*

World War II
– Grand Strategy

MAP: The new Europe as created by the post-World War I treaties. The creation of the 'Polish corridor,' giving the new Poland access to the sea through Danzig, the loss of Alsace and Lorraine in the west, and the forced demilitarization of the Rhineland were three provisions which aroused great resentment among Germans, many of whom believed that the war had not been their country's fault and that they had never really been defeated.

Left: *Europe's troubles also affected the US domestically. Here, members of the pro-Nazi German-American Bund parade in Madison Square Gardens in 1939.*

Below left: *Rationing, even before Pearl Harbor, August 1941.*

Below: *Hitler and Mussolini, the architects of World War II.*

PRE–1914 BOUNDARIES
BOUNDARIES AFTER TREATY OF VERSAILLES, 1919
TERRITORIES LOST BY GERMANY
UNDER LEAGUE OF NATIONS CONTROL
DEMILITARISED ZONE

© Richard Natkiel, 1982

MAP: Hitler's Germany asserts itself. Before the start of World War II, Hitler had already undone many of the Versailles Treaty provisions. He had remilitarized the Rhineland, peacefully re-acquired the Saarland, taken over Czechoslovakia, a state created by the Treaty, and annexed Austria and also a small part of Lithuania, another of the post-war states. The final seizure of what remained of Czechoslovakia in March 1939 convinced Britain and France that they must stand up to Hitler.

Right: *President Roosevelt and Soviet leader Marshal Stalin at a wartime conference.*

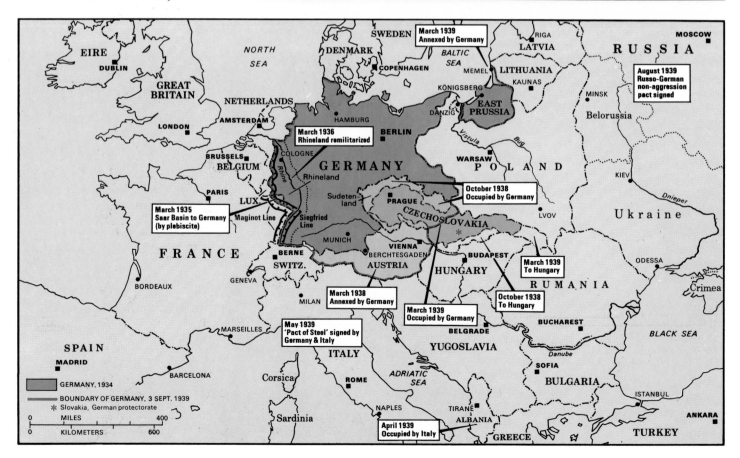

SWEDEN

March 1939
Annexed by Germany

MOSCOW

EIRE

DUBLIN

NORTH SEA

DENMARK

COPENHAGEN

BALTIC SEA

MEMEL

RIGA

LATVIA

LITHUANIA

RUSSIA

KAUNAS

GREAT BRITAIN

NETHERLANDS

AMSTERDAM

HAMBURG

KÖNIGSBERG

DANZIG

EAST PRUSSIA

MINSK

August 1939
Russo-German
non-aggression
pact signed

LONDON

BERLIN

Belorussia

BRUSSELS

BELGIUM

COLOGNE

March 1936
Rhineland remilitarized

GERMANY

Vistula

Bug

WARSAW

P O L A N D

KIEV

Rhine

PARIS

Rhineland

Sudeten-
land

PRAGUE

October 1938
Occupied by Germany

LVOV

Ukraine

Dnieper

LUX.

March 1935
Saar Basin to Germany
(by plebiscite)

Maginot Line

Siegfried
Line

CZECHOSLOVAKIA

MUNICH

F R A N C E

BERNE

SWITZ.

GENEVA

BORDEAUX

MILAN

VIENNA

BERCHTESGADEN

AUSTRIA

BUDAPEST

HUNGARY

March 1939
To Hungary

ODESSA

R U M A N I A

Crimea

March 1938
Annexed by Germany

October 1938
To Hungary

March 1939
Occupied by Germany

BELGRADE

BUCHAREST

May 1939
'Pact of Steel' signed by
Germany & Italy

MARSEILLES

ITALY

YUGOSLAVIA

Danube

SOFIA

BLACK SEA

SPAIN

MADRID

BARCELONA

Corsica

ROME

ADRIATIC
SEA

BULGARIA

ISTANBUL

Sardinia

NAPLES

TIRANE

ALBANIA

GREECE

ANKARA

TURKEY

April 1939
Occupied by Italy

GERMANY, 1934

BOUNDARY OF GERMANY, 3 SEPT. 1939

✳ Slovakia, German protectorate

0 — MILES — 400

0 — KILOMETERS — 600

MAP: The first year of World War II. Nazi Germany occupies much of Europe, Communist Russia takes back much of the territory lost after World War I, and Fascist Italy strikes at easy targets. The predominant factor in this transformation of Europe was the apparently unbeatable *blitzkrieg* style of warfare adopted by the Germans, in which highly mechanized formations with massive air support made rapid and deep advances on narrow fronts, thereby shattering the defensive plans of their opponents. After this first year, however, *blitzkrieg* methods became less effective because Germany's enemies learned from experience and were better prepared for them.

ARCTIC OCEAN
Barents Sea

	GERMAN OCCUPIED, 1 JAN 1941
	ALLIED WITH AXIS
	GERMAN OCCUPIED, 1 JAN – 29 MAY 1941 22 JUNE 1941 – 19 NOV 1942

GERMAN FRONT LINES
————— 16 JULY 1941
– – – – 5 DECEMBER 1941
· · · · · END-APRIL 1942
–·–·– 19 NOVEMBER 1942

MILES 0 ———— 500
KILOMETERS 0 ———— 800

REYKJAVIK ICELAND

PETSAMO MURMANSK

NARVIK

White Sea ARCHANGEL

TRONDHEIM

N O R W A Y S W E D E N FINLAND

PETROZAVODSK

15 Sept 1941
Siege of Leningrad
begins

BERGEN VIIPURI L. Ladoga

OSLO HELSINKI

STOCKHOLM LENINGRAD DEMYANSK

5/6 Dec 1941–end April 1942
Russian counteroffensive
on Moscow axis

TALLINN MOSCOW

ATLANTIC NORTH PSKOV

EDINBURGH SEA RIGA R U S S I A

EIRE GREAT DENMARK COPENHAGEN KAUNAS SMOLENSK TULA

OCEAN DUBLIN LIVERPOOL Baltic Sea KONIGSBERG **19 Nov 1942**
High-tide of German expansion,
Russian counteroffensive begins

BRITAIN **22 June 1941** MINSK VORONEZH

NETH. ("Barbarossa") DANZIG STALINGRAD

AMSTERDAM Germany invades E.PRUSSIA Volga

LONDON Russia HAMBURG Vistula KIEV KHARKOV

BERLIN WARSAW Don Caspian

BRUSSELS BELG. G E R M A N Y P O L A N D Dnieper ZAPOROZHYE Sea

COLOGNE Rhine ROSTOV

PARIS LUX. **6-17 April 1941** ODESSA GROZNY

Germany invades
Yugoslavia

F R A N C E SLOVAKIA NOVOROSSIISK

Bay of BERNE MUNICH VIENNA BUDAPEST BLACK SEA SEVASTOPOL TIFLIS

Biscay VICHY SWITZ. H U N G A R Y

MILAN R U M A N I A IRAN

BORDEAUX TURIN BUCHAREST

VENICE BELGRADE Danube

PORTUGAL MADRID FLORENCE I T A L Y YUGOSLAVIA BULGARIA ANKARA

LISBON **11 November 1942** Corsica ROME SOFIA ISTANBUL T U R K E Y

Germans occupy
Vichy France

SPAIN ALBANIA SYRIA IRAQ

NAPLES GREECE (Free French) (Br)

8 Nov 1942 Sardinia **9 Nov 1942** **6-28 April 1941** Cyprus DAMASCUS

US/British forces land **German forces** **Germany invades** (Br)

in Morocco & Algeria M E D I T E R R A N E A N **land in Tunisia** **Greece** ATHENS

GIBRALTAR Dodecanese PALESTINE AMMAN

PORT (Br) (Italian) (Br) TRANSJORDAN

LYAUTEY SP.MOR. ORAN ALGIERS BÔNE TUNIS MALTA (Br) **20-29 May 1941** JERUSALEM (Br)

CASABLANCA **Crete invaded** Crete S E A

SAFI ALGERIA **1941-1942** ALEXANDRIA Suez SAUDI

(Vichy French) TUNISIA **Axis forces & Brit Eighth Army** Canal CAIRO ARABIA

MOROCCO (Vichy French) **engaged in battles across the desert**

(Vichy French) TRIPOLI TRIPOLI EL ALAMEIN Nile

BENGHAZI

SIRTE **23 Oct-4 Nov 1942**

EL AGHEILA **Battle of El Alamein**

L I B Y A E G Y P T

(Italian)

© Richard Natkiel. 1982

MAP: The war in Europe, 1941-42. This was the crucial period of World War II. Germany, it seemed, was triumphant in mid-1941. Having digested the conquests of 1939-40, she advanced into the Balkans, into Egypt, and then into Russia. Her crushing defeats of the Russian army obscured the reality of Russia's potential strength, while Hitler's decision to declare war on the USA after Japan's attack at Pearl Harbor ranged against him a second enemy of enormous potential. Britain remained undefeated, although by early 1942 her Far Eastern empire was being devoured by the Japanese onslaught. In late 1942 there were clear signs that the tide was turning. The highly professional German Army, pushed into too many campaigns, was defeated by the Russians at Stalingrad and by the British at Alamein, while US industry and manpower made possible the Allied landing in North Africa, threatening the Axis presence there and opening a way to the invasion of Italy.

Right: *The symbol of German success 1939-41; a Ju-87 Stuka begins its attack dive.*

Far right: *USAAF B-17 Flying Fortresses set out to bomb Germany.*

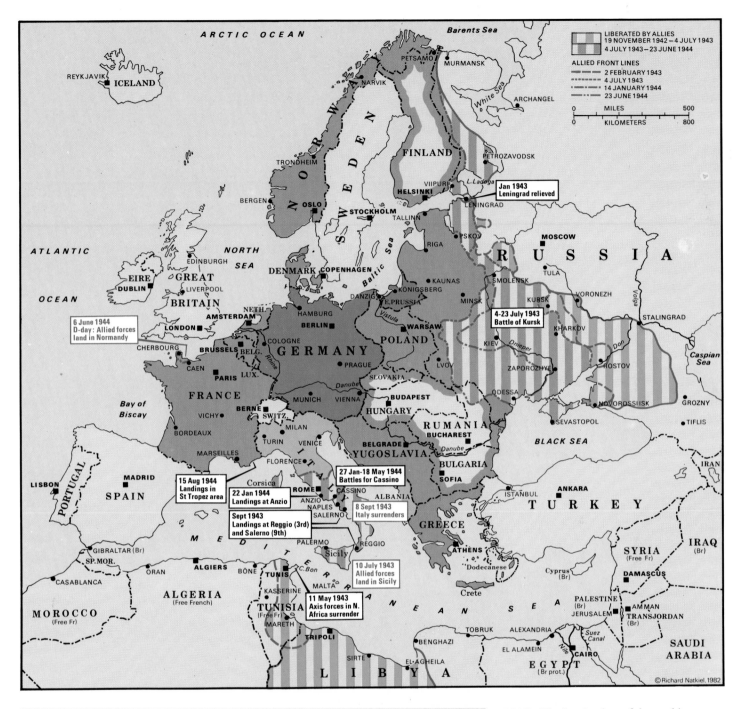

MAP LEGEND:

LIBERATED BY ALLIES
19 NOVEMBER 1942 – 4 JULY 1943
4 JULY 1943 – 23 JUNE 1944

ALLIED FRONT LINES
2 FEBRUARY 1943
4 JULY 1943
14 JANUARY 1944
23 JUNE 1944

MILES 500
KILOMETERS 800

Map annotations:
- Jan 1943 Leningrad relieved
- 4-23 July 1943 Battle of Kursk
- 6 June 1944 D-day: Allied forces land in Normandy
- 15 Aug 1944 Landings in St Tropez area
- 22 Jan 1944 Landings at Anzio
- Sept 1943 Landings at Reggio (3rd) and Salerno (9th)
- 27 Jan-18 May 1944 Battles for Cassino
- 8 Sept 1943 Italy surrenders
- 10 July 1943 Allied forces land in Sicily
- 11 May 1943 Axis forces in N. Africa surrender

© Richard Natkiel, 1982

MAP: The beginning of the end in Europe. The failure of the Germans at the great tank battle of Kursk in summer 1943 signified the start of a long retreat. This defeat coincided with the Anglo-US landings in Sicily, which later developed into the Italian campaign. The Germans were then faced with a third front when Allied forces achieved the technically difficult task of landing their huge invasion army in northern France. Meanwhile, the Battle of the Atlantic against German submarines was being won, and Allied bombers were making numerous, overwhelming, and murderous raids on German cities and industries.

MAP: The end of the war in Europe. Both Hitler and the Allies were prepared to fight on until Germany's total destruction, and were not interested in a negotiated surrender. The German Army conducted a magnificent, if useless, fighting retreat on three fronts and even managed, in the winter of 1944-45, to carry out a dangerous counterattack, known as the Battle of the Bulge, against the advancing Americans in Belgium. Devastating air attacks directed at the German population failed to break morale, and Germany surrendered only after the Red Army stormed Berlin and Hitler had killed himself. By previous arrangement, the advancing American and Russian armies had already met on the Elbe, somewhat to the west of Berlin. Arrangements had already been made at the wartime conferences between Roosevelt, Churchill and Stalin which effectively gave the Soviets complete control of Eastern Europe.

Right: *General Jodl signs the German surrender at Eisenhower's headquarters at Reims, 7 May 1945.*

Opposite bottom left: *An ammunition dump at a US bomber station.*

Opposite, center right: *General Eisenhower (second right) at the final German surrender in Berlin.*

Bottom, far right: *US troops in a landing craft on D-Day.*

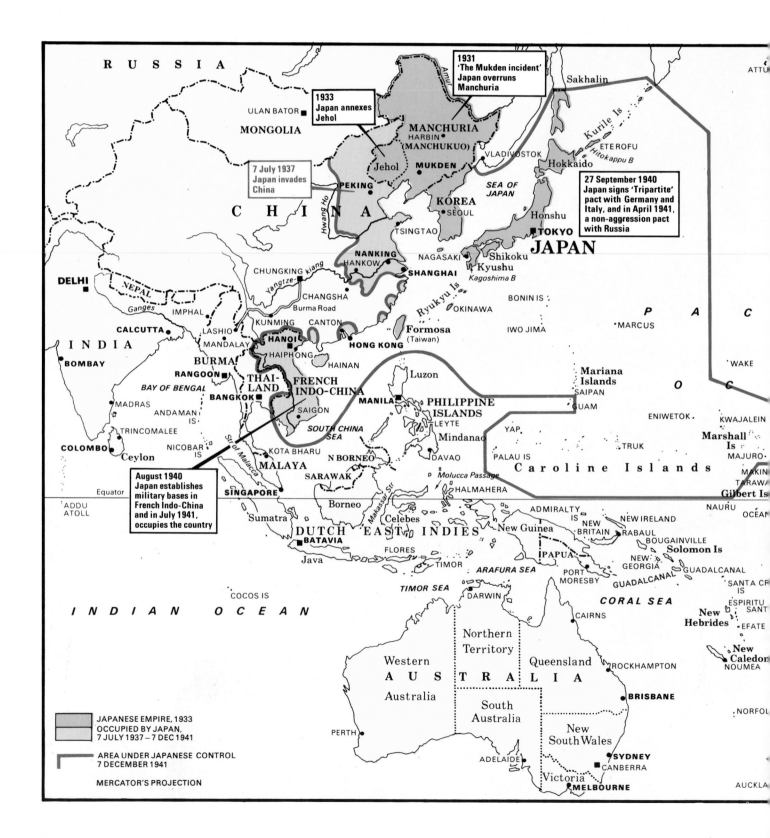

RUSSIA

ULAN BATOR

MONGOLIA

1931
'The Mukden incident'
Japan overruns
Manchuria

Sakhalin

ATTU

1933
Japan annexes
Jehol

MANCHURIA
HARBIN
(MANCHUKUO)

Amur

Kurile Is

ETEROFU
Hitokappu B

Hokkaido

7 July 1937
Japan invades
China

Jehol

MUKDEN

VLADIVOSTOK

PEKING

KOREA

SEOUL

SEA OF
JAPAN

Honshu

27 September 1940
Japan signs 'Tripartite'
pact with Germany and
Italy, and in April 1941,
a non-aggression pact
with Russia

C H I N A

Hwang Ho

TSINGTAO

NANKING
HANKOW

NAGASAKI

Kyushu
Kagoshima B

Shikoku

TOKYO

JAPAN

DELHI

NEPAL

Ganges

CHUNGKING kiang

Yangtze

CHANGSHA
Burma Road

SHANGHAI

Ryukyu Is

OKINAWA

BONIN IS

P A C

MARCUS

CALCUTTA

IMPHAL

KUNMING

CANTON

OKINAWA

Formosa
(Taiwan)

IWO JIMA

O

C

WAKE

I N D I A

LASHIO

MANDALAY

HANOI

HAIPHONG

HONG KONG

HAINAN

Luzon

Mariana
Islands

SAIPAN

BOMBAY

RANGOON

BURMA

THAI-
LAND

FRENCH
INDO-CHINA

MANILA

PHILIPPINE
ISLANDS

LEYTE

GUAM

ENIWETOK

KWAJALEIN

BAY OF BENGAL

BANGKOK

SAIGON

SOUTH CHINA
SEA

Mindanao

YAP

TRUK

Marshall
Is

MAJURO

MADRAS

ANDAMAN
IS

DAVAO

PALAU IS

C a r o l i n e   I s l a n d s

MAKIN

TARAWA

TRINCOMALEE

NICOBAR
IS

Str of Malacca

KOTA BHARU

MALAYA

SARAWAK

N BORNEO

Molucca Passage

Makassar Str

HALMAHERA

Gilbert Is

COLOMBO

Ceylon

August 1940
Japan establishes
military bases in
French Indo-China
and in July 1941,
occupies the country

Equator

NAURU

OCEAN

ADDU
ATOLL

SINGAPORE

Borneo

ADMIRALTY
IS

NEW
IRELAND

NEW
BRITAIN

RABAUL

Sumatra

DUTCH   EAST   INDIES

BATAVIA

Java

Celebes

FLORES

TIMOR

PAPUA

NEW
GEORGIA

Solomon Is

BOUGAINVILLE

GUADALCANAL

SANTA CR
IS

ARAFURA SEA

PORT
MORESBY

GUADALCANAL

New Guinea

COCOS IS

TIMOR SEA

DARWIN

CORAL SEA

CAIRNS

ESPIRITU
SANT

New
Hebrides

EFATE

I N D I A N   O C E A N

Northern
Territory

Western
Australia

Queensland

ROCKHAMPTON

New
Caledon

NOUMEA

A U S T R A L I A

South
Australia

New
South Wales

BRISBANE

NORFOL

PERTH

ADELAIDE

Victoria

SYDNEY

CANBERRA

MELBOURNE

AUCKLA

JAPANESE EMPIRE, 1933
OCCUPIED BY JAPAN,
7 JULY 1937 – 7 DEC 1941

AREA UNDER JAPANESE CONTROL
7 DECEMBER 1941

MERCATOR'S PROJECTION

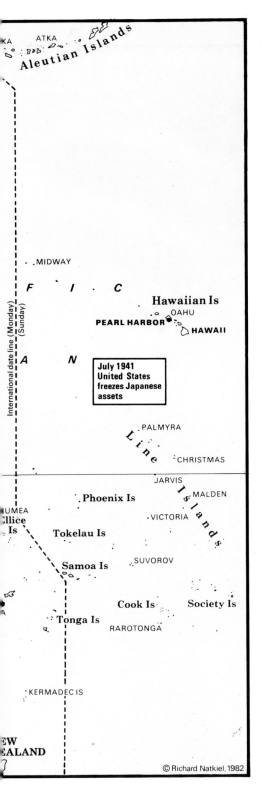

ATKA
Aleutian Islands

MIDWAY

F I C

Hawaiian Is
OAHU
PEARL HARBOR
HAWAII

International date line (Monday) (Sunday)

A N

July 1941
United States
freezes Japanese
assets

PALMYRA

Line

CHRISTMAS

JARVIS

Phoenix Is
MALDEN

UMEA
Ellice
Is
VICTORIA

Tokelau Is

SUVOROV

Samoa Is

Islands

Cook Is
Society Is

Tonga Is
RAROTONGA

KERMADEC IS

EW
EALAND

© Richard Natkiel, 1982

MAP: Prelude to war in the Pacific. Japan, like Germany in the nineteenth century, arrived late as an empire-building great power and, like Germany, was prepared to fight for her 'place in the sun.' This quest for greatness both inspired and enabled the Japanese officer corps to grasp political power in the years after World War I while maintaining, ostensibly, the authority of the Emperor. Suspicion of Japanese intentions on the part of the USA and the Western powers led to various measures which persuaded the Japanese government that no time was to be lost in asserting itself in the Far East. The beginning of the slide into war was the 'Mukden incident' of 1931, when the Japanese officer corps on its own initiative began the seizure of Manchuria. This was followed by further campaigns against China, culminating in an invasion of the Chinese homeland in 1937. Such moves could only arouse hostility and anxiety, especially in the USA and Britain, and Japan's occupation of French Indo-China, after France had been defeated by Hitler, and her joining in a Tripartite Pact with Italy and Germany, made clear her bellicose intentions. US trade restrictions were imposed, and these seemed to threaten Japan's oil imports in 1941; to the militarized Japanese government, this embargo seemed to make war not only desirable, but urgent. The attack on Pearl Harbor followed.

Below: *Flight deck activities aboard the aircraft carrier USS* Wasp, *1941-42. Naval aviation played a dominant role in the Pacific War but the* Wasp *was in fact sunk by a Japanese submarine in the Solomons area in September 1942.*

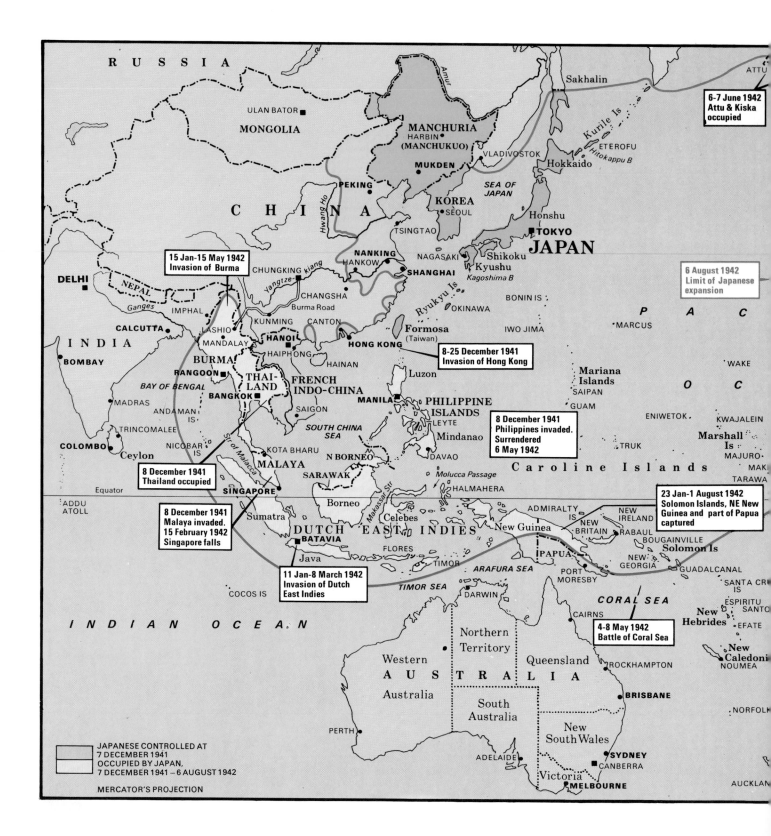

R U S S I A

Sakhalin

ATTU

**6-7 June 1942
Attu & Kiska
occupied**

ULAN BATOR

MONGOLIA

MANCHURIA
(MANCHUKUO)

HARBIN

Amur

Kurile Is

ETEROFU

Hitokappu B

MUKDEN

VLADIVOSTOK

Hokkaido

PEKING

KOREA

*SEA OF
JAPAN*

SEOUL

Honshu

C H I N A

TSINGTAO

NAGASAKI

TOKYO

JAPAN

Hwang Ho

**6 August 1942
Limit of Japanese
expansion**

**15 Jan-15 May 1942
Invasion of Burma**

NANKING

CHUNGKING

kiang

HANKOW

SHANGHAI

Shikoku

Kyushu

Kagoshima B

BONIN IS

P A C

DELHI

NEPAL

Yangtze

CHANGSHA

Burma Road

Ganges

IMPHAL

KUNMING

CANTON

Ryukyu Is

OKINAWA

IWO JIMA

MARCUS

O C

CALCUTTA

LASHIO

Formosa
(Taiwan)

**8-25 December 1941
Invasion of Hong Kong**

MANDALAY

HANOI

I N D I A

HAIPHONG

HONG KONG

BOMBAY

BURMA

HAINAN

Luzon

**Mariana
Islands**

WAKE

RANGOON

THAI-
LAND

FRENCH
INDO-CHINA

SAIPAN

BAY OF BENGAL

BANGKOK

MANILA

**PHILIPPINE
ISLANDS**

GUAM

ENIWETOK

KWAJALEIN

MADRAS

ANDAMAN
IS

SAIGON

LEYTE

**8 December 1941
Philippines invaded.
Surrendered
6 May 1942**

**Marshall
Is**

TRINCOMALEE

*SOUTH CHINA
SEA*

Mindanao

TRUK

MAJURO

COLOMBO

NICOBAR
IS

KOTA BHARU

DAVAO

C a r o l i n e   I s l a n d s

MAK

Ceylon

Str of Malacca

MALAYA

N BORNEO

Molucca Passage

TARAWA

**8 December 1941
Thailand occupied**

SARAWAK

Makassar Str

HALMAHERA

**23 Jan-1 August 1942
Solomon Islands, NE New
Guinea and part of Papua
captured**

Equator

SINGAPORE

Borneo

Celebes

ADMIRALTY
IS

NEW
IRELAND

ADDU
ATOLL

**8 December 1941
Malaya invaded.
15 February 1942
Singapore falls**

Sumatra

D U T C H   E A S T   I N D I E S

New Guinea

NEW
BRITAIN

RABAUL

BOUGAINVILLE

Solomon Is

BATAVIA

FLORES

TIMOR

ARAFURA SEA

PAPUA

NEW
GEORGIA

GUADALCANAL

Java

**11 Jan-8 March 1942
Invasion of Dutch
East Indies**

TIMOR SEA

PORT
MORESBY

SANTA CRU
IS

COCOS IS

DARWIN

CORAL SEA

ESPIRITU
SANTO

I N D I A N   O C E A N

Northern
Territory

CAIRNS

**4-8 May 1942
Battle of Coral Sea**

**New
Hebrides**

EFATE

Western

Queensland

ROCKHAMPTON

**New
Caledoni**

Australia

A U S T R A L I A

NOUMEA

PERTH

South
Australia

New
South Wales

BRISBANE

NORFOLK

ADELAIDE

SYDNEY

CANBERRA

Victoria

MELBOURNE

AUCKLAN

JAPANESE CONTROLLED AT
7 DECEMBER 1941,
OCCUPIED BY JAPAN,
7 DECEMBER 1941 – 6 AUGUST 1942

MERCATOR'S PROJECTION

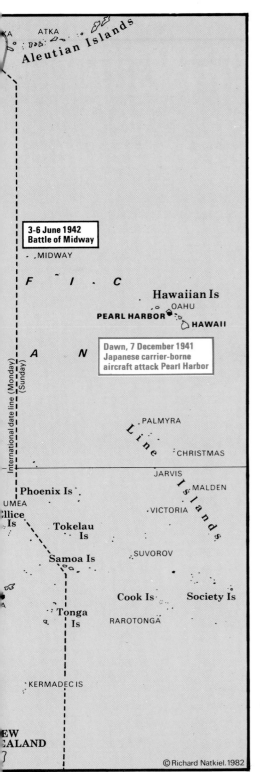

**3-6 June 1942
Battle of Midway**

MIDWAY

F I C

Hawaiian Is

OAHU

PEARL HARBOR **HAWAII**

A N

**Dawn, 7 December 1941
Japanese carrier-borne
aircraft attack Pearl Harbor**

PALMYRA

Line Islands

CHRISTMAS

JARVIS
MALDEN

Phoenix Is
UMEA
VICTORIA
Ellice
Is
Tokelau
Is

SUVOROV

Samoa Is

Cook Is Society Is

Tonga
Is
RAROTONGA

KERMADEC IS

EW
ZEALAND

© Richard Natkiel. 1982

International date line (Monday)
(Sunday)

ATKA
Aleutian Islands

MAP: A new Japanese Empire takes shape. Japan had for years sought its 'Co-prosperity Zone,' a novel euphemism for the much-desired empire, and early victories in the Pacific War seemed to make this a reality. The crippling of US naval power by the surprise attack on Pearl Harbor; the humiliation of British power by the destruction of two capital ships, the conquest of Malaya and the capture of Singapore and Hong Kong; and the occupation of the Dutch East Indies did seem to create a Japanese-controlled zone that could supply the needs of the domestic economy. But the crucial missing ingredient of this recipe was the acquiescence of the USA and Britain, and neither of these powers, though reeling from defeats, had any thought of abandoning the struggle. In the end, the dream lasted less than six months. At the Battle of the Coral Sea the naval advance was held and then, at the Battle of Midway, the Japanese bubble was pricked; no longer fighting an unprepared and surprised enemy, the Japanese Navy was defeated by the US Navy and lost the most important element of its recent successes, superiority in naval aviation. Although much hard fighting was to follow, US war production and manpower would now overtake the Japanese.

Below: *US Marine artillery in action on Bougainville in December 1943.*

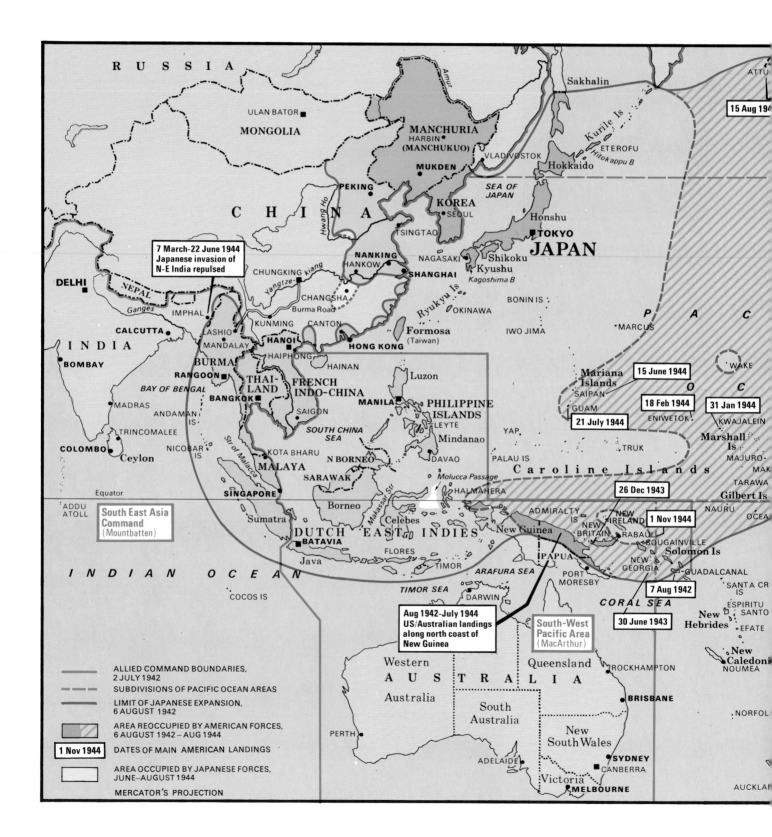

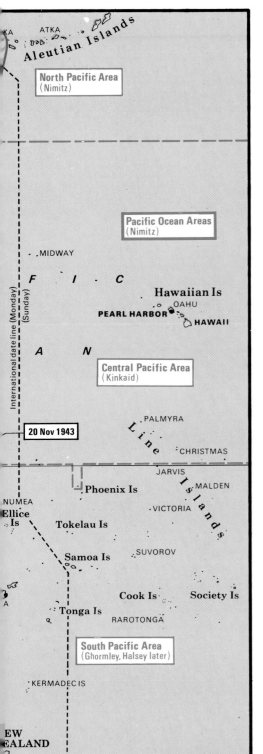

North Pacific Area
(Nimitz)

Pacific Ocean Areas
(Nimitz)

·MIDWAY

F I C

Hawaiian Is

OAHU

PEARL HARBOR ● HAWAII

A N

Central Pacific Area
(Kinkaid)

PALMYRA

Line Islands

20 Nov 1943

CHRISTMAS

JARVIS

Phoenix Is MALDEN

NUMEA

Ellice Is ·VICTORIA

Tokelau Is

SUVOROV

Samoa Is

Cook Is Society Is

Tonga Is

RAROTONGA

South Pacific Area
(Ghormley, Halsey later)

·KERMADEC IS

EW EALAND

International date line (Monday) (Sunday)

Aleutian Islands

ATKA

KA

© Richard Natkiel, 1982

MAP: The tide turns in the Pacific War. The Battle of Midway hastened, rather than initiated, the eventual Japanese defeat. Like Nazi Germany, Japan faced enemies with greatly superior potential resources, and had begun a war which would have to be won fast, or not at all. Like Germany, she discovered that early and crushing victories did not bring the surrender of her chosen enemies, who adopted a holding strategy while accumulating resources. The USA, in particular, quickly adopted a war economy which supplied not only her own expanding forces but also, to a considerable degree, those of her allies. In the Pacific, as US strength steadily overtook that of Japan, there remained the problem of deciding the best strategy for pushing back the Japanese line of conquest to the point where the Japanese homeland could be attacked. The solution was 'island-hopping,' a campaign in which, island by island, the Japanese defenders would be crushed and a slow, bitterly-fought, roll-back achieved. The instrument for this campaign was the task force, a self-contained naval squadron containing the necessary elements of air power and supply and repair facilities to enable it to win local superiority and protect troop landings. A route through the central Pacific islands was chosen, Tarawa being an initial, partly experimental, and rather costly target in this strategy. Meanwhile, in the South-West Pacific General MacArthur directed a US/Australian campaign against the Japanese in New Guinea while, far to the west, the British held and threw back the Japanese in the jungles of Burma.

Below: *Navy pilots aboard the carrier* Lexington *are briefed by their squadron commander during the operations in the Gilbert Islands in late 1943.*

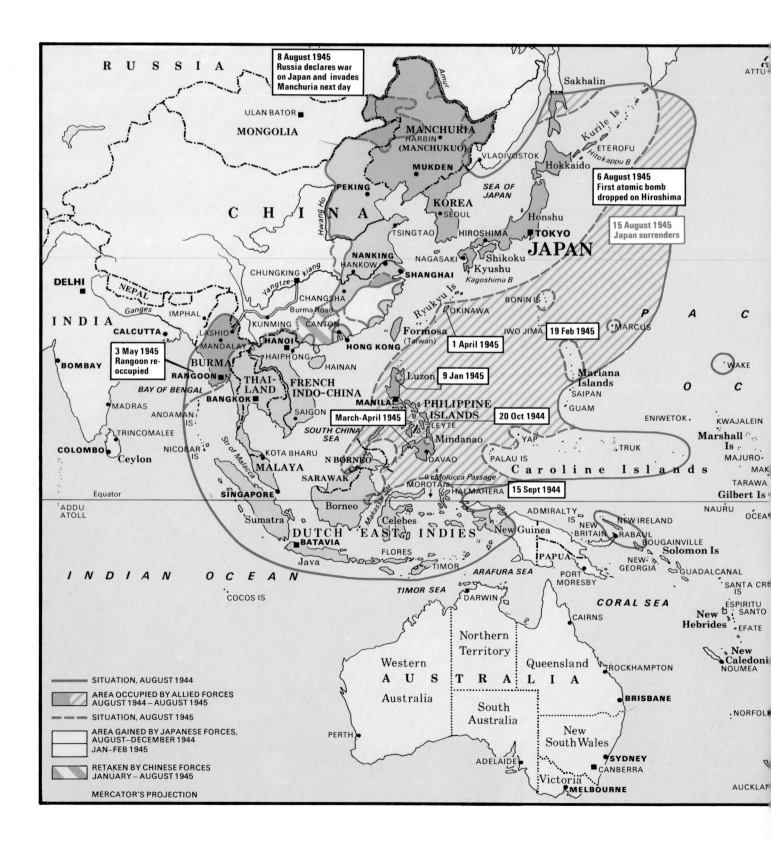

8 August 1945
Russia declares war
on Japan and invades
Manchuria next day

6 August 1945
First atomic bomb
dropped on Hiroshima

15 August 1945
Japan surrenders

3 May 1945
Rangoon re-
occupied

1 April 1945

19 Feb 1945

9 Jan 1945

20 Oct 1944

March-April 1945

15 Sept 1944

RUSSIA

ULAN BATOR
MONGOLIA
MANCHURIA
HARBIN
(MANCHUKUO)
VLADIVOSTOK
MUKDEN
PEKING
KOREA
SEOUL
SEA OF
JAPAN
Sakhalin
ATTU
Kurile Is
ETEROFU
Hitokappu B
Hokkaido
Honshu
TOKYO
JAPAN
HIROSHIMA
NAGASAKI
Shikoku
Kyushu
Kagoshima B

C H I N A
Hwang Ho
TSINGTAO
NANKING
CHUNGKING
kiang
HANKOW
SHANGHAI
Yangtze
CHANGSHA
Burma Road

DELHI
NEPAL
Ganges
IMPHAL
I N D I A
CALCUTTA
LASHIO
MANDALAY
KUNMING
CANTON
HANOI
HAIPHONG
HONG KONG
HAINAN
Ryukyu Is
OKINAWA
Formosa
(Taiwan)
BONIN IS
IWO JIMA
MARCUS
P A C
O C

BOMBAY
BURMA
RANGOON
THAI-
LAND
BANGKOK
FRENCH
INDO-CHINA
SAIGON
BAY OF BENGAL
MADRAS
ANDAMAN
IS
Luzon
MANILA
PHILIPPINE
ISLANDS
LEYTE
Mariana
Islands
SAIPAN
GUAM
WAKE
ENIWETOK
KWAJALEIN
Marshall
Is
MAJURO
MAK

COLOMBO
TRINCOMALEE
Ceylon
NICOBAR
IS
KOTA BHARU
MALAYA
SARAWAK
N BORNEO
SOUTH CHINA
SEA
Str of Malacca
Mindanao
DAVAO
YAP
PALAU IS
TRUK
Caroline Islands
TARAWA
Gilbert Is

Equator
ADDU
ATOLL
Sumatra
SINGAPORE
Borneo
Makassar Str
Molucca Passage
MOROTAI
HALMAHERA
Celebes
ADMIRALTY
IS
NEW
BRITAIN
NEW IRELAND
RABAUL
BOUGAINVILLE
Solomon Is
NAURU
OCEA

I N D I A N   O C E A N
COCOS IS
DUTCH   EAST   INDIES
BATAVIA
Java
FLORES
TIMOR
ARAFURA SEA
New Guinea
PAPUA
PORT
MORESBY
NEW
GEORGIA
GUADALCANAL
SANTA CR
IS
New
Hebrides
ESPIRITU
SANTO
EFATE

TIMOR SEA
CORAL SEA
DARWIN
CAIRNS
NORFOL
New
Caledoni
NOUMEA

Northern
Territory
Western
Australia
Queensland
ROCKHAMPTON
BRISBANE
A U S T R A L I A
South
Australia
New
South Wales
PERTH
ADELAIDE
Victoria
SYDNEY
CANBERRA
MELBOURNE
AUCKLAN

SITUATION, AUGUST 1944

AREA OCCUPIED BY ALLIED FORCES
AUGUST 1944 – AUGUST 1945

SITUATION, AUGUST 1945

AREA GAINED BY JAPANESE FORCES,
AUGUST–DECEMBER 1944
JAN–FEB 1945

RETAKEN BY CHINESE FORCES
JANUARY – AUGUST 1945

MERCATOR'S PROJECTION

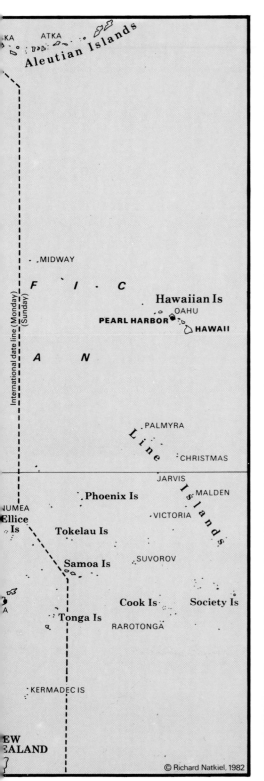

MAP: The assault on Japan. US forces recaptured the Philippines in April 1945, but far more important, strategically, was the capture of the island of Okinawa. The last remaining strength of the Japanese Navy had been dissipated in the Philippines, at the Battle of Leyte Gulf, and in vainly defending the Marianas, so the main opposition to the landings at Okinawa were suicide missions by individual Japanese pilots. On land, the situation was different, with the Japanese army, as ever, fighting bitterly and, usually, to the last man. Iwo Jima was a necessary preliminary for the conquest of Okinawa, whose proximity to the Japanese homeland made it an essential stepping stone for the anticipated invasion of Japan. But this invasion, which would have been long and costly, was rendered unnecessary by the dropping of two atomic bombs on Hiroshima and Nagasaki. This terrible new weapon in the hands of their enemies strengthened the arguments of those in the Japanese government who favored peace, and in mid-August Japan surrendered. Meanwhile, in the last week of war, the Red Army joined in, sweeping through Manchuria.

Below left: *Admiral Oldendorf who commanded US Navy battleship groups, notably in the Battle of Leyte Gulf.*

Below: *Admiral Mitscher commanded the carrier task forces in many of the later battles.*

Top: *Fighter aircraft are prepared for a mission, aboard the USS* Monterey, *Pacific 1943.*

Above: *US Army Sherman tanks in the Ardennes area, Europe winter 1944-45.*

Left: *America's service chiefs. Left to right, General Arnold (USAAF), Admiral Leahy (Chief of Staff to the President), Admiral King (USN) and General Marshall (USA).*

Right: *A US Ranger battalion on the advance in Tunisia, January 1943.*

World War II
– Battles and Campaigns

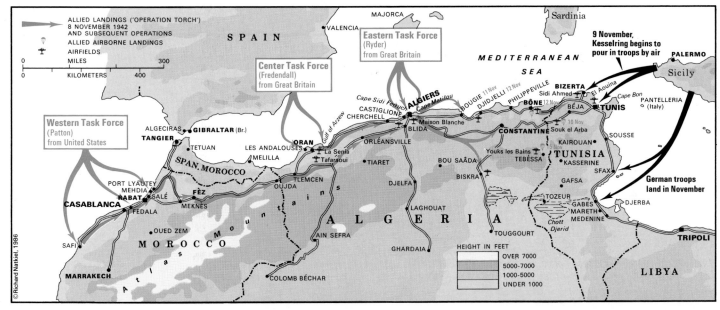

MAP: Operation Torch, the landings in North Africa. This landing, in November 1942, was the first of the big Allied counter-offensives; it was the Allies, not the Axis Powers, who would henceforth have the initiative. This landing in French North Africa was expected to make untenable the situation of the Afrika Korps, then occupied in fighting the British in Libya. It was also a promising stepping stone on the way to Italy. American efforts, before the landing, to persuade the local (Vichy) French command to offer no resistance were only partially successful, but the landing was achieved and French resistance soon ceased. However, the German reaction, a quick despatch of troops from Sicily into Tunisia, was not foiled and heavy fighting was subsequently required to dislodge them; it was only in May that Bizerta was captured by the Americans and Tunis by the British. 'Operation Torch,' apart from its strategic aims, was also the first major test of Anglo-US planning procedures. The transportation of such a large force over so great a distance was itself an achievement. That it was managed by two Allies working in co-ordination was even more impressive.

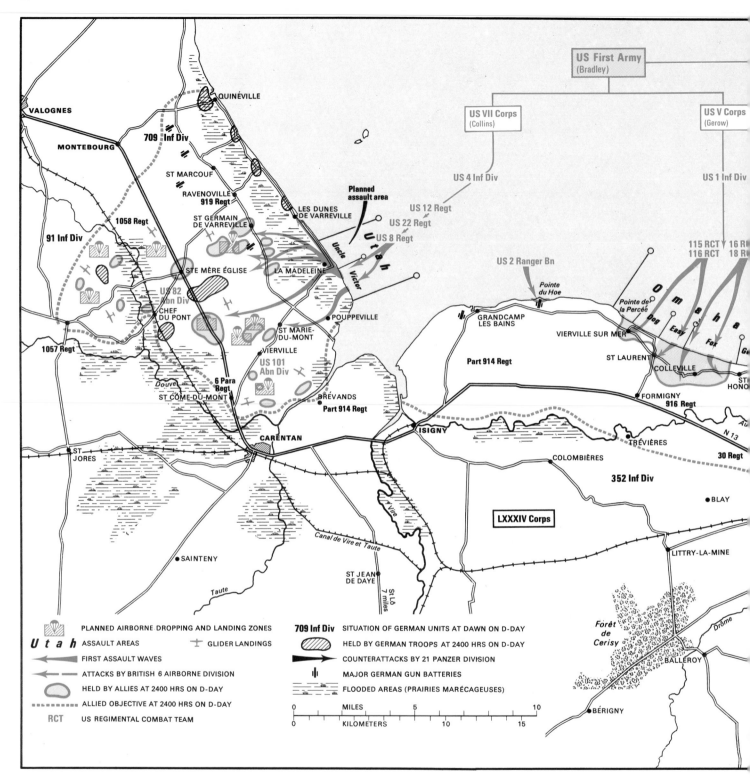

MAP: Operation Overlord, the Allied landings in Normandy. The long-awaited opening of the so-called Second Front occurred in June 1944, with the technically difficult landing on defended beaches in Normandy by the US First Army and the British Second Army. Airborne divisions made the first landings, to cover the chosen beaches, and then the main assault force was taken ashore in landing craft. Unfavorable weather improved, tactical surprise was achieved, and the landings were successfully made on the five chosen beaches. Only at one beach, *Omaha*, where rough seas disrupted the intended use of amphibious tanks, were the Germans able effectively to resist the landings, and even here the American troops were pinned down for only a few hours. By the end of the first day the US VII Corps, in the west, was already breaking out from the coast, while the British and Canadian troops, more slowly, were consolidating and expanding the deep bridgeheads that had already been successfully consolidated.

Far right: *Supplies and troops come ashore on a Normandy beach.*

Right: *The Allied D-Day commanders. From left, General Bradley, Admiral Ramsay, Air Marshal Tedder, General Eisenhower, General Montgomery, Air Marshal Leigh-Mallory and General Bedell Smith.*

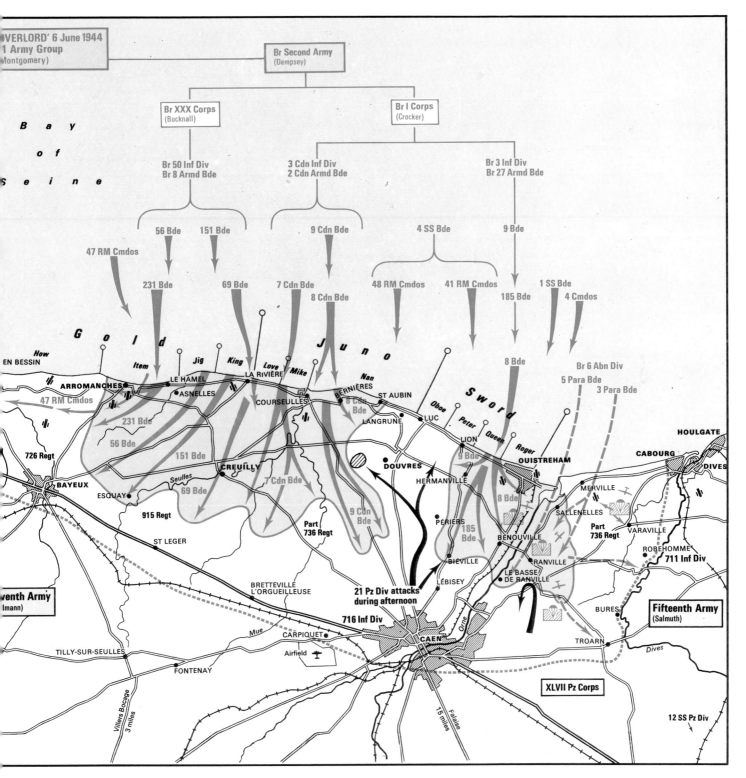

'VERLORD' 6 June 1944
1 Army Group
(Montgomery)

Br Second Army
(Dempsey)

Br XXX Corps
(Bucknall)

Br I Corps
(Crocker)

Br 50 Inf Div
Br 8 Armd Bde

3 Cdn Inf Div
2 Cdn Armd Bde

Br 3 Inf Div
Br 27 Armd Bde

56 Bde

151 Bde

9 Cdn Bde

4 SS Bde

9 Bde

47 RM Cmdos

231 Bde

69 Bde

7 Cdn Bde

48 RM Cmdos

41 RM Cmdos

1 SS Bde

4 Cmdos

8 Cdn Bde

185 Bde

8 Bde

Br 6 Abn Div
5 Para Bde   3 Para Bde

Bay

of

Seine

Gold

How
EN BESSIN

Juno

Nan

Sword

HOULGATE

Item

Jig   King   Love   Mike

ARROMANCHES

LE HAMEL
ASNELLES

LA RIVIÈRE

COURSEULLES

BERNIÈRES
ST AUBIN
8 Cdn Bde

Oboe   Peter   Queen   Roger

LUC

LION

OUISTREHAM

CABOURG

DIVES

47 RM Cmdos

231 Bde

56 Bde

151 Bde

LANGRUNE

9 Bde

DOUVRES

HERMANVILLE

MERVILLE

726 Regt

BAYEUX

CREUILLY

Seulles

69 Bde

7 Cdn Bde

PÉRIERS

185 Bde

8 Bde

BENOUVILLE

RANVILLE

SALLENELLES

VARAVILLE

ESQUAY

9 Cdn Bde

BIÉVILLE

LE BASSE
DE RANVILLE

Part
736 Regt

ROBEHOMME

711 Inf Div

915 Regt

Part
736 Regt

ST LEGER

LÉBISEY

BURES

enth Army
(mann)

BRETTEVILLE
L'ORGUEILLEUSE

21 Pz Div attacks
during afternoon

716 Inf Div

CAEN

Orne

TROARN

Dives

Fifteenth Army
(Salmuth)

Mue

CARPIQUET

Airfield

XLVII Pz Corps

TILLY-SUR-SEULLES

FONTENAY

Villers Bocage
3 miles

Falaise
15 miles

12 SS Pz Div

MAP: The Italian campaign. The Allies had first landed in Italy directly from their conquest of Sicily, which in turn had been attained after Tunisia had been occupied. At the beginning of 1944 the Allied advance was held up around Cassino by a combination of determined German resistance and unfavorable terrain. To relieve the pressure and release the power behind the advance, a landing was made at Anzio, in the German rear. However, this landing, accomplished at the expense of considerable naval losses, only resulted in the assaulting troops themselves being pinned down and threatened with destruction. Luckily, an Allied breakthrough at Cassino relieved this threat and the Germans, having lost their fortified Gustav Line, retired northward to their Gothic Line, allowing the Allies to enter Rome in June 1944. By that time Anglo-American resources were being largely devoted to the battles in France. The northern advance continued in Italy but the lack of resources and the difficult terrain and stubborn German defense ensured that progress was slow until the German collapse in April-May 1945.

Below: *Men of the US 82nd Airborne Division load a Jeep onto their glider before the attack on Sicily.*

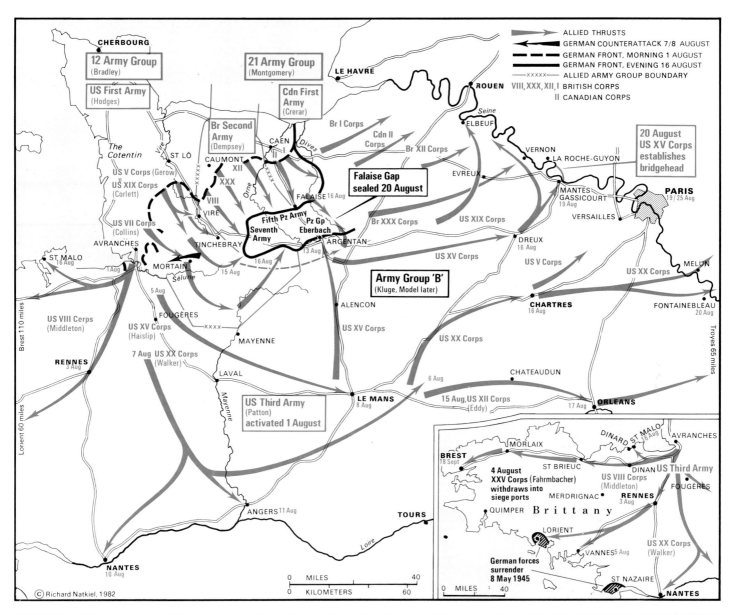

MAP LEGEND:
- ALLIED THRUSTS
- GERMAN COUNTERATTACK 7/8 AUGUST
- GERMAN FRONT, MORNING 1 AUGUST
- GERMAN FRONT, EVENING 16 AUGUST
- ALLIED ARMY GROUP BOUNDARY
- VIII, XXX, XII, I BRITISH CORPS
- II CANADIAN CORPS

Map labels:
CHERBOURG · 12 Army Group (Bradley) · US First Army (Hodges) · 21 Army Group (Montgomery) · Cdn First Army (Crerar) · LE HAVRE · ROUEN · Seine · ELBEUF · Br I Corps · Cdn II Corps · Br XII Corps · VERNON · LA ROCHE-GUYON · 20 August US XV Corps establishes bridgehead · The Cotentin · ST LÔ · Br Second Army (Dempsey) · CAUMONT · XII · CAEN · Dives · EVREUX · MANTES GASSICOURT 19 Aug · PARIS 19/25 Aug · US V Corps (Gerow) · US XIX Corps (Corlett) · XXX · Orne · VIII · FALAISE 16 Aug · Falaise Gap sealed 20 August · VERSAILLES · US VII Corps (Collins) · VIRE · Fifth Pz Army · Pz Gp Eberbach · Br XXX Corps · US XIX Corps · DREUX 16 Aug · AVRANCHES · TINCHEBRAY · Seventh Army · ARGENTAN · 13 Aug · US XV Corps · US V Corps · US XX Corps · MELUN · ST MALO 16 Aug · 1 Aug · MORTAIN · 16 Aug · 15 Aug · Army Group 'B' (Kluge, Model later) · US XX Corps · FONTAINEBLEAU 20 Aug · Sélune · 5 Aug · ALENCON · CHARTRES 16 Aug · Brest 110 miles · US VIII Corps (Middleton) · FOUGÈRES · US XV Corps (Haislip) · xxxx · MAYENNE · US XV Corps · US XX Corps · Lorient 60 miles · RENNES 3 Aug · 7 Aug US XX Corps (Walker) · LAVAL · Mayenne · LE MANS 8 Aug · 15 Aug, US XII Corps (Eddy) · CHATEAUDUN · 6 Aug · 17 Aug · ORLEANS · Troyes 65 miles · US Third Army (Patton) activated 1 August · ANGERS 11 Aug · TOURS · Loire · NANTES 10 Aug · © Richard Natkiel, 1982

MILES 0 — 40 · KILOMETERS 0 — 60

Inset map (Brittany):
MORLAIX · DINARD · ST MALO 6 Aug · AVRANCHES · BREST 18 Sept · ST BRIEUC · DINAN · US Third Army · 4 August XXV Corps (Fahrmbacher) withdraws into siege ports · US VIII Corps (Middleton) · FOUGÈRES · MERDRIGNAC · RENNES 3 Aug · QUIMPER · Brittany · LORIENT · VANNES 5 Aug · US XX Corps (Walker) · German forces surrender 8 May 1945 · ST NAZAIRE · NANTES

MILES 0 — 40

MAP: The US sweep toward Paris. Seven weeks after the Normandy landings, the Allies held Cherbourg and the Cotentin Peninsula. A gap formed in the German line and through it poured General Patton's US Third Army, making first for Brittany and then turning its main strength southeast toward Paris. German counterattacks caused only slight delay to the US advance, and while the Third Army tanks approached Fontainebleau two German panzer armies were cut off and then destroyed by US, British and Canadian forces which closed the gap behind them at Falaise. With the German armies in disarray, the US Third Army bridged the Seine on 20 August, and five days later US and Free French troops entered Paris.

Right: *A German prisoner in Normandy.*

MAP below: The Battle of the Bulge. This critical battle, fought in hilly and wooded terrain in winter, was Hitler's unexpected last throw. Having secured the port of Antwerp, the Allies were pressing eastward and preparing for the difficult Rhine crossing. Hitler, having assembled all available reserves (which were few, because he was also hard-pressed by the Russians) decided to use them in a thrust through southern Belgium which, reaching the coast, would cut off the more advanced Allied formations. Bad weather compensated for the German weakness in the air, because Allied aircraft were grounded, and the thrusting panzer divisions achieved complete tactical surprise. Some US units disintegrated, but here and there courageous pockets of resistance gave the American command time to stabilize the situation. The defense of Bastogne by beleaguered US

airborne troops slowed the Germans, and prevented their capture of the fuel supplies on which their further advance depended. When US air operations recommenced the German offensive, already held, degenerated into a retreat. The Allied command quickly sent reinforcements to halt the advance. General Patton's Third Army, in particular, rapidly switched forces from their previous positions to the south.

MAP right: The final Allied offensive in Germany. Having crossed the Rhine, the Allied advance met only sporadic resistance from last-ditch stands by veteran troops supported by raw young conscripts. In misinformed anticipation of a Nazi last stand in the mountainous south, much of the US strength was initially sent in that direction, but the decision not to press on to Berlin and Prague was a consequence of previous agreements with the Russians. After the capture of Berlin by the Russians, and the suicide of Hitler, the German command surrendered to the British, who were advancing in the northern sector, at Luneberg Heath, south of Hamburg, on 4 May 1945.

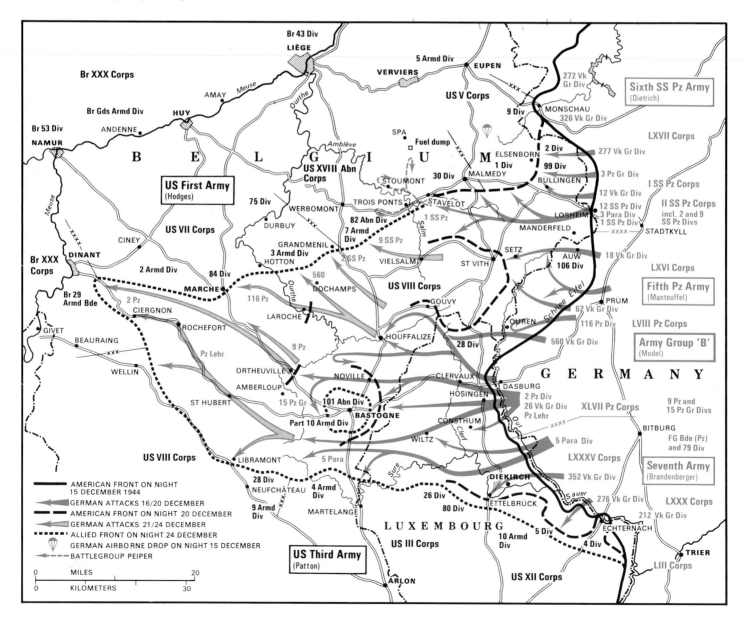

DENMARK

BALTIC SEA

NORTH SEA

FLENSBURG

RÜGEN

KIEL

ROSTOCK

STETTIN

Kiel Canal

LÜBECK

WISMAR

7 May

SCHWERIN

NEUSTRELITZ

STARGAR

HAMBURG
3 May

WILHELMSHAVEN

BREMERHAVEN

18 Apr

Elbe

DANNENBERG

DÖMITZ

WITTENBERG

Oder

KÜSTR

EMDEN

GRONINGEN

OLDENBURG

BREMEN
26 Apr

ÜLZEN

Lüneberg

Belsen

Heath

TANGERMÜNDE

BERLIN

POTSDAM

FRANKFURT

AMSTERDAM

NETHERLANDS

Army Group 'H'
(Blaskowitz)

OSNABRÜCK

4 Apr

HANNOVER
10 Apr

US Ninth Army

BRUNSWICK

MAGDEBURG

Twelfth Army

BARBY

Twenty-fifth Army

ARNHEM

MINDEN

HAMELN

ROSSLAU

COTTBUS

Teutoburger Wald

Weser

G E R M A N Y

MÜNSTER

First Para Army

PADERBORN

Eleventh Army

Harz Mts

Brocken Pk

BLANKENBURG

DESSAU
24 Apr

Cdn First Army
(Crerar)

Br Second Army
(Dempsey)

WESEL

HAMM

LIPPSTADT

US First Army

HALLE

Leine

GÖTTINGEN

NORDHAUSEN

US Ninth Army
(Simpson)

ESSEN

DORTMUND

BOCHUM

Ruhr

KASSEL
4 Apr

MERSEBURG

LEIPZIG

Saale

21 Army Group
(Montgomery)

DUISBURG

WUPPERTAL

Sauerland

Army Group 'B'
(Model)

WEISSENFELS

DRESDEN

GÖRLITZ

DÜSSELDORF

Fifteenth Army

COLOGNE

Fifth Pz Army

BUCHENWALD

ERFURT

GOTHA

WEIMAR

JENA

ZEITZ

COLDITZ

LIEGE

BONN

MARBURG

OHRDRUF

Thüringian Forest

US Third Army

Mulde

CHEMNITZ

USTÍ

REMAGEN

Sieg

Dill

GIESSEN

Rhine

US First Army
(Hodges)

BELGIUM

KOBLENZ

Lahn

FULDA 2 Apr

Seventh Army

HOF

Erzgebirge

KARLOVY VARY

12 Army Group
(Bradley)

WIESBADEN

FRANKFURT

Main

HANAU

BAD ORB

Seventh Army

LUX

MAINZ

US Third Army
(Patton)

HAMMELBURG

SCHWEINFURT

BAYREUTH

Bohemian Forest

CZECHOSLOVAKIA

PRAGU

LUXEMBOURG

TRIER

OPPENHEIM

ASCHAFFEN-
BURG

Spessart Mts

WÜRZBURG

BAMBERG

Odenwald

WORMS

KITZINGEN 5 Apr

PILSEN

THIONVILLE

US Seventh Army
(Patch)

MANNHEIM

4 Apr

NÜREMBERG
20

Franconian Jura

18 Apr

7 May

6 Army Group
(Devers)

SAARBRÜCKEN

First Army

HEILBRONN

FÜRTH

ANSBACH

ČESKE
BUDEJOVICE

Fr First Army
(de Lattre de Tassigny)

KARLSRUHE
4 Apr

PFORZHEIM

Löwenstein
Hills

REGENSBURG 26 Apr

Danube

NANCY

8 Apr

STUTTGART

US Seventh
Army

Franconian

Isar

LANDAU

PASSAU

STRASBOURG

ESSLINGEN

KIRCHHEIM

INGOLSTADT

LANDSHUT
30 Apr

LINZ
5 May

Schwarzwald

TÜBINGEN

Swabian Highlands

DILLINGEN

First Army

AUGSBURG

Inp

BRAUNAU

US Third Army

Nineteenth
Army

ULM 23 Apr

Dachau

COLMAR

SIGMARINGEN

EHINGEN

LANDSBERG

MUNICH
30 Apr

FREIBURG

MEMMINGEN

US Seventh Army

ROSENHEIM

SALZBURG
4 May

Fr First Army

Lake
Constance

OBERAMMERGAU

FÜSSEN

GARMISCH-
PARTENKIRCHEN

BERCHTESGADEN
4 May

Enns

BASLE

BREGEN

Oberjoch
Pass

Fern
Pass

KUFSTEIN

KITZBÜHEL

SWITZERLAND

IMST

INNSBRUCK

A U S T R I A

Aarlberg
Pass

T y r o l

LANDECK

A L P S

TAMSWEG

L

Brenner
Pass

4 May

Resia
Pass

KLAGENFURT

BOLZANO

ITALY

YUGOSLAVIA

US Fifth Army

OCCUPIED BY ALLIED FORCES, 28 MARCH 1945

BRITISH ATTACKS

US ATTACKS

FRENCH ATTACKS

GERMAN POCKETS

OCCUPIED BY RUSSIAN FORCES, 16 APRIL

CONCENTRATION CAMPS

0   MILES   120

0   KILOMETERS   200

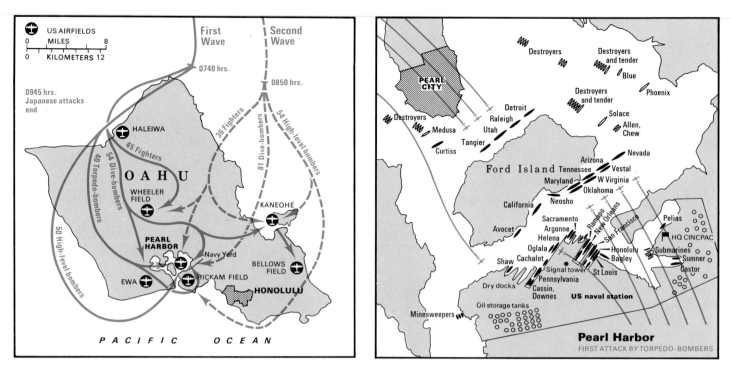

MAP above: The attack on Pearl Harbor. The Japanese aircraft carriers, which had approached undetected to within about 250 miles from Hawaii, launched two waves of aircraft. The first wave, which took the Americans by surprise, consisted of 189 aircraft, including torpedo bombers. The second wave, an hour later, was a bombing mission and attacked from another direction. The attackers lost about thirty aircraft, whereas four fifths of the US aircraft were destroyed on the ground and eight US battleships sunk or badly damaged.

MAP above right: The first attack on Pearl Harbor. This shows the route taken by the torpedo bombers. The line of US battleships was an ideal target, and suffered accordingly. By chance, the US aircraft carriers were at sea, and escaped damage. Given the crucial importance of aircraft carriers in the Pacific campaign, it can be argued that the escape of the US carriers meant that Japan had lost the war on its very first day.

MAP right: The Battle of the Coral Sea. The Japanese aimed at extending their control in the south-west Pacific by setting up bases in the Solomons, and landing in southern New Guinea. The Allies were aware of these movements and sent an Anglo-American cruiser squadron to attack the invasion group on its way to Port Moresby. Meanwhile the opposing carriers launched attacks against each other; the Americans lost their large *Lexington*, while the Japanese lost the smaller *Shoho*. This reduced US carrier strength to a dangerously low level, but the Japanese thrust had been blocked, and was never repeated. The Battle of the Coral Sea was the first important naval battle in which the opposing fleets never came into visual contact.

Left: *A Japanese torpedo strikes home on the battleship* West Virginia *during the attack on Pearl Harbor.*

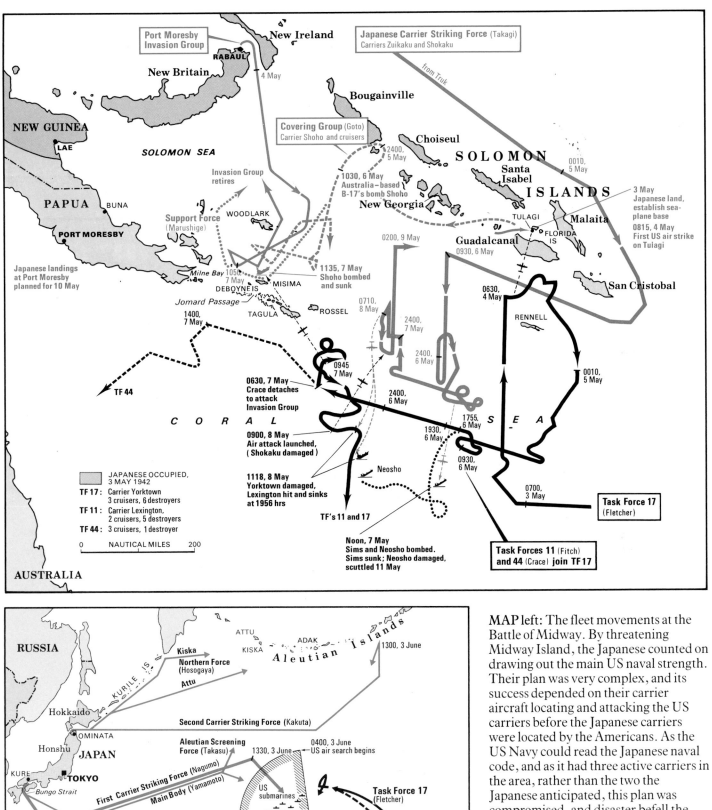

Port Moresby Invasion Group

RABAUL

4 May

New Ireland

New Britain

Japanese Carrier Striking Force (Takagi)
Carriers Zuikaku and Shokaku

from Truk

NEW GUINEA

LAE

SOLOMON SEA

Bougainville

Choiseul

SOLOMON

Santa Isabel

0010, 5 May

Covering Group (Goto)
Carrier Shoho and cruisers

PAPUA

BUNA

Invasion Group retires

2400, 5 May

1030, 6 May
Australia-based
B-17's bomb Shoho

New Georgia

ISLANDS

3 May
Japanese land, establish sea-plane base

PORT MORESBY

Support Force (Marushige)

WOODLARK

TULAGI

FLORIDA IS

Malaita

0815, 4 May
First US air strike on Tulagi

0200, 9 May

Guadalcanal

0930, 6 May

San Cristobal

Japanese landings at Port Moresby planned for 10 May

Milne Bay 1050, 7 May

DEBOYNE IS

MISIMA

1135, 7 May
Shoho bombed and sunk

0630, 4 May

RENNELL

0010, 5 May

Jomard Passage

TAGULA

ROSSEL

0710, 8 May

0710, 8 May

2400, 7 May

2400, 6 May

1400, 7 May

0945, 7 May

0630, 7 May
Crace detaches to attack Invasion Group

2400, 6 May

1755, 6 May

S E A

TF 44

C O R A L

1930, 6 May

0900, 8 May
Air attack launched,
(Shokaku damaged)

0930, 6 May

0700, 3 May

1118, 8 May
Yorktown damaged,
Lexington hit and sinks
at 1956 hrs

Neosho

JAPANESE OCCUPIED, 3 MAY 1942

TF 17: Carrier Yorktown
3 cruisers, 6 destroyers

TF 11: Carrier Lexington,
2 cruisers, 5 destroyers

TF 44: 3 cruisers, 1 destroyer

TF's 11 and 17

Task Force 17 (Fletcher)

0 NAUTICAL MILES 200

Noon, 7 May
Sims and Neosho bombed.
Sims sunk; Neosho damaged, scuttled 11 May

Task Forces 11 (Fitch)
and 44 (Crace) join **TF 17**

AUSTRALIA

RUSSIA

ATTU

ADAK

1300, 3 June

KISKA

A l e u t i a n   I s l a n d s

Kiska

Northern Force (Hosogaya)

KURILE IS

Attu

Second Carrier Striking Force (Kakuta)

Hokkaido

OMINATA

Aleutian Screening Force (Takasu)

0400, 3 June
US air search begins

Honshu

JAPAN

1330, 3 June

KURE

TOKYO

First Carrier Striking Force (Nagumo)

US submarines

Task Force 17 (Fletcher)

Bungo Strait

Main Body (Yamamoto)

MIDWAY

Night, 29 May

Second Fleet Covering Group

IWO JIMA

Midway Occupation Force (Kondo)

Task Force 16 (Spruance)

Transport Group (Tanaka)
and Support Group (Kurita)

FRENCH FRIGATE SHOALS

OAHU

Marianas Islands

WAKE

Minesweeping Group

PEARL HARBOR

HAWAII

SAIPAN

GUAM

0900, 3 June
Sighted

Japanese submarine cordon

JAPANESE FORCES SAIL BETWEEN 25-28 MAY (DATES ARE THOSE AT MIDWAY)

MAP left: The fleet movements at the Battle of Midway. By threatening Midway Island, the Japanese counted on drawing out the main US naval strength. Their plan was very complex, and its success depended on their carrier aircraft locating and attacking the US carriers before the Japanese carriers were located by the Americans. As the US Navy could read the Japanese naval code, and as it had three active carriers in the area, rather than the two the Japanese anticipated, this plan was compromised, and disaster befell the Japanese when their carriers, in the act of rearming and refuelling their aircraft, were themselves attacked by US carrier aircraft. Four Japanese carriers were sunk against a US loss of one.

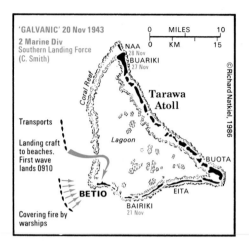

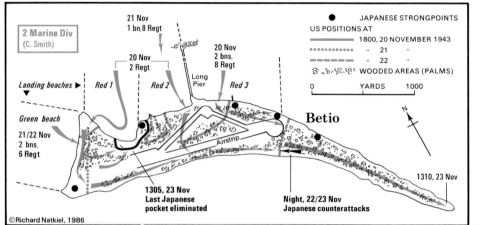

MAP above: Tarawa Atoll. The US amphibious landing on Tarawa Atoll was a trial-and-error project, lessons expensively learned proving valuable for future attacks on Japanese-held islands. The attack was fairly conventional, with a heavy naval bombardment preceding the landing of troops on the beaches. Japanese resistance was unyielding, elaborate defenses having been built, and casualties were heavy.

MAP above: The key action of the Tarawa operation. The islet of Betio, forming part of the reef, was the main objective of the American assault. The Japanese, taking advantage of the terrain, were able to hold out for several days even though considerably outnumbered. The main lesson of the Tarawa operation was that capturing Japanese-held islands would be costly, and that tracked amphibious landing

craft were the most useful vehicles for such actions. In proportion to the forces engaged, the casualties (nearly 1000 dead) were the heaviest in US military history.

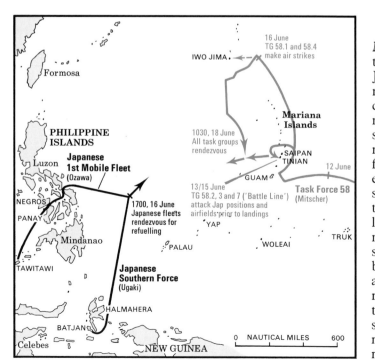

MAP left: The prelude to the Battle of the Philippine Sea. In June 1944 the Japanese naval command sought to restore the balance by luring US aircraft carriers into mass attacks by Japanese naval aircraft. Advancing from the south-west with several newly-built and newly-converted carriers, the Japanese force was divided into two groups, in the expectation that the Americans would spot and attack the smaller group and thereby become good targets for the larger group. The Japanese had the misfortune of losing two carriers to US submarines before the battle began and, being picked up by US radar, their attacking aircraft stood little chance. The result of the two-day engagement was that Japanese naval air power was finally shattered, not so much because it lost so many aircraft, but because it lost so many irreplaceable trained aircrews.

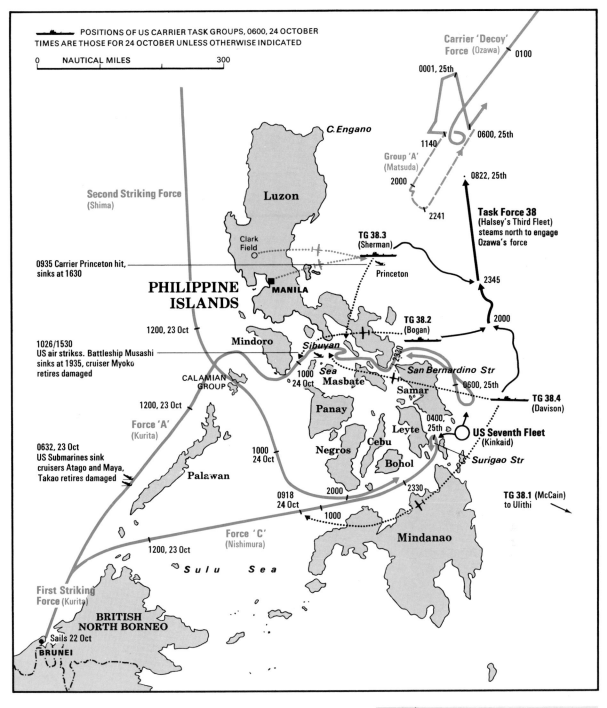

POSITIONS OF US CARRIER TASK GROUPS, 0600, 24 OCTOBER
TIMES ARE THOSE FOR 24 OCTOBER UNLESS OTHERWISE INDICATED

0   NAUTICAL MILES   300

Carrier 'Decoy' Force (Ozawa) 0100

0001, 25th

1140

0600, 25th

Group 'A' (Matsuda)

2000

0822, 25th

2241

Task Force 38 (Halsey's Third Fleet) steams north to engage Ozawa's force

2345

2000

C. Engano

Luzon

Second Striking Force (Shima)

Clark Field

0935 Carrier Princeton hit, sinks at 1630

TG 38.3 (Sherman)

Princeton

PHILIPPINE ISLANDS

MANILA

TG 38.2 (Bogan)

1200, 23 Oct

Mindoro

1026/1530 US air strikes. Battleship Musashi sinks at 1935, cruiser Myoko retires damaged

Sibuyan

San Bernardino Str

0600, 25th

1000 24 Oct

Sea Masbate

Samar

TG 38.4 (Davison)

CALAMIAN GROUP

1200, 23 Oct

Panay

Leyte

0400, 25th

US Seventh Fleet (Kinkaid)

Force 'A' (Kurita)

1000 24 Oct

Negros

Cebu

Bohol

Surigao Str

0632, 23 Oct US Submarines sink cruisers Atago and Maya, Takao retires damaged

Palawan

2000

2330

TG 38.1 (McCain) to Ulithi

0918 24 Oct

1000

Force 'C' (Nishimura)

1200, 23 Oct

Mindanao

Sulu   Sea

First Striking Force (Kurita)

BRITISH NORTH BORNEO

Sails 22 Oct

BRUNEI

MAP above: The Battle of Leyte Gulf. This was probably the biggest naval battle ever fought, and resulted from a Japanese endeavor to attack US troops landing in the Philippines. Having few naval aircraft, the Japanese relied on heavy-gun ships and approached in three groups of which one, a carrier group with almost no aircraft, was to act as a decoy, drawing off US forces so that the main group of battleships and cruisers could fall upon undefended US transports. The plan almost worked, for despite setbacks and losses Kurita's Force A did get within range of the vulnerable US transports. But for some

unexplained reason, Kurita withdrew on being attacked by destroyers and did little damage. Meanwhile, submarine attacks, torpedo boat attacks, air attacks, and the gunfire of US battleships took their toll in the San Bernardino and Surigao Straits, Japanese losses were heavy, including one new and two old battleships.

Right: *General MacArthur fulfils his famous promise to return to the Philippines, Leyte, October 1944.*

MAP: The bombing of Japan. There had been occasional, symbolic, bombing raids on Japan earlier in the war, from aircraft carriers or from China, but these had little military significance. After the capture of the Mariana Islands and the enlargement of their airfields it was possible for the US to send Superfortress bombers to raid specific targets in Japan; the first such raid was against a key Tokyo aircraft factory in November 1944. Bombing accuracy was not high, and General LeMay's 20th Bomber Command soon adopted the British technique of nocturnal fire raids, in which massive incendiary attacks on cities, with the aim of incinerating civilians by the tens of thousand, gave bombing aircraft the opportunity of wreaking destruction without the necessity of precise bomb-aiming. The great fire raid on Tokyo produced about 200,000 casualties, of which about 80,000 were deaths. With the capture of the Iwo Jima airfields, it became possible to provide fighter escorts, making daylight raids less vulnerable to Japanese fighters. Daylight, and the virtual disappearance of Japanese fighters, enabled the bombers, in the months preceding the nuclear attacks on Hiroshima and Nagasaki, to resume, with some hope of success, the bombing of specific industrial targets.

B-29 TARGETS IN JAPAN: FEB/AUGUST 1945

MAIN INCENDIARY (FIRE RAID) TARGETS *

OTHER INCENDIARY TARGETS *

XXX MINE LAYING AREAS

ATOMIC BOMB ATTACK

* FIGURES SHOW PERCENTAGE OF URBAN AREA DESTROYED

0 MILES 150

0 KILOMETRES 200

KOREA

Second atomic bomb dropped on 9 August (over 60,000 casualties)

SHIMONOSEKI

UBE 23

MOJI 27

YAWATA 36 KOKURA 21

FUKUOKA 22

SASEBO 48

OMUTA 42

OI

KUMAMOTO 20

NAGASAKI

Kyush

IZUMI

KAGOSHIMA 44

Top: *General MacArthur, commander of the Allied occupation forces, and Emperor Hirohito after the Japanese surrender.*

Above right: *The atomic bomb explosion over Nagasaki.*

Right: *General Chennault talks with a group of pilots from the US Fourteenth Air Force. The Fourteenth AF attacked Japan from bases in China before the Marianas were captured and airfields built there.*

Far right: *The B.29 Superfortress* Enola Gay *which carried the Hiroshima bomb.*

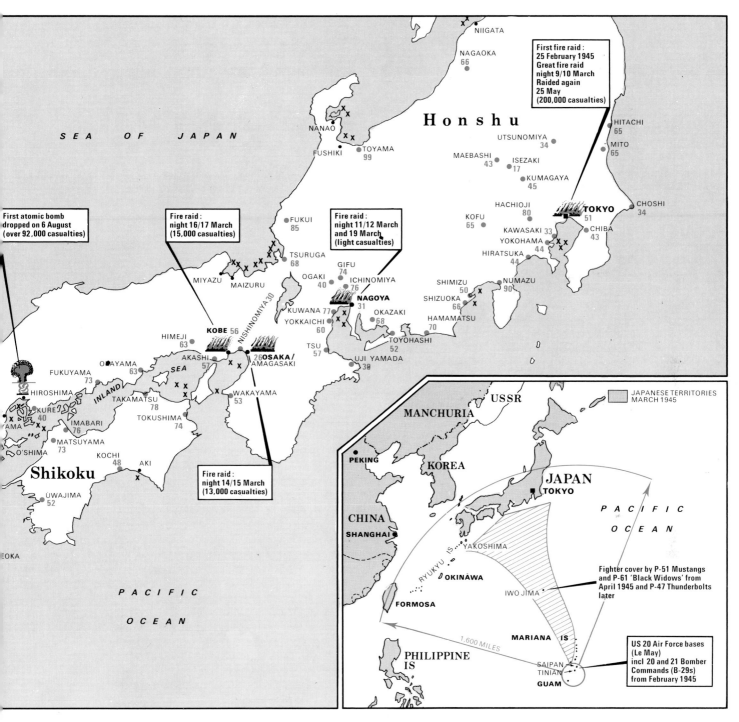

SEA OF JAPAN

NIIGATA

NAGAOKA
66

First fire raid :
25 February 1945
Great fire raid
night 9/10 March
Raided again
25 May
(200,000 casualties)

Honshu

HITACHI
65

UTSUNOMIYA
34

MITO
65

NANAO

MAEBASHI
43

ISEZAKI
17

KUMAGAYA
45

CHOSHI
34

FUSHIKI

TOYAMA
99

HACHIOJI
80

TOKYO
51

KOFU
65

KAWASAKI 33

CHIBA
43

First atomic bomb
dropped on 6 August
(over 92,000 casualties)

Fire raid :
night 16/17 March
(15,000 casualties)

FUKUI
85

Fire raid :
night 11/12 March
and 19 March
(light casualties)

YOKOHAMA
44

HIRATSUKA
44

TSURUGA
68

GIFU
74

SHIMIZU
50

NUMAZU
90

MIYAZU

MAIZURU

OGAKI
40

ICHINOMIYA
76

SHIZUOKA
66

NAGOYA
31

NAGOYA

KUWANA 77

OKAZAKI
68

HAMAMATSU
70

YOKKAICHI
60

KOBE 56

NISHINOMIYA 30

HIMEJI
63

TSU
57

TOYOHASHI
52

AKASHI
57

**OSAKA/
AMAGASAKI**
26

UJI YAMADA
30

FUKUYAMA
73

OKAYAMA
63

SEA

WAKAYAMA
53

INLAND

HIROSHIMA

TAKAMATSU
78

KURE
40

TOKUSHIMA
74

IMABARI
76

MATSUYAMA
73

O'SHIMA

KOCHI
48

AKI

Fire raid :
night 14/15 March
(13,000 casualties)

Shikoku

UWAJIMA
52

PACIFIC OCEAN

USSR

MANCHURIA

JAPANESE TERRITORIES
MARCH 1945

PEKING

KOREA

JAPAN
TOKYO

PACIFIC OCEAN

CHINA

SHANGHAI

RYUKYU IS

YAKOSHIMA

Fighter cover by P-51 Mustangs
and P-61 'Black Widows' from
April 1945 and P-47 Thunderbolts
later

OKINAWA

IWO JIMA

FORMOSA

1,600 MILES

MARIANA IS

PHILIPPINE
IS

SAIPAN
TINIAN
GUAM

US 20 Air Force bases
(Le May)
incl 20 and 21 Bomber
Commands (B-29s)
from February 1945

America
in a Divided World

Near Khe San in the Vietnam War. Precision bombing by US ground support aircraft is directed against enemy positions close to the US line.

The Allied problems of peacetime appeared at first to be simple compared to those of the war years. Postwar events would disprove this optimistic forecast. The occupation of Germany and of Austria (which was separated immediately from Hitler's Germany) had been planned in a series of meetings in Britain and approved at the Yalta Conference. Austria was ruled jointly by the three major occupying forces, and Germany was partitioned in such a way that, according to a contemporary joke, Britain got the industry (the Ruhr and northwestern Germany), the Soviet Union got the agriculture (eastern Germany), and the United States got the scenery (Bavaria). Berlin, although deep within the Soviet occupation zone, was apportioned into sectors, each sector governed by an Allied Power. The Western Allies promptly arranged for division of their allotments so that the reconstituted government of France would receive a zone and a sector. Government of all Germany, meanwhile, had been vested, according to a Yalta accord, in an Allied Control Commission. These arrangements, of course, were pending a European peace conference, which, as time would reveal, was never to meet.

Asia had been conquered largely by the forces of the United States, assisted by British troops. The Soviets had occupied only half of Korea and most of Chinese Manchuria, which gave them little say in peace arrangements for Asia. The United States awarded the Soviets membership in a nominal Far Eastern Commission, but its authority was negligible in Japan – the crucial occupation zone. There General Douglas MacArthur, who controlled the occupation, was empowered to make interim decrees that effectively bypassed the Far Eastern Commission. MacArthur's headquarters in Tokyo ruled Japan until a conference in San Francisco in 1951, which drew up a treaty signed by the governments allied against Japan during the war, except for the Soviet Union. The Japanese peace treaty entered into force in 1952, and the Soviet Union eventually recognized the new Japanese Government.

The Soviets were dissatisfied with the territorial arrangement in the Far East, but they were more concerned about Europe. There the rivalries with Western nations that had been largely dormant during World War II surfaced and reached crisis proportions in the years immediately after 1945. The new status quo, just short of open war itself, became known as the cold war – a phrase popularized by the American financier-statesman Bernard Baruch in 1946.

It was inevitable that the Soviet Union would seek to dominate the small nations of Eastern Europe along its borders in the last days of World War II. As the Soviet troops poured into those countries, they were followed by political cadres that took over or reconstituted national governments. Most observers believed that the Red Army was simply trying to guarantee internal order and protect its supply lines as troops moved farther west. But Soviet troops did not leave Eastern Europe when the war ended. Instead, local opposition parties were systematically destroyed and supplanted by single-party arrangements whereby the local communists dominated the government. This became the political pattern in Eastern Europe, where the last semi-independent regime, that of Czechoslovakia, passed behind the 'iron curtain' as Winston Churchill called it, in 1948.

The United States, Britain, and the weak government of postwar France protested the communization of Eastern Europe, but there was little they could do about it, short of starting World War III: the Soviet Army dominated the Eastern European countries. The fate of Germany, then under Allied occupation, soon became a much larger issue. Would

Germany too pass behind the iron curtain, with it all its military resources?

Uncertain of Soviet intentions, the United States Government sought to negotiate German and other issues in 1945-6. Confrontation was avoided until the spring of 1947, when Greek and Turkish independence were threatened by the USSR. The Greek economy was failing, and Turkey faced military invasion along its lengthy border with the Soviet Union. On 12 March 1947 President Truman announced to Congress the policy that became known as the Truman Doctrine: that the United States would aid any country threatened by international communism.

Shortly thereafter, it became clear that all of Western Europe was in serious economic straits. It was feared that one country after another would pass to communism without economic assistance, which the US offered in June 1947 in a speech by Secretary of State George C Marshall. Interim aid was followed by passage through Congress in 1948 of the first appropriation for what became known as the Marshall Plan. By 1950 it would comprise $13 billion worth of aid to Western Europe.

The final US defense against communism in Western Europe followed logically upon the policies embodied in the Truman Doctrine and the Marshall Plan. This was a military alliance, the North Atlantic Treaty, signed in April 1949 and organized as NATO. Its initial membership was 12 nations: the US, Britain, France, the Netherlands, Belgium, Luxembourg, Canada, Iceland, Norway, Denmark, Portugal, and Italy. Greece and Turkey joined in 1952, West Germany in 1955, and Spain in 1982. NATO military forces average 25 combat-ready divisions, continuously on the alert for hostile incursions into Western territory. Their equipment includes the new 'smart' weapons for use against tanks and planes and communications media by which to differentiate accidental from intentional incursions.

In the Far East, postwar developments were as unexpected as those in the West. The rapid deterioration of the Nationalist Chinese government of General Chiang Kai-shek led to the 1949 victory, almost by default, of Mao Tse-tung's communist regime. The United States sought halfheartedly to support Chiang, but this impossible task was virtually abandoned after 1946, and Chiang and his supporters finally left the Chinese mainland for the island of Formosa (Taiwan).

The unexpected happened again in 1950, when the troops of North Korea, a Soviet satellite, moved across the 38th parallel against the weak forces of South Korea, which had neither planes nor tanks. The Soviets doubted that the US would try to defend the South Korean regime, as the Americans largely abdicated their responsibility to the United Nations. However, President Truman and his advisers discerned a Soviet effort to change the rough alignment of peoples and territories that had coalesced after World War II, when Korea had been divided. Now it seemed that force was to reunite Korea, so the Truman Administration moved American troops in to take part in a war that eventually cost 35,000 American lives.

At the outset, the oncoming North Korean forces appeared unstoppable. Only with great difficulty did the combined troops of General Douglas MacArthur (sent over from Japan) and those dispatched from the United States establish a perimeter around the South Korean port of Pusan. In September 1950, in a surprise move, UN troops seized the port of Inchon, high up on Korea's west side, and soon retook the South Korean capital of Seoul. (At the outset the US co-ordinated its strategy with the UN, which became possible

through the absence of the Soviet representative from the Security Council who was protesting the presence of a Nationalist Chinese representative.) McArthur's forces then surged across the 38th parallel into North Korea.

The decision to move into North Korea was an error comparable to that made by the Soviets in their initial invasion: both strategies sought to change the post-World War II borders. Soon the Communist Chinese intervened; UN forces reeled back, and only after hectic weeks in early 1951 were lines stabilized by troops under command of General Matthew B Ridgway. Ridgway then took the offensive, recaptured Seoul (which had been lost a second time), and established a line against the North Koreans and their Chinese allies that was roughly at the 38th parallel. This line has held to the present day – reinforced by the presence of 40,000 American troops.

The Middle East needed a defense arrangement comparable to NATO, and here the American Government assumed an obligation under the Baghdad Pact. The pact began in 1955 as an alliance between Iraq and Turkey, but soon included Britain, Iran, and Pakistan in what appeared to be an anti-communist front. Actually, the pact represented the remnants of a British project for organizing the Arab nations of the Middle East, which had foundered in political problems attendant upon the emergence of Israel and the declining British influence in the region. In 1958 the United States joined the military committee of the Baghdad Pact; in 1959 it signed executive agreements with Iran, Turkey, and Pakistan. That year the pact's name was changed to Central Treaty Organization (CENTO).

A third overarching agreement was the Southeast Asia Treaty Organization (SEATO), established in 1954. It consisted of the United States, Britain, France, Australia, New Zealand, the Philippines, Thailand, and Pakistan. A special protocol included Cambodia, Laos, and South Vietnam by assuring these formerly French-ruled states of protection without obligation. SEATO was formally dissolved in the early 1980s.

The fourth arrangement of multilateral treaties by which the United States gathered allies was the Rio Pact of 1947, which joined the 21 American republics of that time in formal alliance. The Rio Pact looked more to hemispheric problems than to the question of communism and has never possessed the slightest military meaning.

By the mid-1950s, the United States had enlisted some 43 countries on its side. Later defections, such as that of Cuba, reduced this total, as did the dissolution of SEATO and the disintegration of the Central Treaty Organization in the early 1980s during the ongoing war between Iran and Iraq. Several bilateral alliances wrought further changes in the United States' international position, including those with the Philippines and Australia-New Zealand in 1951; Japan in 1952; Korea in 1953; and Nationalist China (Taiwan) in 1954. It is difficult to believe that until the late 1940s America had formed only one alliance in all its history (with monarchical France, from 1778 until 1800).

After 1945 the United States became involved in Indochina and ended as a leading protagonist in the Vietnam War. French Indochina – with its provinces of Vietnam, Laos, and Cambodia – had been the scene of an ill-fated effort by the French Government to hold back the anticolonial tide. The struggle between the French Army and the revolutionaries of Vietnamese nationalist Ho Chi Minh lasted from 1946 until 1954, when the French withdrew after the defeat and capture of 10,000 of their troops in Dien Bien Phu. The Americans, who had been supporting the French military effort financially, undertook to preserve the independence of what became four separate states – North Vietnam (north of the 17th parallel), South Vietnam, Laos, and Cambodia – in the Geneva Conference of 1954.

Initial American efforts to shore up South Vietnam took the form of massive economic and military assistance to reconstruct the southern half of the divided nation and to train and equip a South Vietnamese Army. By the end of the 1950s, however, North Vietnamese infiltrators began to come out in the open, pushing for unification under Hanoi's procommunist regime. They supported the anti-Saigon guerrillas and soon threw South Vietnam into turmoil; South Vietnamese President Ngo Dinh Diem seemed unable to command loyalty or to exert authority. He was assassinated in 1963 during a coup by his generals.

The Americanization of the Vietnam War really began with the rapid increase in US Army forces, which had totaled only 800 at the end of the Eisenhower Administration in 1961. By the time of Diem's death (soon followed by the assassination of President John F Kennedy), those forces had increased to 15,000. The new American president, Lyndon B Johnson, moved cautiously until after his election in 1964. Meanwhile, however, after the apparent North Korean attack on two American destroyers in the Gulf of Tonkin, Johnson obtained from Congress a massive vote of support – the Tonkin Resolution. By a vote of 416-0 in the House and 88-2 in the Senate, the president was empowered to 'take all necessary measures to repel any armed attack against the forces of the United States and to prevent further aggression.' Beginning in 1965 President Johnson reinforced American troops at an ever-growing rate: by 1968 they numbered 540,000.

What turned the Vietnam War around was the US Army's inability to defeat the communist guerrillas without still more troops; after the North Vietnamese 'Tet' or Lunar New Year offensive in January 1968, it became politically impossible to obtain them. The president had a mandate for action in the Tonkin Resolution, but the scope of the war had outstripped his mandate. Public turmoil swept the United States – resistance to the draft by college students, demonstrations, popular alarm and disgust at televised accounts from the scene of battle. It became evident to the Johnson Administration, and especially to the new secretary of defense, Clark Clifford (appointed in March of 1968) that there could be no end to the Vietnam War, short of negotiation and withdrawal of US troops under whatever conditions could be obtained. Johnson signaled

cessation of the United States effort in a public address at the end of March. The negotiations that followed went on not for months but for years, and throughout the first administration of Johnson's successor, Richard M Nixon. The new president announced his plan for Vietnamization soon after taking office: US troops would be gradually replaced by South Vietnamese soldiers. However, anti-war feeling in the United States grew stronger with the disclosure of secret US air and ground support of South Vietnamese drives against Cambodia, napalm bombings, and the My Lai massacre. Publication of the Pentagon Papers beginning in June 1971 heightened anti-war sentiment. On 23 January 1973 an agreement on ending the war and restoring peace in Vietnam arranged for American military withdrawal, whereupon North Korea released hundreds of American prisoners. Two years later the South Vietnamese regime in Saigon collapsed, after a short military campaign by North Vietnam. The Vietnam War had cost close to 50,000 American lives, and well over $100 billion. Its deleterious effects on the US economy and national morale are still felt today.

American policy in the Middle East was less disastrous than in Indochina, but by the 1980s it had hardly proved a triumph. This crossroad of three continents – Europe, Asia, Africa – had become the focus of international attention in 1948, with the independence of the State of Israel. The Jews of Palestine asserted their status as a nation against their Arab neighbors in

Right: *Infantrymen of the Army of the Republic of Vietnam, which fought alongside the US Army in Vietnam.*

Below: *President Kennedy announces to Congress, in May 1961, the US intention to land a man on the moon.*

Syria, Jordan, and Egypt, and the first Arab-Israeli War ran on until 1949. It ended in an armistice that has never turned into peace – with the sole exception of the Israeli-Egyptian treaty resulting from the Camp David accords of President James E Carter in 1978.

The sequel to Israeli independence comprised four additional wars. In 1956 the Israeli Army attacked Egypt as part of an Anglo-French effort to get back the Suez Canal, nationalized by President Gamal Abdel Nasser of Egypt. This war closed uneasily after the United States and the Soviet Union took the issue to the United Nations and the UN installed a peacekeeping force.

In 1967, after border incursions inspired by Egypt, the Israelis suddenly attacked again and in a lightning campaign seized the Gaza Strip below Haifa, all of Jerusalem, and parts of the west bank of the Jordan River. The UN refused to recognize these territorial acquisitions, but Israel rejected its resolution and remained in occupation.

The fourth Arab-Israeli War came in 1973, with an Egyptian attack on the Jewish State. Using new Russian equipment, including 'smart' weapons, the Egyptians and their Syrian allies inflicted serious losses upon the Israelis, who managed nevertheless to push back the invaders.

In 1982 the Israelis sought to extend their northern border by interfering in the already heated civil war in Lebanon. This brought in more Syrian troops, reinforced with Soviet arms, and a short-term force of US Marines and other Western troops. After the shocking deaths by truck bomb of over 200 Marines, the Americans and other Western troops withdrew; Lebanon seemed likely to become a no-man's land between Syria and Israel. There had been a precedent for American military intervention in Lebanon. In 1958, after revolution in Iraq and impending revolution in Jordan and Lebanon, a division of US Marines and Army troops occupied Lebanon for a short time. The reoccupation of 1983-4, on a much smaller scale, seemed far less successful.

During the cold war years, unsettling events also occurred within the Western Hemisphere. The Monroe Doctrine had remained an unspoken tenet of US foreign policy vis-à-vis neighboring nations. Hence when communism seemed to threaten Guatemala in 1954, the Eisenhower Administration moved decisively, if with small supplies of money and munitions, for the area of revolution was minuscule. In 1959 the new regime of Fidel Castro in Cuba began to raise apprehensions, and in 1961 the Central Intelligence Agency did its best to overthrow it. The failure of the Bay of Pigs invasion, and the Soviet Union's desire to redress its arms inferiority by emplacing intermediate-range missiles on Cuban territory, led to the Cuban missile crisis of 1962. By the mid-1980s, US-Cuban relations had warmed to the point of establishing low-level diplomatic missions, but the Castro regime remained unrecognized. Meanwhile, a 1964 revolution in the Dominican Republic involving 4000 Dominicans brought intervention by 20,000 American troops and assurance of a regime friendly to the United States.

In the 1980s the administration of President Ronald Reagan discerned communist involvement in revolutionary situations in Costa Rica, El Salvador, and Nicaragua. Ongoing diplomatic and military efforts to bring peace to the region have

Left: *The Apollo 13 space vehicle is launched from the Cape Canaveral (Cape Kennedy) space center in 1970, the third US lunar mission. No moon landing was made because of a fire but the astronauts were able to return safely.*

included special ambassadors, the training of local troops with American advisers, and joint military maneuvers. Many believe that the United States should have stayed out of Central America, allowing the people of that region to resolve their own difficulties. Other observers suggest that nearby Latin American nations like Mexico, whose borders are closer to those of the protagonists, could have intervened diplomatically. In any event, the revolutions continue at this writing, taking their principal toll among the impoverished lower classes of these troubled countries.

In fact, the present situation in Latin America recalls the emergence of the United States from colonial status to nationhood. Recent US policy in Latin America has been affected by the spread of nationalism, an idea exemplified by the American Revolution. Nationalism's emergence in Central America has been marked by guerrilla warfare, a tactic used in the Revolutionary War. It would be surprising if US policy toward Latin America, traditionally paternalistic, were not colored now by ambivalence. The New World nations may be moving toward greater awareness of their deep affinities.

American history has been characterized by movement – the touchstone of America's past. Thus nothing, or very little, was fixed irrevocably in the national configuration of the 1980s. The condition of the nation's blacks is a case in point. It had changed markedly with freedom during the Civil War, only to enter upon the stasis established by the Supreme Court decision *Plessy v Ferguson* (1896), according to which facilities for black Americans could be 'separate but equal.' World War I brought migration of perhaps half a million Southern blacks into the industrial North and Middle West, and many of the emigrants remained. World War II engendered a new wave of black mobility. Then came the Supreme Court case of 1954, *Brown v Board of Education of Topeka*, which found that separate educational facilities were inherently unequal and mandated the desegregation of public schools. In the ensuing 'black revolution,' millions of citizens sought their civil rights, and black Americans made significant progress toward economic and social equality.

Another instance of mobility is in the shift of population centers since 1940. The city of New York kept its primacy as the nation's most populous city, while Los Angeles vied with Chicago for second place; early in the 1980s, the sprawling West Coast metropolis achieved its goal. Other urban centers increased or declined in population with the movement of Americans to the West and the Southwest – the so-called Sunbelt. As a result, the national center of population moved from Indiana, where it had remained for decades, to the otherwise obscure hamlet of DeSoto, Missouri, across the Mississippi.

Steel and automobile production – traditionally the prime indices of the American economy – went up for years after World War II, then declined in the face of foreign competition. Smaller cars and alternative construction materials also affected the steel industry. But by any measure, and despite the downturns, American consumption of these key industrial products remained the highest in the world.

In the years since 1940, the drift in population has been increasingly from country to city, rural to urban. This movement first accelerated in the late nineteenth century. The huge immigration from the turn of the twentieth century to World War I increased its momentum, and the trend continued until most Americans lived in towns or urban areas of more than 2500 people. Part of this influx to cities was a result of increased efficiency on the farm – far more production from far fewer people. Part was due to a desire for the cultural and other attractions of city life, and for the wages of urban business and industry.

Births, deaths, marriages, and divorces took on new proportions in the twentieth century. The birth rate dropped sharply from that of the nineteenth century, and the death rate was down, reflecting better health and hence longevity. Marriages were numerous, but then so were divorces, for reasons best known to those who undertook one or both. Some observers attribute the rising divorce rate to an erosion of traditional values and beliefs and the breakup of the extended family. Others see it as a sign of liberation from unhealthy moral and social constraints on personal life styles.

Income taxes had become the mainstay of the twentieth-century government, following passage of the Sixteenth Amendment in 1913. From the beginning of the Republic in the late eighteenth century, the principal source of federal revenue had been the tariff on imports. At the beginning of the present century, however, it became clear that tariffs would not support the increasing projects of government. When the income tax system went into effect in 1916, collections were very low; much more money was derived from excise taxes. Gradually, collections of individual and corporate taxes went up – individual far more than corporate – until the individual (or family) taxpayer became the mainstay of the federal budget.

The dissemination of ideas in America has been transformed by radio and television over the last two generations. These media have become an educational vehicle on a par with formal schooling. Radio 'came in' with a Pittsburgh station, KDKA, just after World War I. For 30 years it had a near monopoly of the airwaves. After 1950, television came into its own and threatened to replace radio as the arbiter of politics, economics, and popular culture. Radio took a new lease on life with 'FM,' and increased use of automobiles ensured a larger radio audience (despite the introduction of tiny car television sets in the 1980s). Radio reached out for those Americans interested in music of all varieties, whose numbers were increasing. By the 1980s it was clear that both radio and television were 'here to stay,' and that each medium most definitely had an influential role to play in forming – and informing – the American mind.

The overriding movement of post-World War II America has been into a dominant position in world affairs. As a postwar power, America has had a primary interest in Western Europe's freedom from Soviet Union control and a secondary interest in the volatile Middle East and its essential oil supplies. In the Far East, the United States has long considered Japan the key to a regional power balance; the opening of unofficial relations with the People's Republic of China in 1972 marked a dramatic change of policy toward this great Eastern nation, the world's most populous communist country.

A concomitant of America's postwar status in international affairs has been the costly and potentially disastrous arms race. The burgeoning military establishment has increasingly skewed the Federal budget toward inflation. More serious still is the threat to humanity of a nuclear war, the dangers of which have become ever more present to public consciousness. In the world today, America is a vital component of the global community that is still struggling toward full consciousness of its interdependence. The responsible exercise of American power in the last years of the twentieth century presents an unprecedented challenge to the government and people of the United States.

Postwar Concerns

MAP below: New states up to 1959. As was to be expected, the remaining territories became states in this period, but the accession of Alaska and Hawaii represented a qualitative and questioned, change. These were not contiguous territories, and Hawaii was even an overseas territory.

MAP top right: The United Nations Organization. This post-war supranational organization, established by the victorious powers, was at first closed to the defeated nations, but they joined in course of time. So did many other new nations, although Switzerland refrained from membership. The USSR had three seats, other nations one each, but permanent membership of the UN's Security Council gave extra authority to the USA, Britain, France, China, and the USSR.

Above: *Harry S. Truman wins the 1948 presidential election. Given little chance of beating the Republican candidate, Dewey, Truman polled a surprisingly high vote and, next day, took delight in the* Chicago Daily Tribune's *premature announcement of his defeat.*

Right: *Inauguration of President Eisenhower in 1957. He is being sworn in by Chief Justice Earl Warren. Richard Nixon, Eisenhower's Vice-President, looks on.*

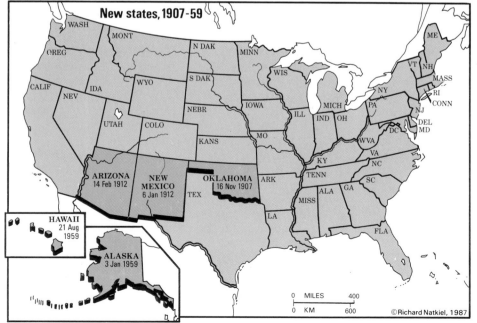

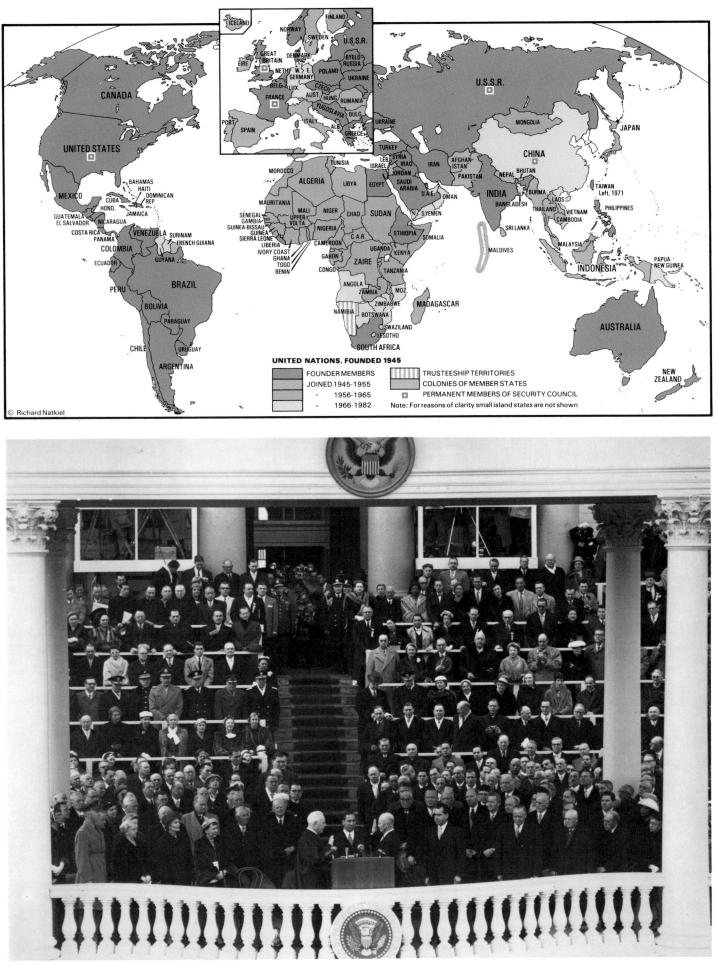

UNITED NATIONS, FOUNDED 1945

FOUNDER MEMBERS
JOINED 1945-1955
"   1956-1965
"   1966-1982

TRUSTEESHIP TERRITORIES
COLONIES OF MEMBER STATES
PERMANENT MEMBERS OF SECURITY COUNCIL

Note: For reasons of clarity small island states are not shown

© Richard Natkiel

152

The Division of Europe

MAP right: The post-war map of central Europe. As agreed at inter-allied wartime conferences, Poland extended its borders westward at the expense of Germany, while sacrificing its eastern region to the USSR. Germany's eastern frontier was henceforth the Oder and Neisse rivers.

MAP below: The partition of Berlin. By previous agreement Berlin, situated in the Soviet-occupied part of Germany, was administered by four powers, but as time passed it became clear that, in fact, it was divided into the Russian sector and what became known as West Berlin, made up of the three sectors administered by the USA, Britain, and France.

Below: *Inside the Russian sector of Berlin at the Potsdammer Platz, where the Russian, US, and British sectors met, 1948.*

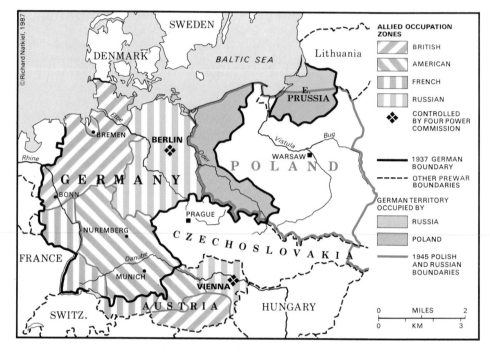

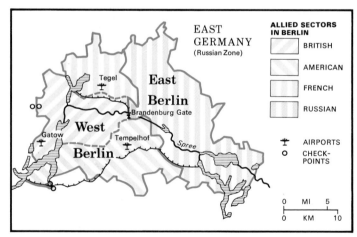

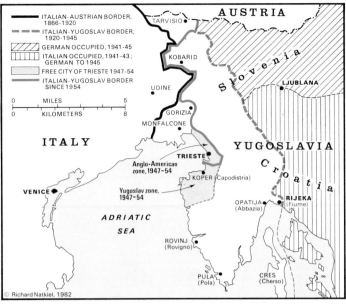

MAP above: Access routes to Berlin. Although the wartime agreements prescribed free access by the western powers to their sectors of Berlin, the vulnerability of their routes through Soviet-controlled eastern Germany was too great a temptation for Stalin. All kinds of interference were attempted, as a means of putting pressure on the West, and in 1948 the Russians mounted a full blockade of West Berlin which, however, failed in the face of a massive year-long airlift organized by the western occupying powers.

MAP above: The Trieste problem. With the defeat of Italy the Italian annexation of western Slovenia and Croatia was terminated and the port of Trieste temporarily taken under Anglo-US control. Conflicting claims by Italy and Yugoslavia for this port were eventually settled in 1954, when it was decided it should be returned to Italy. Yugoslavia, weakened diplomatically by its quarrel with the USSR, accepted this decision resentfully but peacefully.

Right: *General Marshal, US Secretary of State after WWII and instigator of the Marshal Plan to aid Europe's recovery from war.*

Below: *The Berlin Wall in its early days.*

The Korean War

MAP right: The initial onslaught against South Korea. The North Koreans sent seven infantry divisions and an armored division across the frontier, with diversionary amphibious landings along the east coast. They captured Seoul within three days and in two months had penned the South Korean and arriving American and Allied forces into a small area around the port of Pusan. The American success in having the United Nations agree to intervene was made possible by the fact that the Soviets were boycotting the UN Security Council in protest over the recognition of Nationalist and not Communist China. The Soviets were thus unable to use their veto to block the move to help South Korea.

MAP below right: The Inchon landing. This surprise amphibious operation, perfectly executed, was 200 miles behind the North Koreans' concentration besieging Pusan, and turned the tide of the Korean War in the Allies' favor. The initial landing was by three US Marine battalions south of the town and by three to the north.

Top right: *Marines go ashore in the remarkably successful Inchon landing operation.*

Right: *General MacArthur, commander-in-chief of the United Nations' forces, visits the front in Korea.*

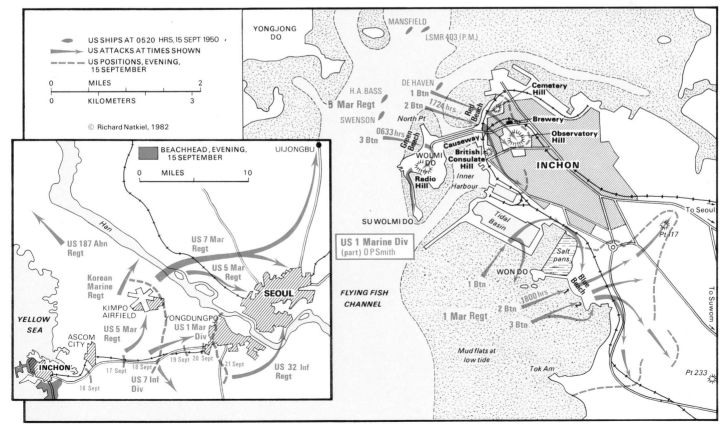

US SHIPS AT 0520 HRS, 15 SEPT 1950
US ATTACKS AT TIMES SHOWN
US POSITIONS, EVENING, 15 SEPTEMBER

0   MILES   2
0   KILOMETERS   3

© Richard Natkiel, 1982

BEACHHEAD, EVENING, 15 SEPTEMBER

0   MILES   10

UIJONGBU

US 187 Abn Regt
Han
US 7 Mar Regt
US 5 Mar Regt
Korean Marine Regt
KIMPO AIRFIELD
SEOUL
YONGDUNGPO
US 5 Mar Regt
US 1 Mar Div
YELLOW SEA
ASCOM CITY
INCHON
16 Sept
17 Sept
18 Sept
19 Sept
20 Sept
21 Sept
US 7 Inf Div
US 32 Inf Regt

YONGJONG DO
MANSFIELD
LSMR 403 (P.M.)
DE HAVEN
H.A.BASS
5 Mar Regt
SWENSON
1 Btn
2 Btn
3 Btn
0633hrs
1724 hrs
North Pt
Green Beach
Red Beach
Cemetery Hill
Brewery
Observatory Hill
INCHON
WOLMI DO
British Consulate Hill
Causeway
Radio Hill
Inner Harbour
SU WOLMI DO
US 1 Marine Div (part) O P Smith
FLYING FISH CHANNEL
Tidal Basin
To Seoul
Pt 117
Salt pans
WON DO
1 Btn
2 Btn
3 Btn
1800hrs
Blue Beach
1 Mar Regt
Mud flats at low tide
Tok Am
Pt 233
To Suwom

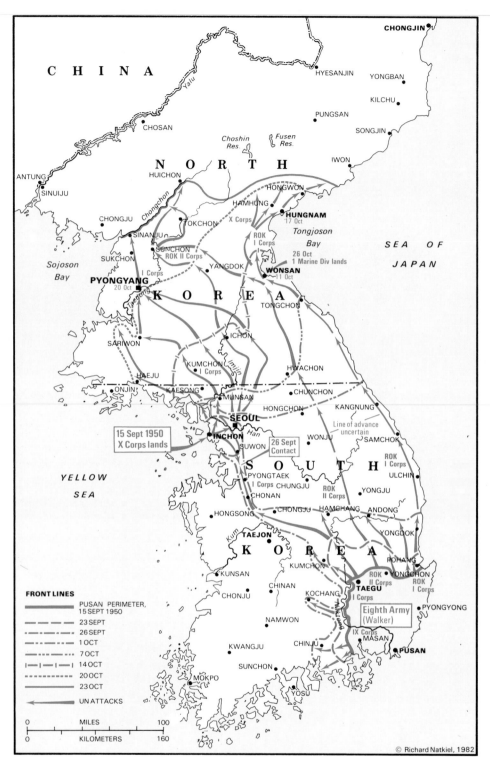

CHINA

CHONGJIN

HYESANJIN
YONGBAN

KILCHU

CHOSAN
PUNGSAN

SONGJIN

Choshin Res.
Fusen Res.

N O R T H
IWON

ANTUNG
HUICHON

SINUIJU
HONGWON

HAMHUNG
CHONGJU

Chongchon
X Corps
HUNGNAM
17 Oct

SINANJU
TOKCHON
ROK
I Corps
Tongjoson Bay

SEA OF JAPAN

Sojoson Bay
SUKCHON
SUNCHON
ROK II Corps
26 Oct
1 Marine Div lands

I Corps
YANGDOK
WONSAN
11 Oct

K O R E A
PYONGYANG
20 Oct
Taedong

TONGCHON

ICHON

SARIWON

Imjin
KUMCHON
I Corps
HWACHON

HAEJU
KAESONG
CHUNCHON

ONJIN
MUNSAN
KANGNUNG

HONGCHON

YELLOW SEA
SEOUL
Han
INCHON

15 Sept 1950
X Corps lands
SUWON
26 Sept
Contact
Line of advance
uncertain

WONJU
SAMCHOK

S O U T H
ROK
I Corps

PYONGTAEK
ULCHIN
I Corps
CHUNGJU

CHONAN
ROK
II Corps
YONGJU

HONGSONG
CHONGJU
HAMCHANG
ANDONG

Kum
YONGDOK

TAEJON

K O R E A
KUMCHON
POHANG

KUNSAN
ROK
II Corps
YONGCHON
ROK
I Corps

CHINAN
TAEGU
I Corps
PYONGYONG

CHONJU
KOCHANG

Naktong
Eighth Army
(Walker)

NAMWON
CHINJU
IX Corps
MASAN

KWANGJU
PUSAN

FRONT LINES

SUNCHON

MOKPO
YOSU

	PUSAN PERIMETER, 15 SEPT 1950
	23 SEPT
	26 SEPT
	1 OCT
	7 OCT
	14 OCT
	20 OCT
	23 OCT
←	UN ATTACKS

0   MILES   100
0   KILOMETERS   160

© Richard Natkiel, 1982

MAP left: The United Nations' Korean offensive of Fall 1950. After the strategic transformation achieved by the Inchon landings, the original intention of the UN Command to throw back the invaders beyond the 38th Parallel was overtaken by a decision to advance into North Korea and, eventually, arrange elections in Korea as a whole. Pyongyang, the North Korean capital, was captured in October but when, in November, the Korea-China frontier was approached, the advancing UN forces found themselves confronted by overwhelming Chinese formations.

Left: US Marines endure the Korean winter, December 1950, during the epic retreat from Koto-Ri.

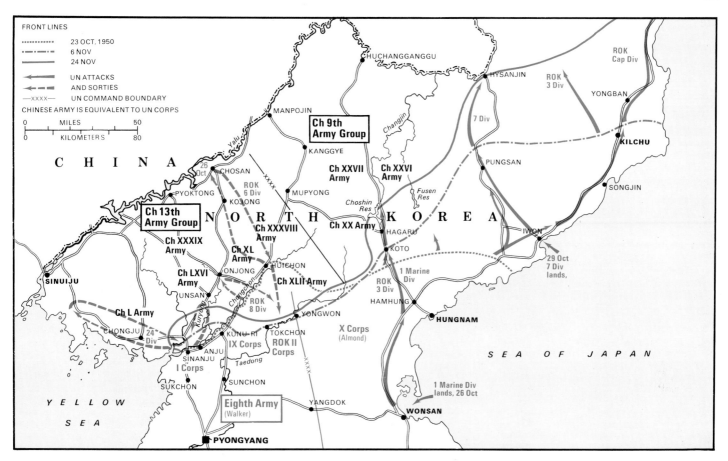

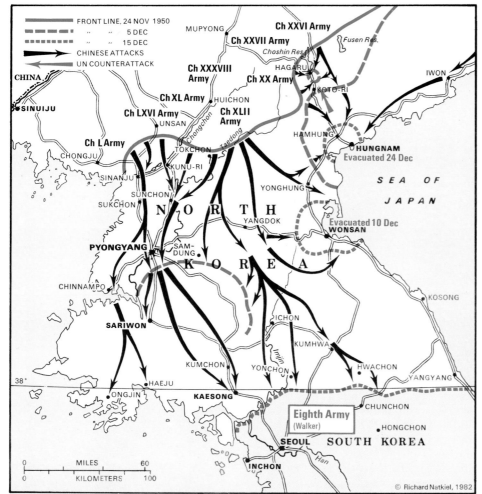

MAP top: The end of the 1950 advance. Initially the Chinese sent two army groups over the frontier to throw back the UN forces.

MAP left: The Chinese counter-offensive in Korea. A rapid retreat, including some evacuations by sea, brought the UN forces back to the 38th Parallel, and in January the Chinese pushed further to capture Seoul.

MAP above: The front is stabilized. The Chinese attempted another offensive in early 1951, which failed, and the UN forces then counterattacked and recovered Seoul. Long-drawn-out armistice discussions then took place, a ceasefire line having been agreed.

158

MAP above: The post-war defensive alliances, or bloc systems. NATO, led by the USA, was a defensive association aimed at checking the USSR, and was countered by the USSR's sponsorship of the Warsaw Pact. Such pacts aimed at coordinating strategy, tactics, weapon design, and diplomacy. The CENTO Pact, organized by the USA and Britain in the Middle East, achieved little, partly because the regimes that joined it tended thereby to speed their own overthrow.

SEATO, a western-sponsored pact for south-east Asia, was little more successful; its adherents often used their membership to win US diplomatic support in local quarrels. The ANZUS alliance, principally linking the USA with Australia and New Zealand, suffered in the mid-1980s when New Zealand refused to accept the presence of nuclear-armed US Navy ships. The map shows the situation in the mid 1950s. Soviet fears of encirclement by the US-

sponsored systems of alliances helped worsen the Cold War tensions between the superpowers.

America as a
World Power

MAP below right: French Indo-China.
France's failure to reimpose her colonial
rule after World War II led to the
Vietnam War, when the USA attempted
to maintain the agreement that
accompanied the French withdrawal and
which split Vietnam into a Communist
North and a non-Communist South.

Right: *Operation Lorraine, a 1953 episode in
France's unsuccessful struggle against the
Vietnam rebellion.*

Below: *A French river patrol in Vietnam, just
prior to the French withdrawal.*

The Vietnam War

MAP right: The Vietnam War. This general situation remained fairly constant right up to the last months of the conflict.

MAP opposite: The air war in Vietnam. Most US air activity was ground-support, which was invaluable even though, because of the terrain and the enemy tactics, damage inflicted was small in proportion to the effort expended. Strategic bombing, as with the 'Rolling Thunder' and 'Flaming Dart' operations, was intended to weaken the North Vietnamese war effort by destroying mainly economic targets. The later Operation 'Linebacker II' was more political than economic, being aimed at strengthening the US negotiating position as the war approached its end.

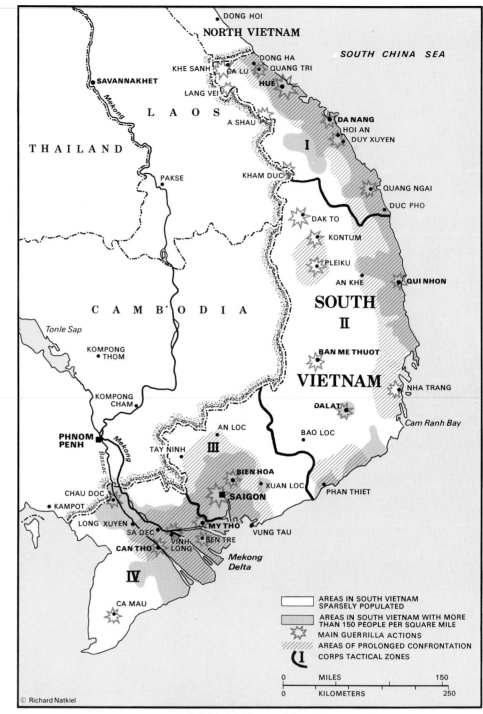

AREAS IN SOUTH VIETNAM SPARSELY POPULATED

AREAS IN SOUTH VIETNAM WITH MORE THAN 150 PEOPLE PER SQUARE MILE

MAIN GUERRILLA ACTIONS

AREAS OF PROLONGED CONFRONTATION

CORPS TACTICAL ZONES

© Richard Natkiel

161

Far left: *The destroyer USS* Everett *provides gunfire support off the Vietnamese coast.*

Left: *Phantom aircraft of the US Navy, which undertook much of the ground-support work.*

MAP right: The end of the Vietnam War. In 1968 the North Vietnamese Tet Offensive, though a failure, had convinced the US public, and much of the US Army, that despite all the American effort and sacrifice the enemy still held the initiative. Public support for the war dropped, and so did the morale of the troops fighting it. American troops were progressively withdrawn, placing more responsibility on the Army of the Republic of Vietnam. In 1972 there was a big Communist offensive, which was successful but not at all decisive except in terms of morale. Then, in late 1974, the last Communist offensive began.

MAP below: The bombing of Hanoi and Haiphong. For much of the war, US aircraft were not permitted to attack the populated areas of Hanoi and Haiphong, for political and humane reasons, but these restrictions were lifted for the final bombing offensive in 1972.

MAP below right: The fighting for Khe Sanh during the 1968 Tet Offensive. The US garrison of the air base held out but the base was abandoned later after the end of the North Vietnamese offensive.

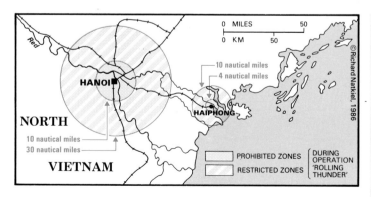

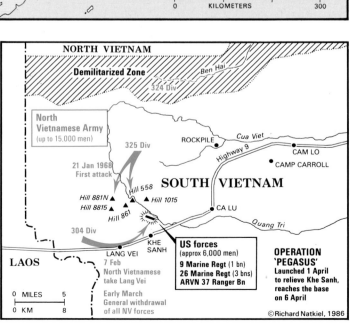

The Caribbean and Central America

MAP below right: The post-war USA and the Caribbean. US intervention in the Caribbean after World War II was almost as frequent as before World War I, although such intervention was mainly diplomatic. Fear of Communist influence in the small states of the region dominated US policy. The emergence of Cuba as a protégé of Moscow alarmed Washington, which tended, more than previously, to suspect any reforming government of Marxist leanings. Critics argued that hostility shown to new radical regimes only served to drive them further toward Soviet patronage.

Above right: *A Soviet ship with a suspicious deck cargo, in the Caribbean during the Cuban Crisis.*

Right: *One of the Soviet missile sites in Cuba that led to the Cuban Missile Crisis of 1962.*

Below: *In happier days: Fidel Castro visits Washington and meets Vice-President Nixon in 1959, before relations deteriorated.*

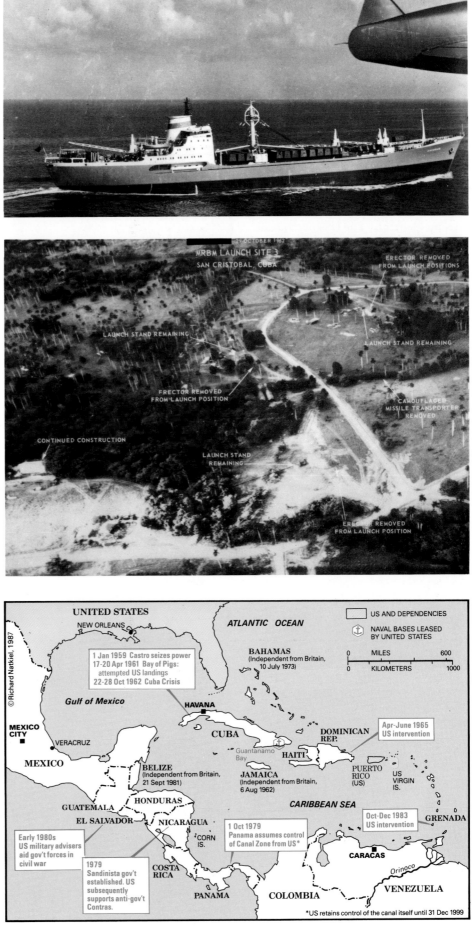

Military Intervention in the 1980s

MAP right: The US invasion of Grenada. In 1983 the moderate Marxist government of the former British West Indian colony of Grenada was overthrown by a coup launched by more extreme elements. The US government decided to intervene, partly because it was anxious about Cuban influence in the island. The landing and the elimination of resistance took two days, with only 18 Americans killed.

Below: *US troops in the Grenada operation.*

Below right: *Field artillery of the 82nd Airborne Division in Grenada.*

Bottom left: *An arranged photograph of Cuban ammunition supplies uncovered in Grenada.*

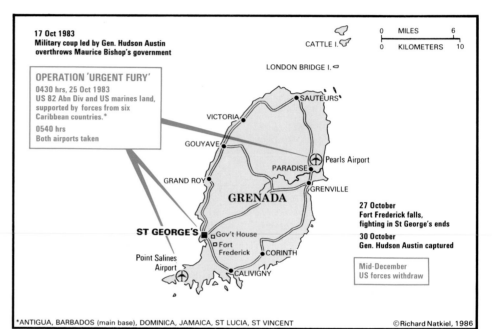

17 Oct 1983
Military coup led by Gen. Hudson Austin overthrows Maurice Bishop's government

OPERATION 'URGENT FURY'
0430 hrs, 25 Oct 1983
US 82 Abn Div and US marines land, supported by forces from six Caribbean countries.*
0540 hrs
Both airports taken

27 October
Fort Frederick falls, fighting in St George's ends

30 October
Gen. Hudson Austin captured

Mid-December
US forces withdraw

*ANTIGUA, BARBADOS (main base), DOMINICA, JAMAICA, ST LUCIA, ST VINCENT

©Richard Natkiel, 1986

MAP right: The USA and Lebanon. Soon after Israel invaded Lebanon in 1982 an international peacekeeping force was organized as part of the plan for an Israeli withdrawal, and US units participated. Arab opinion regarded the USA as Israel's powerful ally, and there were local sporadic attacks on US personnel and property. In April 1983 this violence assumed a large-scale character with a bomb attack on the US embassy. This was followed in October by an attack on the Beirut barracks of the US and French peacekeeping forces. At the US barracks, a truck filled with explosives killed 260 Marines.

MAP below: US aircraft bomb Libya. The Libyan regime of Colonel Qadhafi was associated with several acts of terrorism against US targets in the Middle East, and in April 1986 US aircraft from an aircraft carrier force and from bases in Britain attacked Tripoli and Benghazi. There were civilian casualties, and the attack was widely condemned, but Libyan enthusiasm for terrorism did appear to diminish.

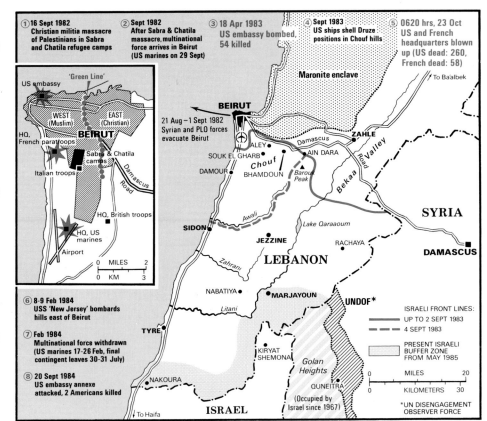

① 16 Sept 1982 Christian militia massacre of Palestinians in Sabra and Chatila refugee camps

② Sept 1982 After Sabra & Chatila massacre, multinational force arrives in Beirut (US marines on 29 Sept)

③ 18 Apr 1983 US embassy bombed, 54 killed

④ Sept 1983 US ships shell Druze positions in Chouf hills

⑤ 0620 hrs, 23 Oct US and French headquarters blown up (US dead: 260, French dead: 58)

⑥ 8-9 Feb 1984 USS 'New Jersey' bombards hills east of Beirut

⑦ Feb 1984 Multinational force withdrawn (US marines 17-26 Feb, final contingent leaves 30-31 July)

⑧ 20 Sept 1984 US embassy annexe attacked, 2 Americans killed

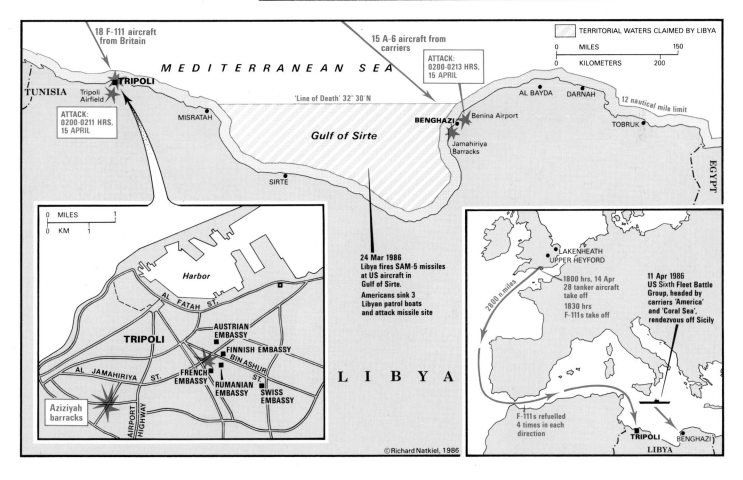

© Richard Natkiel, 1986

Pacific Territory and Influence

MAP right: Post-war US influence in the Pacific. With the defeat of Japan, the USA became clearly dominant in the Pacific, although China and, especially the USSR, were powerful in their own region. Japan was largely demilitarized. The USA continued to administer central Pacific islands and the biggest of its territories there, Hawaii, with its important bases, became a state of the union. The Dutch East Indies gained independence (as Indonesia), and so did several British possessions. The Philippines also gained formal independence and, like Taiwan (where the Chinese Nationalists established themselves after defeat in China proper) became closely linked with the USA.

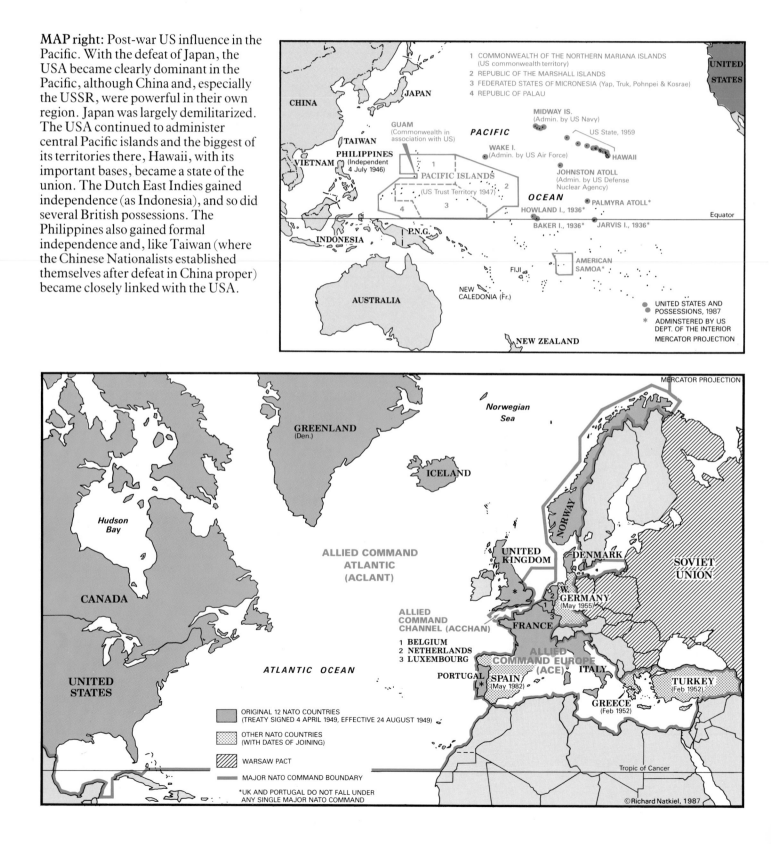

1 COMMONWEALTH OF THE NORTHERN MARIANA ISLANDS (US commonwealth territory)
2 REPUBLIC OF THE MARSHALL ISLANDS
3 FEDERATED STATES OF MICRONESIA (Yap, Truk, Pohnpei & Kosrae)
4 REPUBLIC OF PALAU

CHINA
JAPAN
UNITED STATES
TAIWAN
PHILIPPINES (Independent 4 July 1946)
VIETNAM
GUAM (Commonwealth in association with US)
PACIFIC ISLANDS
(US Trust Territory 1947)
MIDWAY IS. (Admin. by US Navy)
US State, 1959
WAKE I. (Admin. by US Air Force)
HAWAII
JOHNSTON ATOLL (Admin. by US Defense Nuclear Agency)
PACIFIC OCEAN
PALMYRA ATOLL*
HOWLAND I., 1936*
Equator
BAKER I., 1936*
JARVIS I., 1936*
INDONESIA
P.N.G.
FIJI
AMERICAN SAMOA*
NEW CALEDONIA (Fr.)
AUSTRALIA
UNITED STATES AND POSSESSIONS, 1987
* ADMINISTERED BY US DEPT. OF THE INTERIOR
MERCATOR PROJECTION
NEW ZEALAND

MERCATOR PROJECTION
Norwegian Sea
GREENLAND (Den.)
ICELAND
NORWAY
ALLIED COMMAND ATLANTIC (ACLANT)
UNITED KINGDOM
DENMARK
SOVIET UNION
Hudson Bay
CANADA
W. GERMANY (May 1955)
ALLIED COMMAND CHANNEL (ACCHAN)
1 BELGIUM
2 NETHERLANDS
3 LUXEMBOURG
FRANCE
ATLANTIC OCEAN
ALLIED COMMAND EUROPE (ACE)
ITALY
UNITED STATES
PORTUGAL
SPAIN (May 1982)
GREECE (Feb 1952)
TURKEY (Feb 1952)
ORIGINAL 12 NATO COUNTRIES (TREATY SIGNED 4 APRIL 1949, EFFECTIVE 24 AUGUST 1949)
OTHER NATO COUNTRIES (WITH DATES OF JOINING)
WARSAW PACT
MAJOR NATO COMMAND BOUNDARY
*UK AND PORTUGAL DO NOT FALL UNDER ANY SINGLE MAJOR NATO COMMAND
Tropic of Cancer
©Richard Natkiel, 1987

The North Atlantic Alliance

National Parks

MAP below left: The major treaty organizations, the West's NATO and the Soviet bloc's Warsaw Pact. NATO was a product of President Truman's policy (the 'Truman Doctrine') of resisting Communist expansion. Its several national forces were coordinated at its Paris headquarters, SHAPE (Supreme Headquarters, Allied Powers in Europe) which, after France left the Organization, was moved to Brussels. The NATO Supreme Commander is the key military figure, with wide powers in the event of war. He has always been an American, beginning with General Eisenhower. Operationally, the NATO area is split into several military commands, as the map shows. In recent years some Europeans have strongly opposed the deployment by the US of certain new nuclear weapons while in the US this has been viewed in some quarters as an example of Europe's unwillingness to bear a fair share of its own defense. Both strands of opinion have called the future of the alliance into question but support for NATO remains strong in all the member nations.

MAP below: The US National Parks. National Parks, established in order to preserve sites of natural, scientific, or historical importance, are proclaimed by acts of Congress, and administered by a special bureau in the Department of the Interior. The first major Park was the Yellowstone, in Wyoming, established in 1872, and the list is still growing. To a large extent the concept has preserved sites from desecration and damage by commercial interests, at the expense of regulations and restrictions which some Americans find irritating.

© Richard Natkiel, 1987

Selected Statistical Information

Demographics of blacks in US, 1900-1980

1900	8.834 million
1910	9.828
1920	10.463
1930	11.891
1940	12.866
1950	15.042
1960	18.860
1970	22.581*
1980	26.631*

*includes Alaska and Hawaii

Shift of Centers of Population since 1900

1900	Columbus, Indiana
1910	Bloomington, Indiana
1920	Spencer, Indiana
1930	Linton, Indiana
1940	Carlisle, Indiana
1950	Louisville, Illinois*
1960	Centralia, Illinois*
1970	Mascoutah, Illinois*
1980	DeSoto, Missouri*

*includes Alaska and Hawaii

Ranking of Cities by Population (in millions)

1940

1.	New York City	7.455
2.	Chicago	3.397
3.	Philadelphia	1.931
4.	Detroit	1.623
5.	Los Angeles	1.504
6.	Cleveland	.878
7.	Baltimore	.859
8.	St Louis	.816
9.	Boston	.770
10.	Pittsburgh	.672

1950

1.	New York City	9.556
2.	Chicago	5.178
3.	Los Angeles-Long Beach	4.368
4.	Philadelphia	3.671
5.	Detroit	3.016
6.	Boston	2.411
7.	San Francisco-Oakland	2.241
8.	Pittsburgh	2.213
9.	St Louis	1.719
10.	Newark	1.468

1960

1.	New York City	10.695
2.	Los Angeles-Long Beach	6.743
3.	Chicago	6.221
4.	Philadelphia	4.343
5.	Detroit	3.762
6.	San Francisco-Oakland	2.783
7.	Boston	2.589
8.	Pittsburgh	2.405
9.	St Louis	2.060
10.	Washington	2.002

1970

1.	New York City	7.895
2.	Chicago	3.367
3.	Los Angeles	2.816
4.	Philadelphia	1.949
5.	Detroit	1.511
6.	Houston	1.233
7.	Baltimore	.906
8.	Dallas	.844
9.	Washington	.757
10.	Cleveland	.751

1980

1.	New York City	7.072
2.	Chicago	3.005
3.	Los Angeles	2.967
4.	Philadelphia	1.688
5.	Houston	1.595
6.	Detroit	1.203
7.	Dallas	.904
8.	San Diego	.876
9.	Phoenix	.790
10.	Baltimore	.787

Most Populous States (in millions)

1940

1.	New York	13.479
2.	Pennsylvania	9.900
3.	Illinois	7.897
4.	Ohio	6.908
5.	California	6.907
6.	Texas	6.415
7.	Michigan	5.256
8.	Massachusetts	4.317
9.	New Jersey	4.160
10.	Missouri	3.785

1950

1.	New York	14.830
2.	California	10.586
3.	Pennsylvania	10.498
4.	Illinois	8.712
5.	Ohio	7.947
6.	Texas	7.711
7.	Michigan	6.372
8.	New Jersey	4.835
9.	Massachusetts	4.691
10.	North Carolina	4.062

1960

1.	New York	16.782
2.	California	15.717
3.	Pennsylvania	11.319
4.	Illinois	10.081
5.	Ohio	9.706
6.	Texas	9.580
7.	Michigan	7.823
8.	New Jersey	6.067
9.	Massachusetts	5.149
10.	Florida	4.952

1970

1.	California	19.932
2.	New York	18.237
3.	Pennsylvania	11.794
4.	Texas	11.197
5.	Illinois	11.114
6.	Ohio	10.652
7.	Michigan	8.875
8.	New Jersey	7.168
9.	Florida	6.789
10.	Massachusetts	5.689

1980

1.	California	23.771
2.	New York	17.575
3.	Texas	14.321
4.	Pennsylvania	11.880
5.	Illinois	11.433
6.	Ohio	10.800
7.	Florida	9.874
8.	Michigan	9.255
9.	New Jersey	7.377
10.	North Carolina	5.888

Right: *The high school at Little Rock, Arkansas, scene of clashes in 1957 over the desegregation of schools.*

Steel Production since 1910

	(millions of tons)
1910	28.3
1920	46.2
1930	44.6
1940	67.0
1950	96.8
1960	99.3
1970	131.5
1980	111.8
1982	74.6

Automobiles (Factory Sales), 1910-1970

1910	.181 million
1920	1.905
1930	2.787
1940	3.717
1950	6.666
1960	6.675
1970	6.547

Above left: *Duke Ellington and his orchestra, stars of radio in the 1930s.*

Right: *Joseph McCarthy was finally discredited in televised congressional hearings in 1954.*

Left: *The latest in consumer goods, Louisville, Kentucky 1926.*

Population Shift, Rural to Urban, 1900-1980

	(thousands)	
	rural	*urban*
1900	45,835	30,160
1910	49,973	41,999
1920	51,553	54,158
1930	53,820	68,955
1940	57,246	74,425
1950	54,230★	96,468
1960	54,054★★	125,269
1970	53,887★★	149,325

★new 1950 urban definition
★★includes Alaska and Hawaii

Summary of Vital Statistics, 1920-80 (per thousand)

	Births	*Deaths*	*Marriages*	*Divorces*
1920	27.7	13.0	12.0	1.6
1930	21.3	11.3	9.2	1.6
1940	19.4	10.8	12.1	2.0
1950	24.1	9.6	11.1	2.2
1960	23.7★	9.5★	8.5★	2.2★
1970	18.4★	9.5★	10.6★	3.5★
1980	15.9★	8.8★	10.6★	5.2★

★includes Alaska and Hawaii

Income Taxes, 1916-80 (in millions $)

	Individuals	*Corporations*
1916	68	57
1920	(not available)	(not available)
1930	1,147	1,263
1940	982	1,148
1950	17,153	10,854
1960	44,946	22,179
1970	103,652	35,037
1980	285,551	61,137

Spread of Radio and Television Stations, 1945-80

Television

	Commercial	*Noncommercial*
1945	9	–
1950	104	–
1960	579	47
1970	691	190

Radio

	AM	*FM Commercial*	*FM Noncommercial*
1945	955	53	12
1950	2,144	691	62
1960	3,483	741	165
1970	4,288	2,126	416

Territorial Expansion of the USA

Early settlement in what is now the USA was mainly by English colonization. Charters were granted by the King, authorizing private individuals and companies to establish colonies. Many were unsuccessful, for even with the enterprise and endurance shown by early settlers the hostile environment could prove too much; bad weather, unfriendly Indians, and disease could be expected, but bad luck could show itself in a combination of simultaneous afflictions that proved terminal. Walter Raleigh's Roanoke Colony of the late sixteenth century was the most notable of such failures. The Virginia Company of London achieved, in 1607, the first permanent American settlement at Jamestown. A second Virginia Company was thereupon chartered, and for a time almost the entire eastern seaboard was known as Virginia.

At first charters had been issued to trading companies like the Massachusetts Bay Company, and to proprietory colonies like Pennsylvania which were owned and managed by lords proprietors. Such charters, English monarchs discovered, limited their own powers in the New World, and a process of converting the colonies to royal colonies began. At the time of Independence in 1776, of the thirteen colonies only two (Connecticut and Rhode Island) were still commercial (corporate) colonies and two (Maryland and Pennsylvania) proprietory colonies. Massachusetts by that time was an anomaly, retaining a charter but being governed as a royal colony.

The extension of royal control paralleled the transfer of European national rivalries to the new continent. The Spanish had long been involved in Florida, while the French began to settle along the St Lawrence. In the home countries, kings began to think of

Below: *The beginning of New England.*

Page 175: *President Polk and the Oregon question, 1845.*

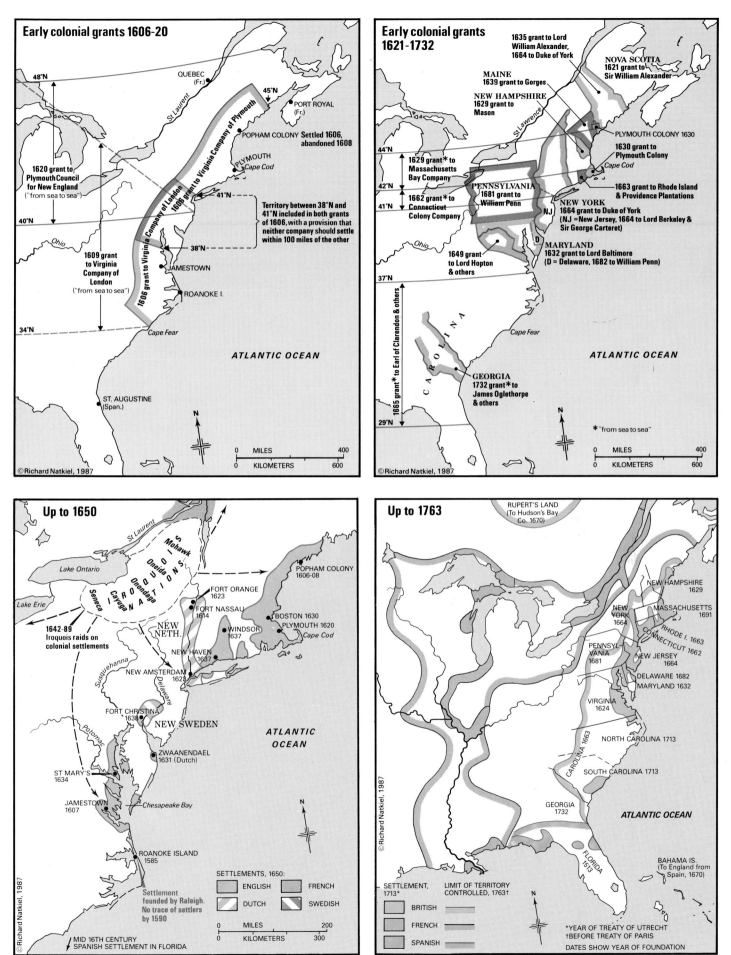

Early colonial grants 1606-20

- 48°N — QUEBEC (Fr.)
- 45°N — PORT ROYAL (Fr.)
- POPHAM COLONY Settled 1606, abandoned 1608
- PLYMOUTH — Cape Cod
- St Laurent
- 1620 grant to Plymouth Council for New England ("from sea to sea")
- 1606 grant to Virginia Company of Plymouth
- 41°N
- 40°N
- Ohio
- 1606 grant to Virginia Company of London
- 38°N
- 1609 grant to Virginia Company of London ("from sea to sea")
- JAMESTOWN
- ROANOKE I.
- Territory between 38°N and 41°N included in both grants of 1606, with a provision that neither company should settle within 100 miles of the other
- 34°N
- Cape Fear
- ATLANTIC OCEAN
- ST. AUGUSTINE (Span.)
- N
- MILES 0 — 400
- KILOMETERS 0 — 600
- © Richard Natkiel, 1987

Early colonial grants 1621-1732

- 1635 grant to Lord William Alexander, 1664 to Duke of York
- NOVA SCOTIA 1621 grant to Sir William Alexander
- MAINE 1639 grant to Gorges
- NEW HAMPSHIRE 1629 grant to Mason
- St Lawrence
- PLYMOUTH COLONY 1630
- 1630 grant to Plymouth Colony
- Cape Cod
- 44°N
- 1629 grant* to Massachusetts Bay Company
- 42°N
- PENNSYLVANIA 1681 grant to William Penn
- 1663 grant to Rhode Island & Providence Plantations
- 41°N
- 1662 grant* to Connecticut Colony Company
- NEW YORK 1664 grant to Duke of York (NJ = New Jersey, 1664 to Lord Berkeley & Sir George Carteret)
- NJ
- Ohio
- D
- MARYLAND 1632 grant to Lord Baltimore (D = Delaware, 1682 to William Penn)
- 1649 grant to Lord Hopton & others
- 37°N
- C A R O L I N A
- Cape Fear
- ATLANTIC OCEAN
- 1665 grant* to Earl of Clarendon & others
- GEORGIA 1732 grant* to James Oglethorpe & others
- 29°N
- *"from sea to sea"
- N
- MILES 0 — 400
- KILOMETERS 0 — 600
- © Richard Natkiel, 1987

Up to 1650

- St Laurent
- Lake Ontario
- Mohawk
- Oneida
- Onondaga
- I R O Q U O I S   N A T I O N S
- Cayuga
- Seneca
- Lake Erie
- POPHAM COLONY 1606-08
- FORT ORANGE 1623
- FORT NASSAU 1614
- BOSTON 1630
- 1642-89 Iroquois raids on colonial settlements
- NEW NETH.
- WINDSOR 1637
- PLYMOUTH 1620
- Cape Cod
- NEW HAVEN 1637
- Susquehanna
- NEW AMSTERDAM 1628
- Delaware
- FORT CHRISTINA 1638
- NEW SWEDEN
- Potomac
- ZWAANENDAEL 1631 (Dutch)
- ST MARY'S 1634
- JAMESTOWN 1607
- Chesapeake Bay
- ATLANTIC OCEAN
- ROANOKE ISLAND 1585
- Settlement founded by Raleigh. No trace of settlers by 1590
- N
- SETTLEMENTS, 1650:
  - ENGLISH
  - FRENCH
  - DUTCH
  - SWEDISH
- MILES 0 — 200
- KILOMETERS 0 — 300
- MID 16TH CENTURY SPANISH SETTLEMENT IN FLORIDA
- © Richard Natkiel, 1987

Up to 1763

- RUPERT'S LAND (To Hudson's Bay Co. 1670)
- NEW HAMPSHIRE 1629
- MASSACHUSETTS 1691
- NEW YORK 1664
- RHODE I. 1663
- CONNECTICUT 1662
- PENNSYLVANIA 1681
- NEW JERSEY 1664
- DELAWARE 1682
- MARYLAND 1632
- VIRGINIA 1624
- CAROLINA 1663
- NORTH CAROLINA 1713
- SOUTH CAROLINA 1713
- GEORGIA 1732
- ATLANTIC OCEAN
- FLORIDA 1513
- BAHAMA IS. (To England from Spain, 1670)
- SETTLEMENT, 1713*
  - BRITISH
  - FRENCH
  - SPANISH
- LIMIT OF TERRITORY CONTROLLED, 1763†
- N
- *YEAR OF TREATY OF UTRECHT
- †BEFORE TREATY OF PARIS
- DATES SHOW YEAR OF FOUNDATION
- © Richard Natkiel, 1987

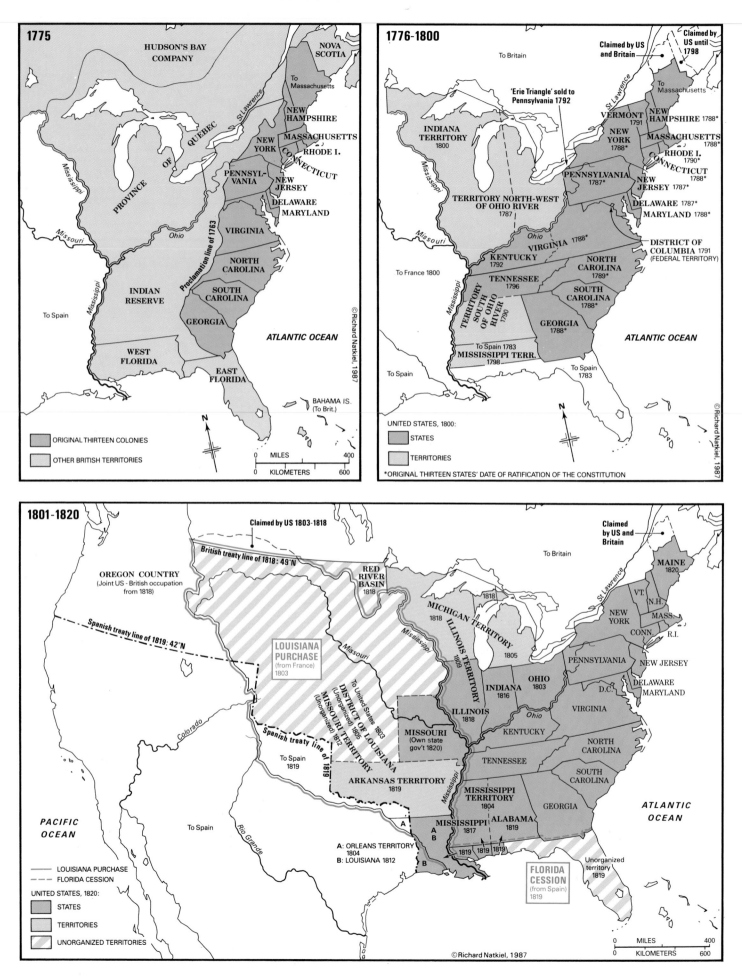

1775

HUDSON'S BAY COMPANY

NOVA SCOTIA

To Massachusetts

PROVINCE OF QUEBEC

St Lawrence

NEW HAMPSHIRE

MASSACHUSETTS

NEW YORK

RHODE I.

CONNECTICUT

PENNSYL-VANIA

NEW JERSEY

DELAWARE

MARYLAND

VIRGINIA

Ohio

Proclamation line of 1763

Mississippi

Missouri

INDIAN RESERVE

NORTH CAROLINA

SOUTH CAROLINA

GEORGIA

To Spain

WEST FLORIDA

EAST FLORIDA

ATLANTIC OCEAN

BAHAMA IS. (To Brit.)

© Richard Natkiel, 1987

ORIGINAL THIRTEEN COLONIES

OTHER BRITISH TERRITORIES

N

MILES 0 — 400
KILOMETERS 0 — 600

1776-1800

To Britain

Claimed by US and Britain

Claimed by US until 1798

St Lawrence

To Massachusetts

INDIANA TERRITORY 1800

'Erie Triangle' sold to Pennsylvania 1792

VERMONT 1791

NEW HAMPSHIRE 1788*

NEW YORK 1788*

MASSACHUSETTS 1788*

RHODE I. 1790*

CONNECTICUT 1788*

PENNSYLVANIA 1787*

NEW JERSEY 1787*

DELAWARE 1787*

MARYLAND 1788*

Mississippi

Missouri

TERRITORY NORTH-WEST OF OHIO RIVER 1787

Ohio

VIRGINIA 1788*

DISTRICT OF COLUMBIA 1791 (FEDERAL TERRITORY)

KENTUCKY 1792

To France 1800

TENNESSEE 1796

NORTH CAROLINA 1789*

TERRITORY SOUTH OF OHIO RIVER 1790

SOUTH CAROLINA 1788*

GEORGIA 1788*

To Spain 1783

MISSISSIPPI TERR. 1798

To Spain

To Spain 1783

ATLANTIC OCEAN

UNITED STATES, 1800:

STATES

TERRITORIES

N

© Richard Natkiel, 1987

*ORIGINAL THIRTEEN STATES' DATE OF RATIFICATION OF THE CONSTITUTION

1801-1820

Claimed by US 1803-1818

British treaty line of 1818: 49°N

Claimed by US and Britain

To Britain

OREGON COUNTRY (Joint US - British occupation from 1818)

RED RIVER BASIN 1818

MAINE 1820

Spanish treaty line of 1819: 42°N

1818

St Lawrence

MICHIGAN TERRITORY 1818

VT.

N.H.

LOUISIANA PURCHASE (from France) 1803

Missouri

ILLINOIS TERRITORY 1809

NEW YORK

MASS.

CONN.

R.I.

To United States 1803

DISTRICT OF LOUISIANA (Unorganized) 1805

MISSOURI TERRITORY (Unorganized) 1812

Mississippi

INDIANA 1816

OHIO 1803

PENNSYLVANIA

D.C.

NEW JERSEY

DELAWARE

MARYLAND

MISSOURI (Own state gov't 1820)

ILLINOIS 1818

Ohio

VIRGINIA

Spanish treaty line of 1819

KENTUCKY

NORTH CAROLINA

To Spain 1819

Colorado

ARKANSAS TERRITORY 1819

TENNESSEE

SOUTH CAROLINA

To Spain

Rio Grande

MISSISSIPPI TERRITORY 1804

Mississippi

GEORGIA

ATLANTIC OCEAN

A

MISSISSIPPI 1817

A B

ALABAMA 1819

A: ORLEANS TERRITORY 1804
B: LOUISIANA 1812

B

1819 1819 1819

FLORIDA CESSION (from Spain) 1819

Unorganized territory 1819

PACIFIC OCEAN

LOUISIANA PURCHASE

FLORIDA CESSION

UNITED STATES, 1820:

STATES

TERRITORIES

UNORGANIZED TERRITORIES

© Richard Natkiel, 1987

MILES 0 — 400
KILOMETERS 0 — 600

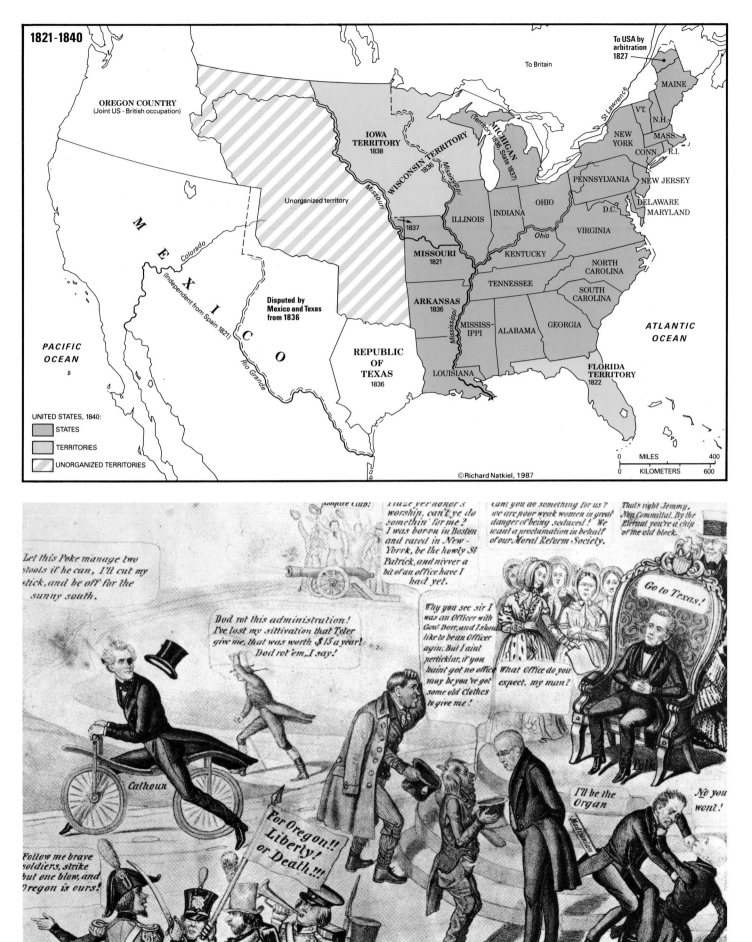

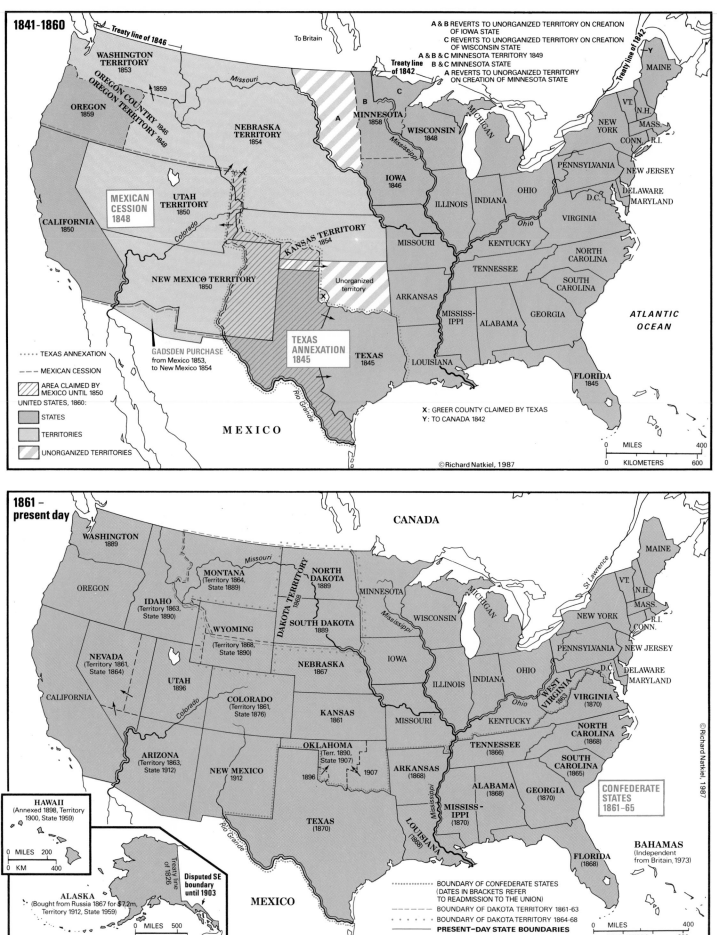

1841-1860

A & B REVERTS TO UNORGANIZED TERRITORY ON CREATION OF IOWA STATE
C REVERTS TO UNORGANIZED TERRITORY ON CREATION OF WISCONSIN STATE
A & B & C MINNESOTA TERRITORY 1849
B & C MINNESOTA STATE
A REVERTS TO UNORGANIZED TERRITORY ON CREATION OF MINNESOTA STATE

Treaty line of 1846

To Britain

Treaty line of 1842

Treaty line of 1842

WASHINGTON TERRITORY 1853

OREGON COUNTRY 1846
OREGON TERRITORY 1848
1859

Missouri

MAINE

OREGON 1859

NEBRASKA TERRITORY 1854

A   B   C

MINNESOTA 1858

WISCONSIN 1848

MICHIGAN

VT.
N.H.

NEW YORK

MASS.

CALIFORNIA 1850

MEXICAN CESSION 1848

UTAH TERRITORY 1850

Colorado

IOWA 1846

ILLINOIS   INDIANA   OHIO

PENNSYLVANIA

CONN. R.I.

NEW JERSEY

D.C.   DELAWARE
MARYLAND

VIRGINIA

KANSAS TERRITORY 1854

MISSOURI

KENTUCKY

NORTH CAROLINA

NEW MEXICO TERRITORY 1850

Unorganized territory

X

ARKANSAS

TENNESSEE

SOUTH CAROLINA

GEORGIA

ATLANTIC OCEAN

GADSDEN PURCHASE from Mexico 1853, to New Mexico 1854

TEXAS ANNEXATION 1845

TEXAS 1845

MISSISS-IPPI   ALABAMA

LOUISIANA

FLORIDA 1845

Rio Grande

········ TEXAS ANNEXATION
— — — MEXICAN CESSION

AREA CLAIMED BY MEXICO UNTIL 1850
UNITED STATES, 1860:
STATES
TERRITORIES
UNORGANIZED TERRITORIES

MEXICO

X: GREER COUNTY CLAIMED BY TEXAS
Y: TO CANADA 1842

©Richard Natkiel, 1987

0   MILES   400
0   KILOMETERS   600

1861 – present day

CANADA

WASHINGTON 1889

OREGON

Missouri

MONTANA (Territory 1864, State 1889)

NORTH DAKOTA 1889

DAKOTA TERRITORY 1868

MINNESOTA

St Lawrence

MAINE

IDAHO (Territory 1863, State 1890)

WYOMING (Territory 1868, State 1890)

SOUTH DAKOTA 1889

WISCONSIN

MICHIGAN

VT.
N.H.

NEW YORK

MASS.
R.I.
CONN.

NEVADA (Territory 1861, State 1864)

UTAH 1896

COLORADO (Territory 1861, State 1876)

NEBRASKA 1867

IOWA

Mississippi

ILLINOIS   INDIANA   OHIO

PENNSYLVANIA

NEW JERSEY

D.C.   DELAWARE
MARYLAND

CALIFORNIA

Colorado

KANSAS 1861

MISSOURI

KENTUCKY

WEST VIRGINIA 1863

VIRGINIA (1870)

ARIZONA (Territory 1863, State 1912)

NEW MEXICO 1912

OKLAHOMA (Terr. 1890, State 1907)

1896   1907

ARKANSAS (1868)

TENNESSEE (1866)

NORTH CAROLINA (1868)

SOUTH CAROLINA (1865)

HAWAII (Annexed 1898, Territory 1900, State 1959)

TEXAS (1870)

MISSISS-IPPI (1870)

ALABAMA (1868)

GEORGIA (1870)

CONFEDERATE STATES 1861-65

0   MILES   200
0   KM   400

Rio Grande

LOUISIANA (1868)

FLORIDA (1868)

BAHAMAS (Independent from Britain, 1973)

Treaty line of 1826

Disputed SE boundary until 1903

ALASKA (Bought from Russia 1867 for $7.2m, Territory 1912, State 1959)

MEXICO

········ BOUNDARY OF CONFEDERATE STATES (DATES IN BRACKETS REFER TO READMISSION TO THE UNION)
— — — BOUNDARY OF DAKOTA TERRITORY 1861-63
·········· BOUNDARY OF DAKOTA TERRITORY 1864-68
——— PRESENT-DAY STATE BOUNDARIES

0   MILES   400
0   KILOMETERS   600

0   MILES   500
0   KM   1000

©Richard Natkiel, 1987

establishing new realms and to view the growth of other kings' overseas possessions with suspicion. During these new conflicts, the Dutch and the Swedes soon withdrew, the Swedish Delaware colony being absorbed by the Dutch who, after an unsuccessful European war, handed over their American colonies, including what was later to be New York, to the British as part of the peace settlement. On the whole, it was the conflict between the French and the British which dominated the territorial development of the continent in the eighteenth century. Associated with this struggle was an extension of the territories claimed by the various colonies. Frontiers were pushed back into the interior not on the basis of settlement, but on claims resulting from exploration and, sometimes, mere speculation. Sometimes, as in 1713, the European powers would formalize treaties which defined, more or less precisely, the frontiers of their respective North American settlements, such agreements being revised at the end of each successive war. Britain's victory in the Seven Years War of 1756-63 determined the final shape of the America that won independence two decades later. The French settlers remained in Quebec but the French flag went home, the British colonies were confirmed, while Spain relinquished Florida to Britain but gained the enormous expanse of largely unexplored western territory known as Louisiana. After American Independence, Spain regained Florida, and began to claim additional territory in the south-west. The new American Confederation, by a succession of ordinances, regularized the territorial situation. It settled conflicting claims between colonies as they each tried to extend westward, it provided for land sales, and land in the public domain was reorganized wherever possible into territories that could subsequently graduate to statehood. In 1787 the North-West Territory was established north of the Ohio and east of the Mississippi to be ruled by a Congress-appointed governor, to be free of slavery, and to evolve into new states.

Then, early in the next century, France acquired Louisiana but Napoleon, putting his own short-term desires before the long-term interests of France, sold it to the US government. Sixteen years later Florida became a smaller but significant acquisition.

In 1848 the Oregon Territory was established, following the settlement in 1846 of a longstanding border dispute caused by conflicting British and American exploration claims. This Territory subsequently became the states of Oregon, Washington, and Idaho.

Purchase and the peaceful settlement of boundary disputes, exemplified also in the 1827 agreement resolving the northern boundaries of Maine, gave way in the south-west to other forms of territorial expansion unforeseen by the Constitution, including aggressive war. Texas was largely settled by American immigrants from the slaveholding southern states, who soon demanded independence from the Mexican government, and in 1836 went to war to achieve this, later joining the USA. The Mexican War (1846-48) followed an unsuccessful attempt by the US government to purchase, at a low price, California and New Mexico from the Mexican government. When negotiations failed, President Polk sent in the US Army to get what he wanted.

By the Civil War, territorial expansion was almost complete, although the unattached territories, later states, of Alaska and Hawaii were still to be acquired. In the ensuing decades the remaining territories achieved populations that entitled them to statehood, the 48th state being Arizona in 1912, with Alaska and Hawaii being the 49th and 50th, in 1959. The peopling of the western territories proceeded rapidly in the post-Civil War decades, aided by the expansion of the railroad system and by the many incentives offered by private and public interests.

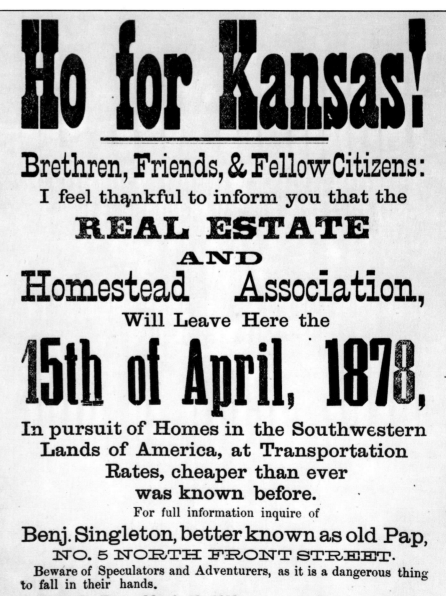

Population of the USA

A shipload of maidens despatched to the Jamestown colony, after it had securely established itself, perhaps marks the take-off of population growth. Estimates suggest that the population of the British colonies of 1610 was in the region of 500, and that the population grew to about 275,000 in 1700, and was over one million by 1750. The first American census was taken in 1790, and registered a population of 3,929,000. Subsequent trends can be seen from the chart.

Helped by immigration, the population rose at the rate of about 30 percent per decade up to about 1910, and then by roughly 15 percent.

The trend of population density can be seen from the maps. The move toward the west can be discerned, although the extensive agricultural and mountainous regions of the Middle and Far West could only support a thin population. The industrial region of the great Lakes and North-East was soon registering a high density, although densities were low by European standards. There had been a constant shift from rural to urban areas. By 1960, 89 percent of the inhabitants of New Jersey were town-dwellers, and New York and California also had urban percentages in the high eighties.

More recently, with the development of new light industries and the relative decline of the old heavy industries, and with a higher proportion of the population not dependent on a fixed place of work, there has been the beginning of a population shift toward what is known as the Sunbelt, embracing California and the South. Americans of European descent made up almost nine-tenths of the total population in 1960, most of the remainder being of African origin. The Hispanic population, largely originating in Mexico, Puerto Rico, the Philippines and Cuba, was increasing, but remained relatively small except in a few localities. There were rather more than half a million Indians in 1960, and they were increasing quite fast. Chinese and Japanese communities were also quite common, especially in the West Coast states.

Below: *The first Thanksgiving is celebrated at Plymouth, 1621.*

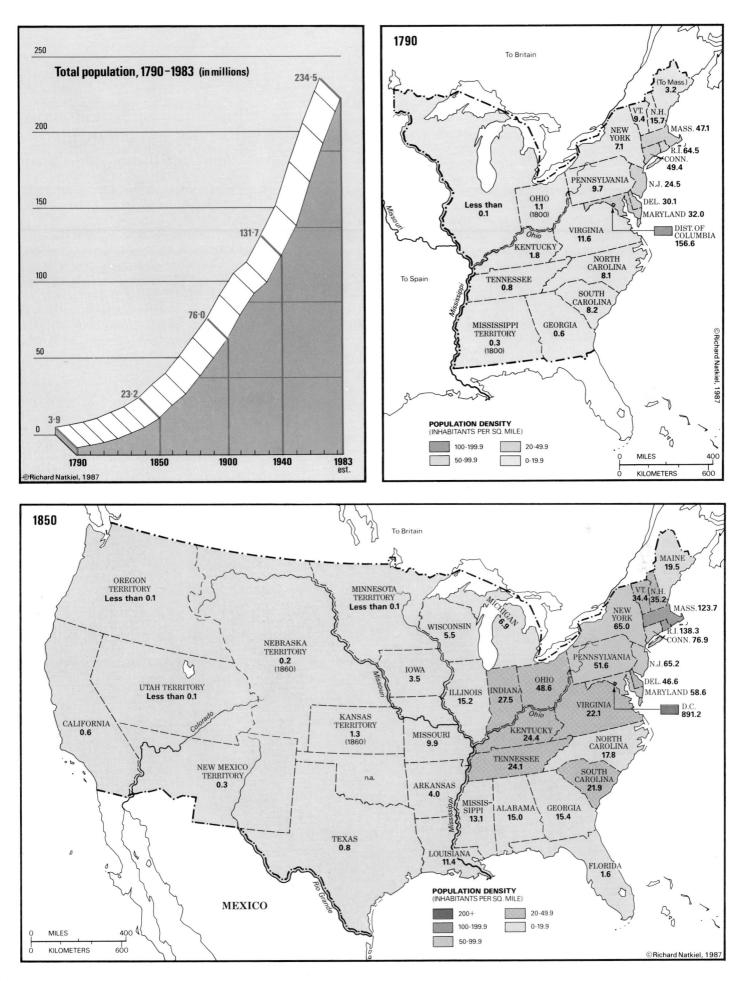

Total population, 1790-1983 (in millions)

250

200

150

100

50

0

234·5

131·7

76·0

23·2

3·9

1790   1850   1900   1940   1983 est.

©Richard Natkiel, 1987

1790

To Britain

(To Mass.) 3.2

VT 9.4   N.H. 15.7   MASS. 47.1

NEW YORK 7.1

R.I. 64.5   CONN. 49.4

PENNSYLVANIA 9.7

N.J. 24.5

DEL. 30.1

MARYLAND 32.0

Less than 0.1

OHIO 1.1 (1800)

Missouri

Ohio

VIRGINIA 11.6

KENTUCKY 1.8

DIST. OF COLUMBIA 156.6

To Spain

TENNESSEE 0.8

NORTH CAROLINA 8.1

SOUTH CAROLINA 8.2

Mississippi

MISSISSIPPI TERRITORY 0.3 (1800)

GEORGIA 0.6

©Richard Natkiel, 1987

POPULATION DENSITY
(INHABITANTS PER SQ. MILE)

100-199.9   20-49.9

50-99.9   0-19.9

MILES 0 — 400

KILOMETERS 0 — 600

1850

To Britain

OREGON TERRITORY Less than 0.1

MINNESOTA TERRITORY Less than 0.1

MAINE 19.5

VT 34.4   N.H. 35.2

MICHIGAN 6.9

WISCONSIN 5.5

NEW YORK 65.0

MASS. 123.7

R.I. 138.3   CONN. 76.9

NEBRASKA TERRITORY 0.2 (1860)

IOWA 3.5

PENNSYLVANIA 51.6

N.J. 65.2

DEL. 46.6

MARYLAND 58.6

UTAH TERRITORY Less than 0.1

Missouri

ILLINOIS 15.2

INDIANA 27.5

OHIO 48.6

Ohio

VIRGINIA 22.1

D.C. 891.2

CALIFORNIA 0.6

Colorado

KANSAS TERRITORY 1.3 (1860)

MISSOURI 9.9

KENTUCKY 24.4

NORTH CAROLINA 17.8

NEW MEXICO TERRITORY 0.3

n.a.

TENNESSEE 24.1

SOUTH CAROLINA 21.9

ARKANSAS 4.0

MISSIS-SIPPI 13.1

ALABAMA 15.0

GEORGIA 15.4

Mississippi

TEXAS 0.8

LOUISIANA 11.4

FLORIDA 1.6

MEXICO

Rio Grande

MILES 0 — 400

KILOMETERS 0 — 600

POPULATION DENSITY
(INHABITANTS PER SQ. MILE)

200+   20-49.9

100-199.9   0-19.9

50-99.9

©Richard Natkiel, 1987

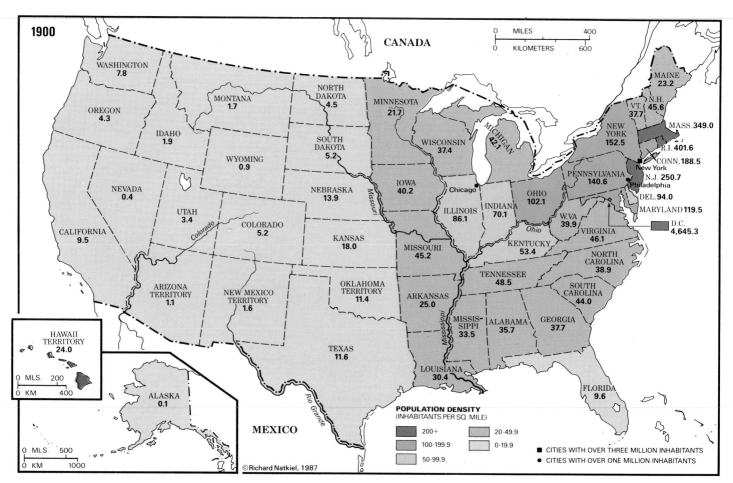

1900

CANADA

	MILES	
0		400
0	KILOMETERS	600

WASHINGTON 7.8

MONTANA 1.7

NORTH DAKOTA 4.5

MINNESOTA 21.7

OREGON 4.3

IDAHO 1.9

SOUTH DAKOTA 5.2

WISCONSIN 37.4

MICHIGAN 42.1

MAINE 23.2

VT. 37.7

N.H. 45.6

NEW YORK 152.5

MASS. 349.0

WYOMING 0.9

IOWA 40.2

R.I. 401.6

CONN. 188.5

NEVADA 0.4

NEBRASKA 13.9

Chicago

ILLINOIS 86.1

INDIANA 70.1

OHIO 102.1

PENNSYLVANIA 140.6

New York

N.J. 250.7

Philadelphia

DEL. 94.0

UTAH 3.4

CALIFORNIA 9.5

COLORADO 5.2

KANSAS 18.0

MISSOURI 45.2

KENTUCKY 53.4

W.VA 39.9

VIRGINIA 46.1

MARYLAND 119.5

D.C. 4,645.3

Colorado

Missouri

Ohio

ARIZONA TERRITORY 1.1

NEW MEXICO TERRITORY 1.6

OKLAHOMA TERRITORY 11.4

ARKANSAS 25.0

TENNESSEE 48.5

NORTH CAROLINA 38.9

SOUTH CAROLINA 44.0

MISSIS-SIPPI 33.5

ALABAMA 35.7

GEORGIA 37.7

HAWAII TERRITORY 24.0

0	MLS.	200
0	KM	400

ALASKA 0.1

TEXAS 11.6

LOUISIANA 30.4

FLORIDA 9.6

Rio Grande

Mississippi

MEXICO

0	MLS.	500
0	KM	1000

©Richard Natkiel, 1987

POPULATION DENSITY
(INHABITANTS PER SQ. MILE)

	200+		20-49.9
	100-199.9		0-19.9
	50-99.9		

■ CITIES WITH OVER THREE MILLION INHABITANTS

● CITIES WITH OVER ONE MILLION INHABITANTS

Right: *Saluting the flag in a New York School of the 1880's. Public elementary schools were established in New York in 1832. Regular rituals like saluting the flag helped to instill in the young a national American consciousness.*

Above: *A cartoon criticizing Tammany Hall, the Democratic Party's political machine in New York, like the city's police Tammany Hall jobs were the preserve of Irish-Americans.*

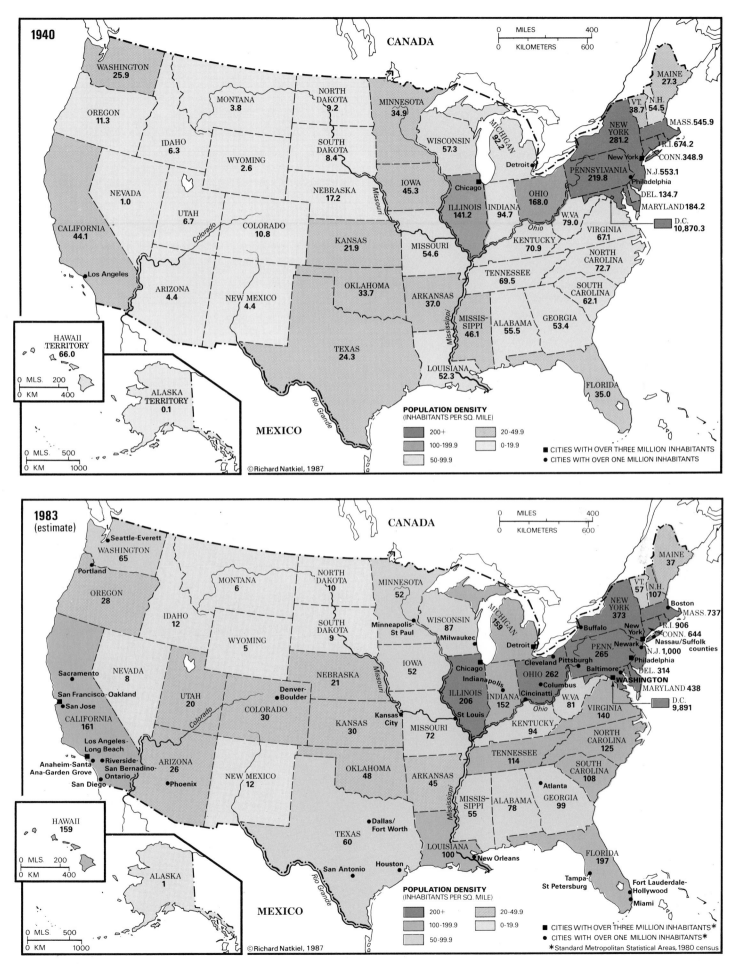

1940

CANADA

MILES 0 — 400
KILOMETERS 0 — 600

WASHINGTON 25.9
MONTANA 3.8
NORTH DAKOTA 9.2
MINNESOTA 34.9
MAINE 27.3
OREGON 11.3
IDAHO 6.3
WYOMING 2.6
SOUTH DAKOTA 8.4
WISCONSIN 57.3
MICHIGAN 92.2
Detroit
VT. 38.7
N.H. 54.5
MASS. 545.9
R.I. 674.2
NEW YORK 281.2
New York
CONN. 348.9
NEVADA 1.0
UTAH 6.7
COLORADO 10.8
NEBRASKA 17.2
IOWA 45.3
Chicago
ILLINOIS 141.2
INDIANA 94.7
OHIO 168.0
PENNSYLVANIA 219.8
N.J. 553.1
Philadelphia
DEL. 134.7
CALIFORNIA 44.1
Los Angeles
KANSAS 21.9
MISSOURI 54.6
KENTUCKY 70.9
W.VA 79.0
VIRGINIA 67.1
MARYLAND 184.2
D.C. 10,870.3
ARIZONA 4.4
NEW MEXICO 4.4
OKLAHOMA 33.7
ARKANSAS 37.0
TENNESSEE 69.5
NORTH CAROLINA 72.7
SOUTH CAROLINA 62.1
MISSISSIPPI 46.1
ALABAMA 55.5
GEORGIA 53.4
TEXAS 24.3
LOUISIANA 52.3
FLORIDA 35.0

HAWAII TERRITORY 66.0
0 MLS. 200
0 KM 400

ALASKA TERRITORY 0.1
0 MLS. 500
0 KM 1000

MEXICO

©Richard Natkiel, 1987

POPULATION DENSITY
(INHABITANTS PER SQ. MILE)
200+
100-199.9
50-99.9
20-49.9
0-19.9
■ CITIES WITH OVER THREE MILLION INHABITANTS
● CITIES WITH OVER ONE MILLION INHABITANTS

1983 (estimate)

CANADA

MILES 0 — 400
KILOMETERS 0 — 600

Seattle-Everett
WASHINGTON 65
Portland
OREGON 28
MONTANA 6
NORTH DAKOTA 10
MINNESOTA 52
MAINE 37
IDAHO 12
SOUTH DAKOTA 9
WISCONSIN 87
Minneapolis-St Paul
Milwaukee
MICHIGAN 159
Detroit
VT. 57
N.H. 107
Boston
MASS. 737
NEW YORK 373
Buffalo
New York
R.I. 906
CONN. 644
Nassau/Suffolk counties
WYOMING 5
NEVADA 8
Sacramento
UTAH 20
Denver-Boulder
COLORADO 30
NEBRASKA 21
IOWA 52
Chicago
ILLINOIS 206
St Louis
Indianapolis
INDIANA 152
OHIO 262
Columbus
Cincinnati
Cleveland
Pittsburgh
PENN. 265
Newark
N.J. 1,000
Philadelphia
DEL. 314
Baltimore
WASHINGTON
MARYLAND 438
D.C. 9,891
San Francisco-Oakland
San Jose
CALIFORNIA 161
Los Angeles-Long Beach
Anaheim-Santa Ana-Garden Grove
Riverside-San Bernardino-Ontario
San Diego
ARIZONA 26
Phoenix
NEW MEXICO 12
KANSAS 30
Kansas City
MISSOURI 72
KENTUCKY 94
W.VA 81
VIRGINIA 140
NORTH CAROLINA 125
TENNESSEE 114
OKLAHOMA 48
ARKANSAS 45
MISSISSIPPI 55
ALABAMA 78
GEORGIA 99
Atlanta
SOUTH CAROLINA 108
Dallas/Fort Worth
TEXAS 60
San Antonio
Houston
LOUISIANA 100
New Orleans
FLORIDA 197
Tampa-St Petersburg
Fort Lauderdale-Hollywood
Miami

HAWAII 159
0 MLS. 200
0 KM 400

ALASKA 1
0 MLS. 500
0 KM 1000

MEXICO

©Richard Natkiel, 1987

POPULATION DENSITY
(INHABITANTS PER SQ. MILE)
200+
100-199.9
50-99.9
20-49.9
0-19.9
■ CITIES WITH OVER THREE MILLION INHABITANTS *
● CITIES WITH OVER ONE MILLION INHABITANTS *
* Standard Metropolitan Statistical Areas, 1980 census

Presidential Elections

The US Constitution laid down principles and procedures which are still followed, even though the rise of the party system was not anticipated. Separation of powers between President, Congress, and Supreme Court was a principle which has always been adhered to, with benefit, but the indirect election of president and vice-president through the Electoral College, though retained, is a weakness, for it can mean the election of a president on a minority vote; in 1824, 1860, 1876, 1888, 1912, and 1948 this did happen.

The procedure is that in each state the voters choose their electors, and it is the electors who, after the election, meet in each state and cast their votes for the president and vice-president. Thus a presidential candidate who receives not quite as many votes as his rival loses all the electoral vote of that state, a winner-takes-all situation. An elector is not legally required to vote for the candidate who had most popular support, but in practice does so. Each state has a number of electors equal to its total of

Congressmen, which means that, quite properly, populous states have more electoral votes than others, but this in turn means that a candidate who captures such a state by a hair's breadth, gaining all its electoral votes, is disproportionately advantaged. Despite its shortcomings, this system has worked insofar as losers have accepted defeat with, usually, good grace. The 1876 election was perhaps the most acrimoniously questioned; the electoral votes of four states being challenged. A commission was set up which awarded the election to Hayes, whose opponent had actually won a majority of the popular vote.

Above left: George Washington in Continental Army uniform, 1780.

Above: Thomas Jefferson, painted by Charles Wilson Peale.

Below right: Abraham Lincoln, photographed by Brady in 1864.

Below, far right: President Coolidge (left), photographed with his successor, Herbert Hoover, in 1928.

The Presidents of the United States

President	Period in Office	President	Period in Office
George Washington (1732-1799)	1789-1797	Chester Alan Arthur (1829-1886)	1881-1885
John Adams (1735-1826)	1797-1801	Grover Cleveland (1837-1908)	1885-1889 and
Thomas Jefferson (1743-1826)	1801-1809		1893-1897
James Madison (1751-1836)	1809-1817	Benjamin Harrison (1833-1901)	1889-1893
James Monroe (1758-1831)	1817-1825	William McKinley (1843-1901)	1897-1901*
John Quincy Adams (1767-1848)	1825-1829	*(assassinated in the first year of his second term)	
Andrew Jackson (1767-1845)	1829-1837	Theodore Roosevelt (1858-1919)	1901-1909
Martin van Buren (1782-1862)	1837-1841	William Howard Taft (1857-1930)	1909-1913
William Henry Harrison (1773-1841)	1841*	Woodrow Wilson (1856-1924)	1913-1921
*(died one month after inauguration)		Warren Gamaliel Harding (1865-1923)	1921-1923
John Tyler (1790-1862)	1841-1845	Calvin Coolidge (1872-1933)	1923-1929
James Knox Polk (1795-1849)	1845-1849	Herbert Hoover (1874-1964)	1929-1933
Zachary Taylor (1784-1850)	1849-1850	Franklin Delano Roosevelt (1882-1945)	1933-1945*
Millard Fillmore (1800-1874)	1850-1853	*(died in the first year of his fourth term)	
Franklin Pierce (1840-1869)	1853-1857	Harry S. Truman (1884-1972)	1945-1953
James Buchanan (1791-1868)	1857-1861	Dwight David Eisenhower (1890-1969)	1953-1961
Abraham Lincoln (1809-1865)	1861-1865	John Fitzgerald Kennedy (1917-1963)	1961-1963
Andrew Johnson (1808-1875)	1865-1869	Lyndon Baines Johnson (1908-1973)	1963-1969
Ulysses Simpson Grant (1822-1885)	1869-1877	Richard Milhous Nixon (1913-)	1969-1974
Rutherford Birchard Hayes (1822-1893)	1877-1881	Gerald Rudolph Ford (1913-)	1974-1977
James Abram Garfield (1831-1881)	1881*	James Earl Carter (1924-)	1977-1981
*(assassinated during his first year in office)		Ronald Wilson Reagan (1911-)	1981-

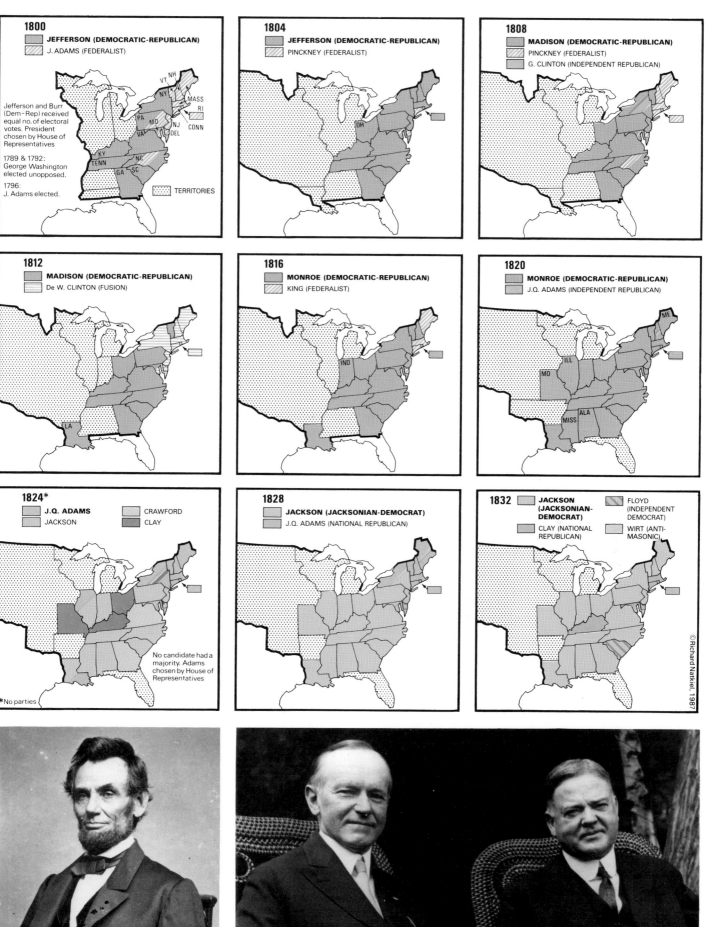

1800

JEFFERSON (DEMOCRATIC-REPUBLICAN)

J. ADAMS (FEDERALIST)

Jefferson and Burr (Dem-Rep) received equal no. of electoral votes. President chosen by House of Representatives

1789 & 1792: George Washington elected unopposed.

1796: J. Adams elected.

VT NH NY MASS RI PA NJ CONN MD DEL VA KY TENN NC SC GA

TERRITORIES

1804

JEFFERSON (DEMOCRATIC-REPUBLICAN)

PINCKNEY (FEDERALIST)

OH

1808

MADISON (DEMOCRATIC-REPUBLICAN)

PINCKNEY (FEDERALIST)

G. CLINTON (INDEPENDENT REPUBLICAN)

1812

MADISON (DEMOCRATIC-REPUBLICAN)

De W. CLINTON (FUSION)

LA

1816

MONROE (DEMOCRATIC-REPUBLICAN)

KING (FEDERALIST)

IND

1820

MONROE (DEMOCRATIC-REPUBLICAN)

J.Q. ADAMS (INDEPENDENT REPUBLICAN)

ME ILL MO MISS ALA

1824*

J.Q. ADAMS

JACKSON

CRAWFORD

CLAY

No candidate had a majority. Adams chosen by House of Representatives

*No parties

1828

JACKSON (JACKSONIAN-DEMOCRAT)

J.Q. ADAMS (NATIONAL REPUBLICAN)

1832

JACKSON (JACKSONIAN-DEMOCRAT)

CLAY (NATIONAL REPUBLICAN)

FLOYD (INDEPENDENT DEMOCRAT)

WIRT (ANTI-MASONIC)

© Richard Natkiel, 1987

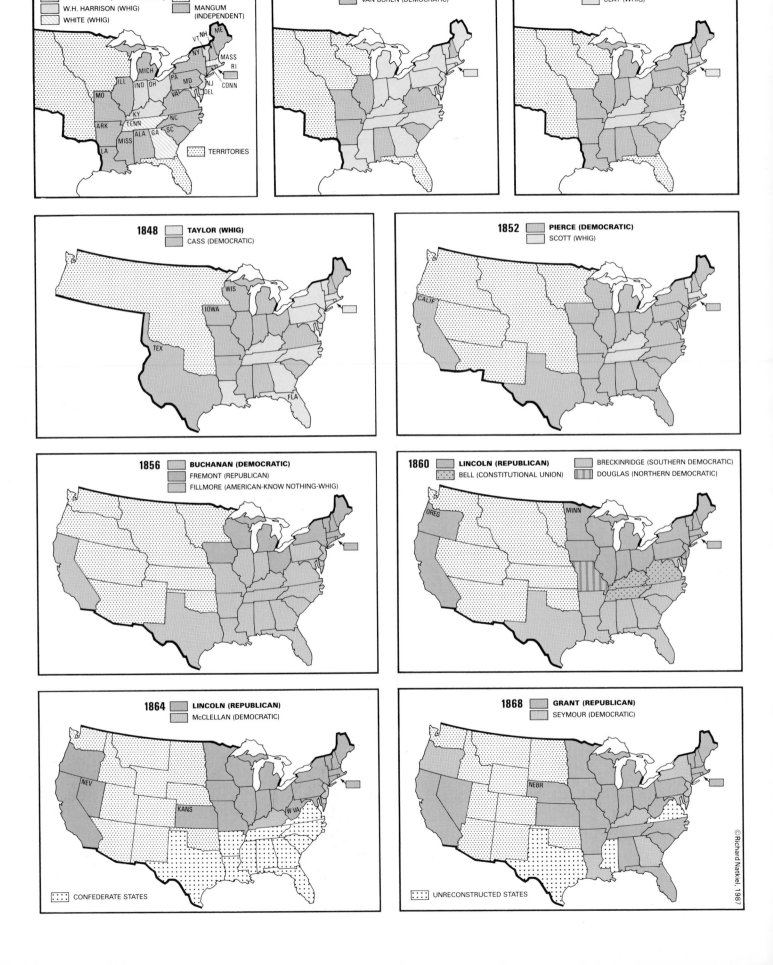

1836 VAN BUREN (DEMOCRATIC) / W.H. HARRISON (WHIG) / WHITE (WHIG) / WEBSTER (WHIG) / MANGUM (INDEPENDENT) / TERRITORIES

1840 W.H. HARRISON (WHIG) / VAN BUREN (DEMOCRATIC)

1844 POLK (DEMOCRATIC) / CLAY (WHIG)

1848 TAYLOR (WHIG) / CASS (DEMOCRATIC)

1852 PIERCE (DEMOCRATIC) / SCOTT (WHIG)

1856 BUCHANAN (DEMOCRATIC) / FREMONT (REPUBLICAN) / FILLMORE (AMERICAN-KNOW NOTHING-WHIG)

1860 LINCOLN (REPUBLICAN) / BELL (CONSTITUTIONAL UNION) / BRECKINRIDGE (SOUTHERN DEMOCRATIC) / DOUGLAS (NORTHERN DEMOCRATIC)

1864 LINCOLN (REPUBLICAN) / McCLELLAN (DEMOCRATIC) / CONFEDERATE STATES

1868 GRANT (REPUBLICAN) / SEYMOUR (DEMOCRATIC) / UNRECONSTRUCTED STATES

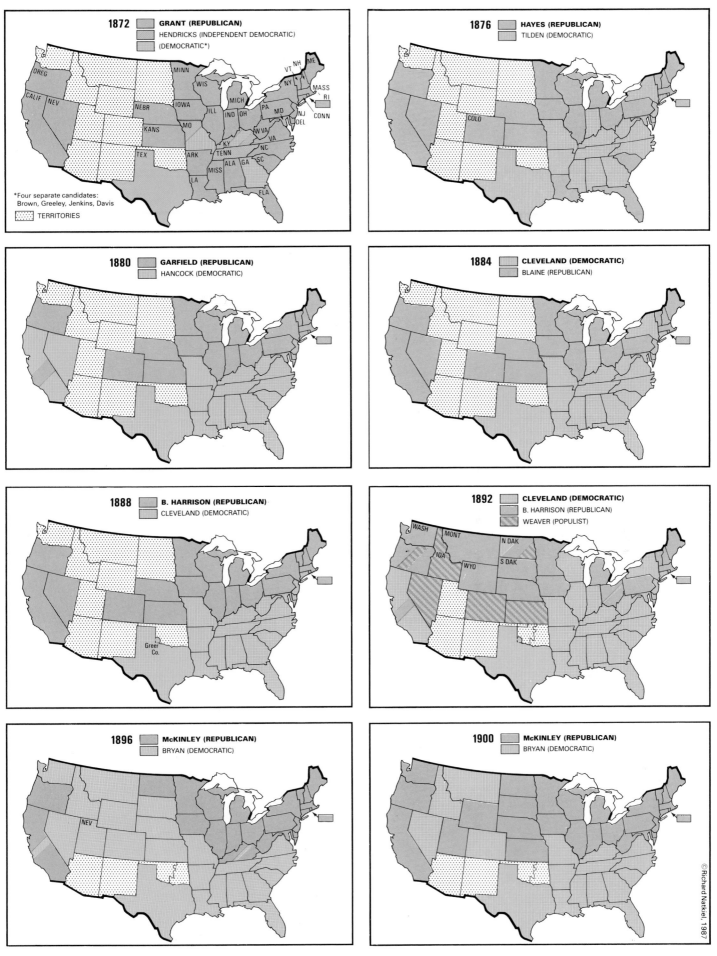

1872
GRANT (REPUBLICAN)
HENDRICKS (INDEPENDENT DEMOCRATIC)
(DEMOCRATIC*)

*Four separate candidates:
Brown, Greeley, Jenkins, Davis
TERRITORIES

1876
HAYES (REPUBLICAN)
TILDEN (DEMOCRATIC)

1880
GARFIELD (REPUBLICAN)
HANCOCK (DEMOCRATIC)

1884
CLEVELAND (DEMOCRATIC)
BLAINE (REPUBLICAN)

1888
B. HARRISON (REPUBLICAN)
CLEVELAND (DEMOCRATIC)

1892
CLEVELAND (DEMOCRATIC)
B. HARRISON (REPUBLICAN)
WEAVER (POPULIST)

1896
McKINLEY (REPUBLICAN)
BRYAN (DEMOCRATIC)

1900
McKINLEY (REPUBLICAN)
BRYAN (DEMOCRATIC)

© Richard Natkiel, 1987

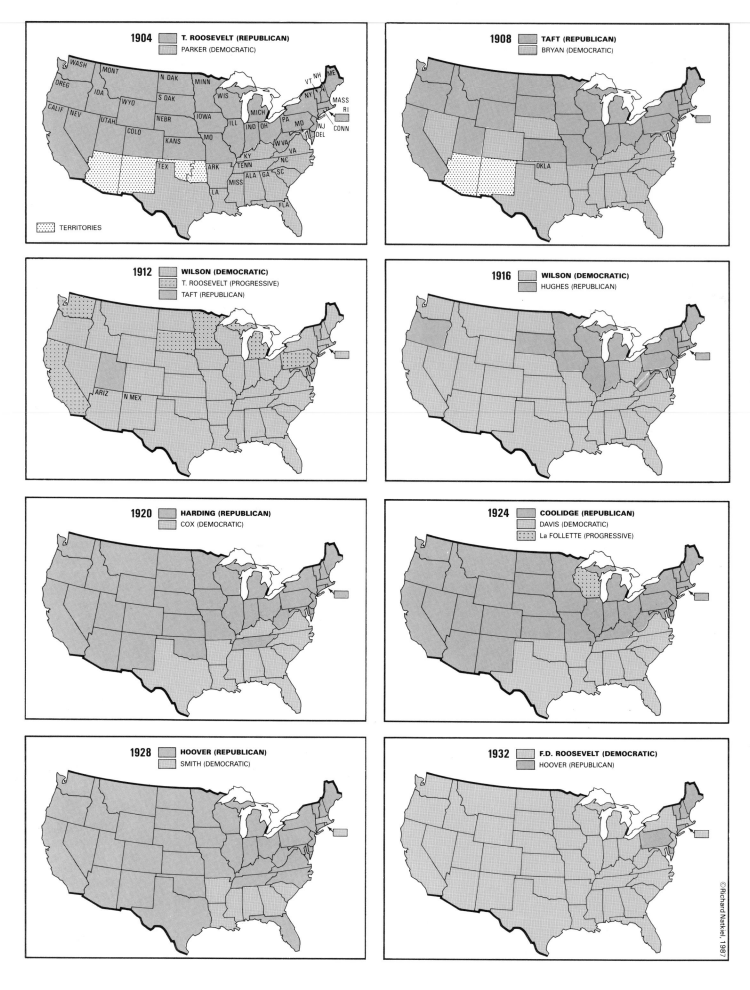

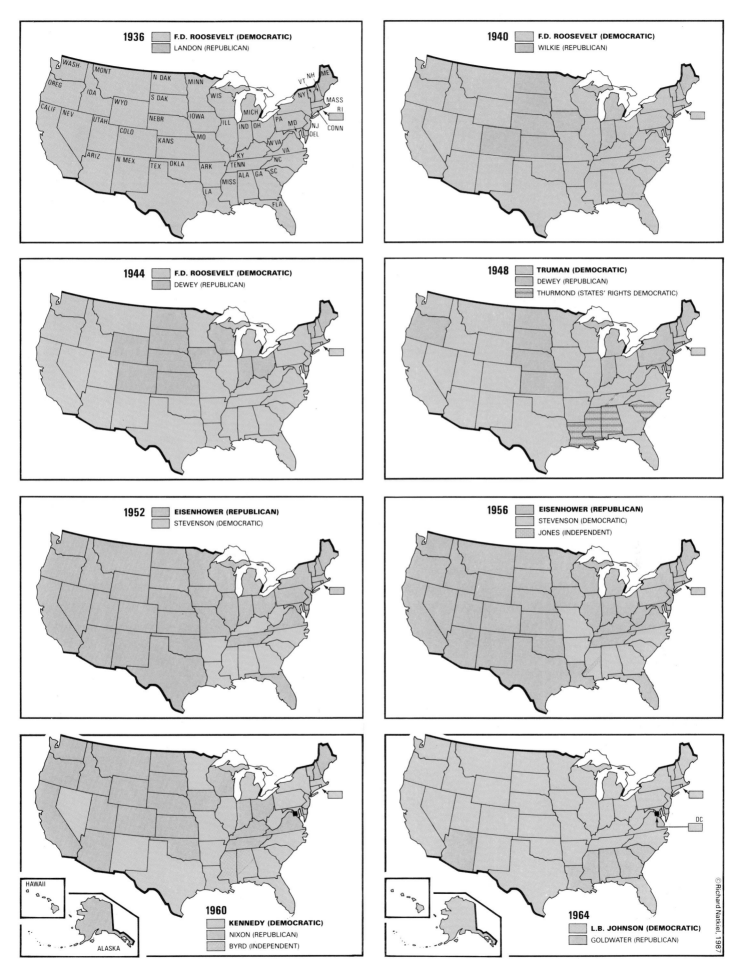

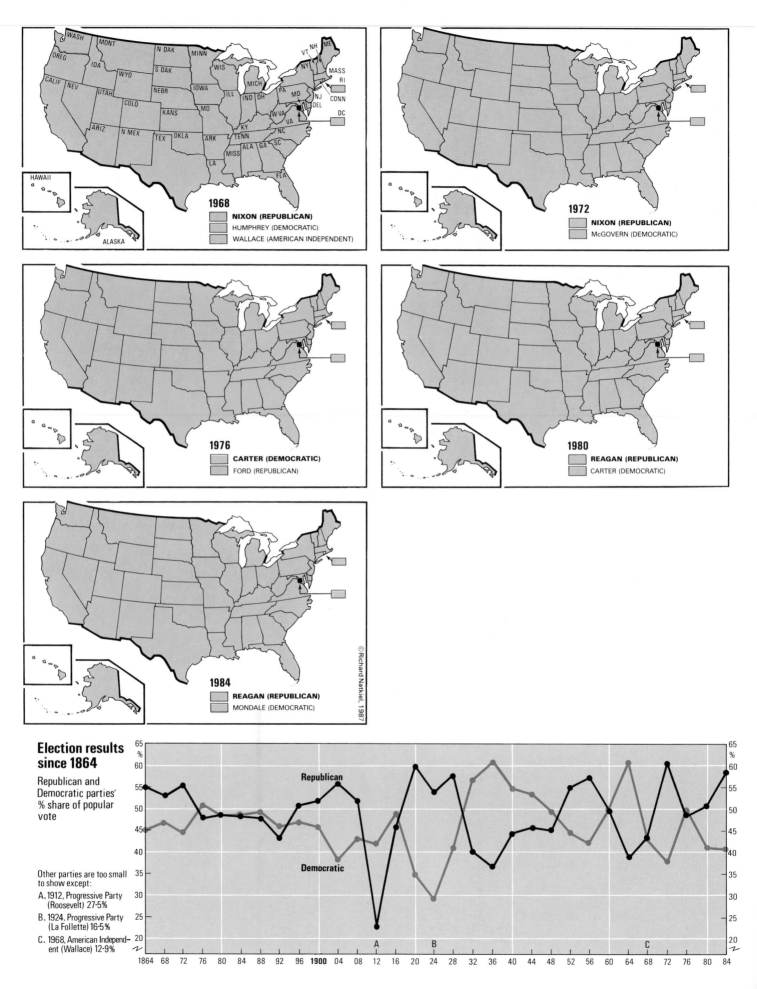

1968

NIXON (REPUBLICAN)
HUMPHREY (DEMOCRATIC)
WALLACE (AMERICAN INDEPENDENT)

1972

NIXON (REPUBLICAN)
McGOVERN (DEMOCRATIC)

1976

CARTER (DEMOCRATIC)
FORD (REPUBLICAN)

1980

REAGAN (REPUBLICAN)
CARTER (DEMOCRATIC)

1984

REAGAN (REPUBLICAN)
MONDALE (DEMOCRATIC)

© Richard Natkiel, 1987

Election results since 1864

Republican and Democratic parties' % share of popular vote

Republican

Democratic

Other parties are too small to show except:

A. 1912, Progressive Party (Roosevelt) 27·5%

B. 1924, Progressive Party (La Follette) 16·5%

C. 1968, American Independent (Wallace) 12·9%

1864 68 72 76 80 84 88 92 96 **1900** 04 08 12 16 20 24 28 32 36 40 44 48 52 56 60 64 68 72 76 80 84

Political parties first appeared, unexpectedly, during the struggle for ratification of the Constitution, the Federalist and Anti-Federalist parties being established in 1781. The former, led by Alexander Hamilton, favored a strong federal government and the latter, led by Thomas Jefferson, emphasized the individual and state's rights, and was therefore opposed to a strong central government. The Federalists progressively lost votes and relevance and put forward a presidential candidate for the last time in 1816. The Anti-Federalists, who soon became known as the Democratic Republicans, came into power with Jefferson's election in 1800, but eventually were split irrevocably between conservative and radical wings. In the 1828 presidential election their radical wing, in the person of Jackson, won the election and became the Democratic Party. The conservative wing, at first called the National Republican Party, soon became known as the Whig Party. The Democratic Party remained dominant, apart from the 1840 and 1848 elections, until it split over the slavery issue and fielded two opposing candidates in 1860. The Republican Party, meantime, had been created in 1854 by the amalgamation of the weak Whigs with dissident Democrats who called themselves Independent Democrats. This new party was against slavery, and in 1860, with Abraham Lincoln, it won the presidency for the first time. Apart from the 1884, 1892, 1912 and 1916 elections it kept power through the Civil War and up to the Depression. It advocated careful finance, protective tariffs, and industrial growth, ambitions that were dear to the heart not only of industrialists, who

Above: From left, Richard Nixon, Ronald Reagan, Gerald Ford and Jimmy Carter.

supplied its funds, but also of industrial workers, who supplied votes. However, the activities of the Republicans in the defeated South after the Civil War, at best tactless and at worst brutal, created a solid pool of Democratic voters in the former slaveholding South. This, and the Republicans' inability to attract the farming vote, accounted for the Democratic victory of 1892. The Republican failure in 1912 was occasioned by a split in the Republican ranks.

The Republican President Hoover had the misfortune to be caught by the Depression and was followed by the Democrat Roosevelt, whose popularity kept him in office until his death, after which legislation was passed making it impossible for a president to be elected for more than two terms. Roosevelt's New Deal attracted votes, and the combination of industrial worker and solid South support proved unbeatable until the Republicans put forward General Eisenhower as their presidential candidate in 1952. In the following

decades the Democratic Party, which received its campaign funds equally from industrialists and unions, was less united than the Republican Party, which was funded almost entirely by industrialists. The Democrats became a conglomeration of minority causes and had great difficulty in selecting candidates acceptable to the Party as a whole. Moreover, the Republican President Reagan had some success in speeding the transformation of southerners and industrial workers into Republican voters. Having to a large extent lost their traditional constituencies, the Democrats' electoral success seemed to depend increasingly on the mistakes and shortcomings of their Republican rivals.

Below left: The Republican Party Convention, 1880, the future President Garfield is speaking.

Below: President Johnson takes the oath following Kennedy's assassination.

Index

Picture Credits

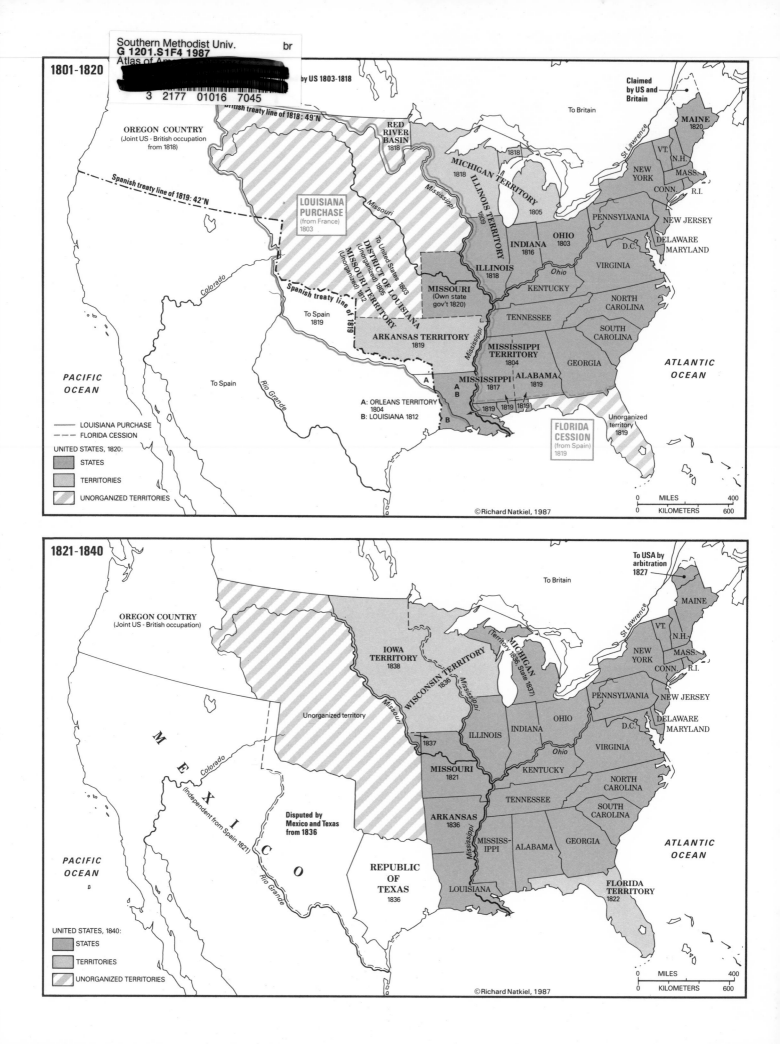

1801-1820

...by US 1803-1818

British treaty line of 1818: 49°N

Claimed by US and Britain

OREGON COUNTRY
(Joint US - British occupation from 1818)

Spanish treaty line of 1819: 42°N

RED RIVER BASIN 1818

To Britain

MICHIGAN TERRITORY 1818

ILLINOIS TERRITORY 1809

1818

1805

MAINE 1820

VT. N.H.

NEW YORK

MASS.

CONN. R.I.

LOUISIANA PURCHASE (from France) 1803

Missouri

To United States 1803

DISTRICT OF LOUISIANA (Unorganized) 1805

MISSOURI TERRITORY (Unorganized) 1812

Mississippi

INDIANA 1816

OHIO 1803

PENNSYLVANIA

NEW JERSEY

D.C.

DELAWARE MARYLAND

ILLINOIS 1818

MISSOURI (Own state gov't 1820)

VIRGINIA

Spanish treaty line of 1819

To Spain 1819

KENTUCKY

NORTH CAROLINA

Colorado

TENNESSEE

Ohio

ARKANSAS TERRITORY 1819

Mississippi

SOUTH CAROLINA

MISSISSIPPI TERRITORY 1804

GEORGIA

ATLANTIC OCEAN

To Spain

Rio Grande

A

MISSISSIPPI 1817 A B

ALABAMA 1819

1819 1819 1819

Unorganized territory 1819

A: ORLEANS TERRITORY 1804
B: LOUISIANA 1812

B

FLORIDA CESSION (from Spain) 1819

PACIFIC OCEAN

— LOUISIANA PURCHASE
--- FLORIDA CESSION

UNITED STATES, 1820:
▨ STATES
▨ TERRITORIES
▨ UNORGANIZED TERRITORIES

0   MILES   400
0   KILOMETERS   600

©Richard Natkiel, 1987

1821-1840

To USA by arbitration 1827

To Britain

OREGON COUNTRY
(Joint US - British occupation)

MAINE

VT. N.H.

IOWA TERRITORY 1838

WISCONSIN TERRITORY 1836

(Territory 1836 State 1837) **MICHIGAN**

NEW YORK

MASS.

CONN. R.I.

Missouri

Mississippi

PENNSYLVANIA

NEW JERSEY

M E X I C O
(Independent from Spain 1821)

Unorganized territory

1837

ILLINOIS

INDIANA

OHIO

D.C.

DELAWARE MARYLAND

Colorado

MISSOURI 1821

KENTUCKY

Ohio

VIRGINIA

Disputed by Mexico and Texas from 1836

NORTH CAROLINA

Rio Grande

ARKANSAS 1836

TENNESSEE

SOUTH CAROLINA

REPUBLIC OF TEXAS 1836

Mississippi

MISSISSIPPI

ALABAMA

GEORGIA

ATLANTIC OCEAN

PACIFIC OCEAN

LOUISIANA

FLORIDA TERRITORY 1822

UNITED STATES, 1840:
▨ STATES
▨ TERRITORIES
▨ UNORGANIZED TERRITORIES

0   MILES   400
0   KILOMETERS   600

©Richard Natkiel, 1987